Directory
of
U.S. Christian Schools

Cleveland C. Matchett, Compiler

BAKER BOOK HOUSE
Grand Rapids, Michigan 49506

Preface

Christian schools have existed in America since the early 1700s. In fact, the earliest schools in our country were parochial, sponsored by churches. Today we witness the mushrooming of Christian schools in all parts of the United States. Various explanations have been offered to account for the phenomenal expansion of the Christian school movement.

Critics sometimes attribute the rapid rise in the number of Christian schools to a desire to avoid integration. Undoubtedly some Christian schools may have been started with such a motive, but objective investigation will show that there are more basic reasons for the proliferation of Christian schools.

Some Christian schools have been organized as an alternative to what churches and parents term as unsatisfactory, even intolerable, conditions in the public schools. Many Christian parents are becoming aware of the need to inculcate spiritual values into the lives of children during their formative years. They realize that education is more than just the three Rs. The moral and ethical problems so prevalent in our society, these parents insist, call for an education with distinctively Christian perspectives. Such an education is not available in public schools.

The potential for transforming our society through Christian education can hardly be overemphasized. Youth today desperately need a faith to live by as well as die by. Christian schools are intended not only to prepare students for combating the secularism and humanism so entrenched in our society, but also to influence young minds and souls for eternity.

Many articles about the Christian school movement have appeared in national periodicals. Some point to the rapid increase in the number of Christian schools and discuss the potential for political clout.

The astounding growth in the number of Christian schools in the United States may be grasped by perusing this directory. Christian schools in each state are grouped according to geographic areas, usually designated by a larger city in the area. Listings cover a wide variety of schools, both denominational and nondenominational.

Families seeking a good Christian school in an area to which they plan to move can by means of this directory correspond with schools in which they are interested. Businesses which provide products used in education will find the listings helpful in their promotion work. Philanthropic organizations and persons may also find this directory useful.

As large as it is, this directory is not complete. The number and location of Christian schools constantly changes. An attempt has been made to be as accurate and up-to-date as possible. Suggestions for corrections, additions, or deletions will gladly be received.

Summary

<u>ALABAMA</u>

BIRMINGHAM AREA:

Alliance Christian School
1289 Montgomery Hwy.
Birmingham, AL   35216

Alliance Christian School
1820 Seventh Ave., N.
Birmingham, AL   35215

Alliance Christian School
230 North 85th St.
Birmingham, AL   35206

Jefferson Christian Academy
3609 Montclair Rd.
Birmingham, AL   35213

Minor Christian High School
McDonald Chapel Rd.
Birmingham, AL   35217

West Birmingham Christian
  School
1120 Apricot Ave.
Birmingham, AL   35214

Maranatha Christian Schools
7921 Fifth Ave., S.
Birmingham, AL   35206

Shades Mountain Christian
  School
2280 Tyler Rd.
Birmingham, AL   35226

Katherwood Christian Schools
600 Roanoke St.
Birmingham, AL   35224

Briarwood Christian School
3005 Highway 280, S.
Birmingham, AL   35243

Briarwood Christian School
6255 Cahaba Valley Rd.
Birmingham, AL   35243

Trinity Christian School
2900 Avenue G
P.O. Box 8221
Ensley, AL   35218

Grace Christian School
1819 First St., N.W.
Birmingham, AL   35215

Bethel Christian Schools
7001 Division Ave.
Birmingham, AL   35206

Cathedral Christian School
1401 Center Point Rd.
Birmingham, AL   35215

Faith Christian School
4601 Valleydale Rd.
Birmingham, AL   35243

Flint Hill Christian School
1630 Powder Plant Rd.
Bessemer, AL   35020

Tabernacle Christian School
2649 Decatur Hwy.
Gardendale, AL   35071

Glen Iris Baptist School
1137 South Tenth Pl.
Birmingham, AL   35205

Berney Points Baptist School
1637 Pearson Ave., S.W.
Birmingham, AL   35211

First Baptist School of
  Pleasant Grove
724 Fourth St.
Pleasant Grove, AL   35127

Palmerdale Baptist School
P.O. Box 156
Palmerdale, AL   35123

Bible Methodist Christian Day
  School
Route 3, Box 543
Pell City, AL   35125

Independent Presbyterian Day
  School
3100 Highland Ave., S.
Birmingham, AL   35205

Southminster Presbyterian
  Day School
1124 Montgomery Hwy.
(Vestavia)
Birmingham, AL   35216

Heritage Academy
  Independent Reformed
808 Chestnut St.
Birmingham, AL   35216

Saint Paul's Inter-Parochial
  School
2121 Fourth Ave., N.
Birmingham, AL   35203

Advent Episcopal Day School
2019 Sixth Ave., N.
Birmingham, AL   35203

All Saints Episcopal School
110 West Hawthorne Rd.
Birmingham, AL   35209

Blessed Sacrament Catholic
  School
1525 Cotton Ave.
Birmingham, AL   35211

MOBILE AREA:

Mobile Christian School
5900 Cottage Hill Rd.
Mobile, AL   36609

Northside Christian High
  School
818 West Turner Rd.
Prichard, AL   36610

Central Baptist School
998 Dauphin Island Pkwy.
Mobile, AL   36605

Trinity Bible School
2420 Shelton Beach Rd.
Mobile, AL   36618

Indian Springs Christian
  School
Lott Rd.
Mobile, AL   36613

Prichard Christian School
418 Edison Dr.
Prichard, AL   36610

Bel Aire Christian School
3590 Pleasant Valley Rd.
Mobile, AL   36609

West End Baptist Christian
  School
2157 Government St.
Mobile, AL   36606

Greystone Christian School
1301 Azalea Rd.
Mobile, AL   36609

Emmanuel Christian School
5601 Zeigler Blvd.
Mobile, AL   36608

Cypress Shores Christian
  School
Higgins Rd.
Mobile, AL   36619

Eastern Shore Christian
  School
Highway 31
Spanish Fort, AL   36527

Plateau First Baptist
  Christian School
514 Telegraph Rd.
Plateau, AL   36610

Magnolia Springs Christian
  School
Route 2, Box 586A
Theodore, AL   36582

Theodore Christian School
Theodore, AL   36582

Satsuma Christian School
Old Highway 43
P.O. Box 428
Satsuma, AL   36572

Fulton Road Christian Grade
  School
1800 Dauphin Island Pike
Mobile, AL   36605

Saint Mark United Methodist
  Day School
439 Azalea Rd.
Mobile, AL   36609

First Independent Methodist
  School
4548 Halls Mill Rd.
Mobile, AL   36609

Faith Lutheran School
1703 Stone St.
Mobile, AL   36617

Cottage Hill Baptist School
4255 Cottage Hill Rd.
Mobile, AL   36609

Evangel Christian School
  Assembly of God
2421 Lott Rd.
Mobile, AL   36613

Shiloh Christian School
717 Cleveland Rd.
Saraland, AL   36571

Evangel Assembly of God
  School
166 Meaher St.
Prichard, AL   36610

Mobile Junior Academy
  Seventh Day Adventist
3200 Pleasant Valley Rd.
Mobile, AL   36606

Saint Paul's Episcopal High
  School
161 Dogwood Ln.
Mobile, AL   36608

Saint Luke's Episcopal School
980 Azalea Rd.
Mobile, AL   36609

Aquinas Catholic Academy
911 Dauphin St.
Mobile, AL   36604

McGill Catholic Institute
1501 Old Shell Rd.
Mobile, AL   36604

Saint Thomas School
253 North Craft Hwy.
Chickasaw, AL   36611

HUNTSVILLE AREA:

Westminster Christian
  Academy
3100 University Dr., N.W.
Huntsville, AL   35805

Lighthouse Christian Academy
2103 Virginia Blvd., N.W.
Huntsville, AL   35811

Madison Academy High
  School
301 Max Luther Dr., N.W.
Huntsville, AL   35811

Randolph School
1005 Drake Ave., Box 919
Huntsville, AL   35802

Kiddie Korner Nazarene
3412 Martin Lake Rd.
Huntsville, AL   35810

Berachah Baptist Academy
3011 Sparkman Dr., N.W.
Huntsville, AL   35810

Triana Village Christian
  School
3217 Village Dr.
Huntsville, AL   35805

Grace Lutheran School
3321 Memorial Pkwy., S.
Huntsville, AL   35801

Evangel Christian School
1400 Evangel Dr., N.W.
Huntsville, AL   35805

Central Seventh Day
  Adventist School
102 Drake Ave., S.E.
Huntsville, AL   35802

Saint Joseph's Catholic
  School
2300 Beasley Ave., N.W.
Huntsville, AL   35805

Holy Spirit Catholic School
Airport Rd., S.W.
Huntsville, AL   35802

TUSCALOOSA AREA:

Tuscaloosa Christian School
Prude Mill Rd.
Cottondale, AL   35453

West End Christian School
700 35th Ave.
Tuscaloosa, AL   35401

Holy Spirit Catholic School
711 37th St., E.
Tuscaloosa, AL   35405

BESSEMER AREA:

Zion Lutheran School
1201 24th St., N.
Bessemer, AL   35020

MONTGOMERY AREA:

Landmark Christian
  Academy
800 Perry Hill Rd.
Montgomery, AL   36109

Trinity Presbyterian School
1700 East Trinity Blvd.
Montgomery, AL   36109

Calvary Christian Academy
Patterson Rd.
Box 23789
Montgomery, AL   36104

Grace Christian School
820 Selma Hwy., Route 6
Prattville, AL   36067

First Seventh Day
  Adventist School
4233 Atlanta Hwy.
Montgomery, AL   36109

Montgomery Catholic High
  School
Vaughn Rd.
Montgomery, AL   36106

Saint James School
2005 North Country Club
  Dr.
Montgomery, AL   36106

GADSDEN AREA:

Westminster Christian
  Secondary School
100 Westminster Dr.
Gadsden, AL   35901

Coosa Christian Academy
1403 Malone St.
Gadsden, AL   35901

Saint James Catholic School
1058 Rainbow Dr.
Gadsden, AL   35901

ANNISTON AREA:

Trinity Christian Academy
Old Coldwater Rd.
Oxford, AL   36203

Faith Christian School
4100 Ronnaki Rd.
Anniston, AL   36201

Sacred Heart Catholic School
1821 McCall Dr.
Anniston, AL   36201

BREWTON AREA:

South Normal School
Brewton, AL   36426

DOTHAN AREA:

Dothan Christian Academy
2215 Mimosa Dr.
Dothan, AL   36301

Emmanuel Christian School
Hartford Hwy.
Dothan, AL   36301

Northside Methodist Academy
2600 Redmond St.
Dothan, AL   36303

Trinity Presbyterian School
1310 South Oates St.
Dothan, AL   36301

Seventh Day Adventist
  School
2210 East Cottonwood Rd.
Dothan, AL   36301

FLORENCE AREA:

Florence Christian Academy
4417 Florence Blvd.
Florence, AL   35630

Lauderdale Christian
  Academy
Hendrix Rd.
Florence, AL   35630

Mars Hill Bible School
698 Cox Creek Pkwy.
Florence, AL   35630

Saint Joseph Catholic School
115 Plum St.
Florence, AL   35630

SELMA AREA:

Meadowview Christian
  School
1512 Old Orrville Rd.
Selma, AL   36701

Stanton Christian Day School
Box 53
Stanton, AL   36709

Perry Christian School
Marion, AL   36756

Alabama Lutheran Academy
1804 Green St.
Selma, AL   36701

Saint Elizabeth's School
1211 Church St.
Selma, AL   36701

Dallas Christian School
Selma, AL   36701

PHENIX CITY AREA:

Woodland Christian School
Layfield Dr.
Phenix City, AL   36867

Saint Patrick Catholic School
Phenix City, AL   36867

ALEXANDER CITY AREA:

Alexander City Christian
  Academy
1307 Hillabee St.
Alexander City, AL   35010

Union Academy
Route 1
Dadeville, AL   36853

ATHENS AREA:

Trinity Christian School
Athens, AL   35611

Athens Bible School
Athens, AL   35611

DECATUR AREA:

Grace Baptist Schools
1312 Riverview Ave., S.E.
  at Sherman St.
Decatur, AL   35601

ANDALUSIA AREA:

Montezuma Christian Academy
Box 277
Andalusia, AL   36420

EUFAULA AREA:

Grace Christian School
Route 4, P.O. Box 47A1
Eufaula, AL   36027

AUBURN AREA:

Lee Academy
2307 East Glenn Ave.
Auburn, AL   36830

THOMASVILLE AREA:

Messiah Lutheran Elementary
  School
Star Route 3, P.O. Box 42
Bashi, AL   36784

CENTREVILLE AREA:

Cahawba Christian Academy
P.O. Box 218
Centreville, AL   35042

ALASKA

ANCHORAGE AREA:

Anchorage Christian Schools
6401 East Northern Lights
  Blvd.
Anchorage, AK   99504

Anchorage Christian Academy
7145 Madelynne Dr.
Anchorage, AK   99504

East Park Christian Schools
  Church of God
1711 South Bragaw St.
Anchorage, AK   99504

Muldoon Christian School
7041 De Barr Rd.
Anchorage, AK   99504

Sonrise Christian School
7020 Foothill Dr.
Anchorage, AK   99508

Harvester Christian Academy
9101 Brayton Dr.
Anchorage, AK   99507

Koinonia Christian School
4601 Garfield St.
Anchorage, AK   99503

Anchorage School of Bible
  Doctrine
7337 Old Seward Hwy.
Anchorage, AK   99502

Abbott Loop Christian School
2626 Abbott Rd.
Anchorage, AK   99507

Lutheran Church of Faith
  Christian School
5200 Lake Otis Pkwy.
Anchorage, AK   99507

Seventh Day Adventist School
O'Malley Rd.
Anchorage, AK

FAIRBANKS AREA:

North Pole Christian Academy
North Pole, AK   99507

Hamilton Acres Baptist
  School
138 Farewell St.
Fairbanks, AK 99701

Lighthouse Christian
  Academy
324 Minnie St.
Fairbanks, AK 99701

Living Word Academy
1379 Alaska Hwy.
Delta Junction, AK 99737

Immaculate Conception
  Catholic School
715 Monroe St.
Fairbanks, AK 99701

PALMER-MATANUSKA AREA:

Matanuska Valley Christian
  Schools
555 North Gulkana St.
Palmer, AK 99645

Alaska Christian Bible
  Institute
P.O. Box 2770
Wasilia, AK 99687

Arctic Bible Institute
Lazy Mountain
Palmer, AK 99645

Eagle River Christian
  Academy
Old Glenn Hwy., Mile 15
Eagle River, AK 99577

Copper Valley Catholic
  School
Glennallen, AK 99588

BETHEL AREA:

Bethel Bible School
  Assembly of God
Bethel, AK 99559

KOTZEBUE AREA:

Friends School
Kotzebue, AK 99752

KODIAK AREA:

Kodiak Christian School
P.O. Box 49
Kodiak, AK 99615

Saint Mary's Catholic
  School
P.O. Box 725
Kodiak, AK 99615

KENAI AREA:

Soldotna-Cook Inlet Academy
Drawer 'A'
Soldotna, AK 99669

Kalifonski Christian School
Route 2, P.O. Box 857
Soldotna, AK 99669

SHUMAGIN ISLAND:

Christian School
Box 67
Sand Point, AK 99661

ARIZONA

PHOENIX AREA:

Phoenix Christian High
  School
1751 West Indian School Rd.
Phoenix, AZ 85015

Phoenix Christian School
2940 West Bethany Home Rd.
Phoenix, AZ 85017

Golden West Christian
  School
9827 North 32nd St.
Phoenix, AZ 85028

Westdale Christian School
3526 West Polk St.
Phoenix, AZ 85009

Westwood Christian School
5020 North 23rd Ave.
Phoenix, AZ 85015

Deer Valley Christian
  School
3302 West Sweetwater Ave.
Phoenix, AZ 85029

Paradise Valley Christian
  School
2401 East Cactus
Phoenix, AZ 85028

Phoenix Christian Grade
  School
2425 North 26th St.
Phoenix, AZ 85008

Light and Life School
  Free Methodist
4002 North 18th Ave.
Phoenix, AZ 85015

American Evangelical
  Lutheran Day School
18300 West Glenrosa Ave.
Phoenix, AZ 85033

Christ the King
  Lutheran School
3190 East Northern Ave.
Phoenix, AZ 85028

Good Shepherd Lutheran
  School
3040 North Seventh Ave.
Phoenix, AZ 85013

All Saints' Episcopal School
6300 North Central Ave.
Phoenix, AZ 85012

Brophy Catholic
  College Preparatory School
4707 North Central Ave.
Phoenix, AZ 85012

Gerard Catholic High School
2252 North 44th St.
Phoenix, AZ 85008

Bourgade Catholic High
  School
4602 North 31st Ave.
Phoenix, AZ 85017

Saint Mary's Catholic High
  School
230 East Polk St.
Phoenix, AZ 85004

TUCSON AREA:

Tucson Christian Schools
2855 North Craycroft St.
Tucson, AZ   85712

Palo Verde Christian School
2151 North Palo Verde Blvd.
Tucson, AZ   85716

Amphitheater Christian
 School
226 West Prince Rd.
Tucson, AZ   85705

Grace Christian School
6180 East Pima St.
Tucson, AZ   85712

Ironwood Hills Church
 School
2245 West Ironwood Hills Dr.
Tucson, AZ   85705

Redeemer Evangelical
 Lutheran School
200 East Yavapai Rd.
Tucson, AZ   85705

Good Shepherd Lutheran
 School
3600 East Pima St.
Tucson, AZ   85716

Faith Lutheran School
3925 East 5th St.
Tucson, AZ   85711

Seventh Day Adventist
 School of Tucson
3225 North Martin Ave.
Tucson, AZ   85719

Saint Michael's Episcopal
 School
Wilmot Rd. & 5th St.
Tucson, AZ   85711

Abbie Loveland Tuller
 Episcopal School
5870 East 14th St.
Tucson, AZ   85711

Suffolk Hills Catholic
 High School
625 East Magee Rd.
Tucson, AZ   85704

Cathedral Religious Education
 Center
415 South 6th Ave.
Tucson, AZ   85701

Saint John the Evangelist
 Catholic School
602 West Ajo Rd.
Tucson, AZ   85713

GLENDALE AREA:

Western Christian School
4030 North 67th Ave.
Glendale, AZ   85301

Northwest Christian Academy
14240 North 43rd Ave.
Glendale, AZ   85306

Grace Lutheran School
7161 North 56th Ave.
Glendale, AZ   85301

Thunderbird Academy
 Seventh Day Adventist
13401 North Scottsdale Rd.
Scottsdale, AZ   85254

Glenview Adventist School
6801 North 43rd Ave.
Glendale, AZ   85301

PRESCOTT AREA:

Prescott Christian School
815 Whipple St.
P.O. Box 1112
Prescott, AZ   86301

Vineyard Christian Academy
Highway 89, Chino Valley
Prescott, AZ   86301

Mountainview Christian
 Academy
394 Iron Springs Rd.
Prescott, AZ   86301

Fellowship Christian School
228 West Alarcon St.
Prescott, AZ   86301

Christian Academy of
 Prescott
P.O. Box 226
Prescott, AZ   86302

First Lutheran School
609 West Gurley St.
Prescott, AZ   86301

Sacred Heart Catholic School
131 North Summit Ave.
Prescott, AZ   86301

TEMPE AREA:

Tri-City Christian Academy
3230 South Price Rd.
Tempe, AZ   85282

Grace Community Christian
 School
3201 South Terrace Rd.
Box 26966
Tempe, AZ   85282

Emmanuel Evangelical
 Lutheran School
715 West Southern Ave.
Tempe, AZ   85282

Seventh Day Adventist School
630 West 17th Pl.
Tempe, AZ   85281

MESA AREA:

Central Christian School
315 North Hobson St.
Mesa, AZ   85203

Trinity Christian School
2402 Usery Pass Rd.
Mesa, AZ   85207

Redeemer Christian School
717 North Stapley Dr.
Mesa, AZ   85203

Phoenix Christian Grade
 School
2667 West Onza Ave.
Mesa, AZ   85202

Christ the King Catholic
 School
1545 East Dana Ave.
Mesa, AZ   85204

FLAGSTAFF AREA:

Flagstaff Christian School
2029 North 2nd St.
Flagstaff, AZ 86001

Nazarene Christian Day
 School
Soliere Blvd.
Flagstaff, AZ 86001

Saint Michael's Catholic
 High School
Saint Michael's, AZ 86511

YUMA AREA:

Yuma Lutheran School
255 South Engler Ave.
Yuma, AZ 85364

Seventh Day Adventist
 School
17th St. & 5th Ave.
Yuma, AZ 85364

Saint Francis of Assisi
 Catholic School
700 West 18th St.
Yuma, AZ 85364

CHANDLER AREA:

Chandler Christian School
301 North Hartford St.
Chandler, AZ 85224

Seton Catholic High School
300 East Williams Field Rd.
Chandler, AZ 85224

NOGALES AREA:

Mission of the Loving
 Shepherd Jr. & Sr. High
 School
Patagonia Rd.
Nogales, AZ 85621

TEEC NOS POS AREA:

Immanuel Mission School
Box 218
Teec Nos Pos, AZ 86514

WINDOW ROCK AREA:

Hilltop Christian School
c/o Navajo Bible School &
 Mission
Drawer F
Window Rock, AZ 86515

ORAIBI AREA:
 (HOPI INDIAN RESERVA-
  TION)

Hopi Mission School
P. O. Box 39
Oraibi, AZ 86039

SUN VALLEY AREA:

Twin Wells Indian School
Sun Valley, AZ 86025

ARKANSAS

LITTLE ROCK AREA:

Little Rock Christian
 Schools
10610 Chicot Rd.
Little Rock, AR 72204

Central Arkansas Christian
 Schools, Inc.
10900 North Rodney Parham
 Rd.
Little Rock, AR 72207

Central Christian Academy
5121 Baseline Rd.
Little Rock, AR 72206

Heritage Christian School
850 Stagecoach Rd.
Little Rock, AR 72204

Pinnacle Christian Academy,
 Inc.
Pinnacle & Guenther Rds.
Little Rock, AR 72207

Calvary Christian School
5924 Woodlawn St.
Little Rock, AR 72205

Jesus Name Christian
 School
P. O. Box 532
Beebe, AR 72012

Maumelle Accelerated
 Christian Education School
Maumelle, AR 72118

Park Place Baptist Academy
2221 South Broadway
Little Rock, AR 72206

First Lutheran School
315 South Hughes St.
Little Rock, AR 72205

Pentecostal Church of God
 School of Rose City
4128 Baucum Pike
North Little Rock, AR 72117

Seventh Day Adventist Jr.
 Academy
8708 North Rodney Parham
 Rd.
Little Rock, AR 72205

The Cathedral School
310 West 17th St.
Little Rock, AR 72206

Catholic High School
6300 Lee Ave.
Little Rock, AR 72205

Holy Souls Catholic School
910 North Tyler St.
Little Rock, AR 72205

FORT SMITH AREA:

Fort Smith Christian School
Windsor & Albert Pike
Fort Smith, AR 72904

Metro Christian Schools
4401 Windsor Dr.
Fort Smith, AR 72904

Victory Christian Academy
5211 South 29th St.
Fort Smith, AR 72901

Northside Christian Academy
  United Pentecostal
3700 Kelley Ave.
Fort Smith, AR   72904

First Lutheran School
2407 Massard Rd.
Fort Smith, AR   72903

Christ the King Catholic
  School
1918 South Greenwood St.
Fort Smith, AR   72901

Saint Boniface Catholic
  School
201 North 19th St.
Fort Smith, AR   72901

HOT SPRINGS AREA:

Hot Springs Christian
  Academy
516 Third St.
Hot Springs, AR   71901

Evangel Christian Academy
  Assembly of God
Mill Creek Rd.
Hot Springs, AR   71901

Sunshine Valley Academy
  Seventh Day Adventist
810 Ware Rd.
Hot Springs, AR   71901

Saint Michael's School
1125 Malvern St.
Hot Springs, AR   71901

EL DORADO AREA:

New Covenant Christian
  Academy
1214 South Washington St.
El Dorado, AR   71730

Seventh Day Adventist
  School
Strong Hwy.
El Dorado, AR   71730

Holy Redeemer Catholic
  School
1103 West Cedar St.
El Dorado, AR   71730

PINE BLUFF AREA:

Pine Bluff Christian School
523 West 6th St.
Pine Bluff, AR   71601

Maranatha Christian School
Lane & Holsey Sts.
Pine Bluff, AR   71602

Victory Baptist Academy
Olive & West 6th Ave.
Pine Bluff, AR   71601

Lutheran Day School
Pine & West 15th Sts.
Pine Bluff, AR   71601

Episcopal Day School
708 West 2nd St.
Pine Bluff, AR   71601

Saint Joseph Catholic
  School
West 7th Ave. at Olive St.
Pine Bluff, AR   71601

Saint Peter's Catholic
  School
Harding & Alabama Sts.
Pine Bluff, AR   71601

WEST MEMPHIS AREA:

West Memphis Christian
  School
1600 North Missouri St.
West Memphis, AR   72301

Tabernacle Baptist
  Academy
521 North Graham St.
West Memphis, AR   72301

Saint Michael's Catholic
  School
405 North Missouri St.
West Memphis, AR   72301

FAYETTEVILLE AREA:

Fayetteville Christian
  Academy
904 West 15th St.
Fayetteville, AR   72701

Benton County Christian
  School
2005 South 12th St.
Rogers, AR   72756

Saint Joseph Catholic School
321 East Lafayette St.
Fayetteville, AR   72701

JONESBORO AREA:

Jonesboro Christian School
2821 Forest Home
Jonesboro, AR   72401

Apostolic Christian School
622 West Oak
Jonesboro, AR   72401

Blessed Sacrament Catholic
  School
720 South Church St.
Jonesboro, AR   72401

TEXARKANA AREA:

Victory Baptist Academy
216 Wake Village Rd.
Texarkana, AR   75501

Seventh Day Adventist School
2422 Texas Blvd.
Texarkana, AR   75501

BLYTHEVILLE AREA:

Apostolic Christian School
P.O. Box F
Leachville, AR   72438

Presbyterian Christian
  Academy
901 Highland St.
Blytheville, AR   72315

Presbyterian Christian Day
  School
West Johnson & Elm St.
Osceola, AR   72370

Immaculate Conception
  Catholic School
103 South 13th St.
Blytheville, AR   72315

SPRINGDALE AREA:

Shiloh Baptist Christian
  Schools
301 Holcomb St.
Springdale, AR　72764

Cookson Hills Christian
  School
Route 4
Siloam Springs, AR　72761

SEARCY AREA:

Harding College Academy
  Church of Christ
South Blakeney St.
Searcy, AR　72143

Morris Catholic School
Box 137
Searcy, AR　72143

FORREST CITY AREA:

Calvary Christian School
1611 North Washington St.
Forrest City, AR　72335

CALIFORNIA

LOS ANGELES AREA:

Pacific Christian High School
625 Coleman Ave.
Los Angeles, CA　90042

Good News Christian School
8015 Sepulveda St.
Los Angeles, CA　90045

Golden West Christian School
1310 Liberty St.
Los Angeles, CA　90026

Faith Christian School
6201 South La Brea St.
Los Angeles, CA　90303

Marina Christian School
12606 Culver Blvd.
Los Angeles, CA　90066

Marshall Keeble Christian
  Institute
2941 West 70th St.
Los Angeles, CA　90043

Grace Christian School
15733 South Orange Ave.
Paramount, CA　90723

Peninsula Christian School
22507 South Figueroa St.
Carson, CA　90745

San Gabriel Christian School
117 North Pine St.
San Gabriel, CA　91775

First Christian Day School
225 South Santa Fe Ave.
Compton, CA　90221

Village Christian School
8930 Village Ave.
Sun Valley, CA　91352

Westminster Academy
1499 Colorado Ave.
Los Angeles, CA　90041

Christian Elementary School
6548 South Newlin Ave.
Whittier, CA　90601

Huntington Park Baptist Day
  School
2662 Clarendon Ave.
Huntington Park, CA　90255

Los Angeles Baptist High
  School
9825 Woodley Ave.
Sepulveda, CA　91343

Miracle Baptist Christian
  School
8314 South Central Ave.
Los Angeles, CA　90001

Mount Calvary Christian
  School
3770 Santa Rosalia Dr.
Los Angeles, CA　90008

Normandie Christian School
6306 South Normandie Ave.
Los Angeles, CA　90044

Nazarene Christian School
3154 East Gage Ave.
Huntington Park, CA　90255

Nazarene Christian School of
  Norwalk
15014 Studebaker Rd.
Norwalk, CA　90050

West Angeles Christian
  Academy
3010 Crenshaw Blvd.
Los Angeles, CA　90016

Pacifica Christian Schools
7547 East Quill Ave.
Downey, CA　90242

Gardena Valley Christian
  School
1473 West 182nd St.
Gardena, CA　90248

Hawthorne Christian School
13600 South Prairie St.
Hawthorne, CA　90250

Inglewood Christian School
215 East Hillcrest Blvd.
Inglewood, CA　90301

New Life Baptist Christian
  Day School
11516 State St.
Lynwood, CA　90262

Acacia Avenue Baptist Day
  School
P.O. Box 185
4712 El Sequndo Blvd.
Hawthorne, CA　90250

Calvary Baptist School
4081 West El Sequndo Blvd.
Hawthorne, CA　90250

Calvary Christian School
2400 West 85th St.
Inglewood, CA　90301

Lockhaven Christian School
3921 West 104th St.
Inglewood, CA　90303

Tarzana - Lindley Avenue
  Baptist Elementary School
5901 Lindley Ave.
Tarzana, CA   91356

Peninsula Baptist School
5640 Crestridge Rd.
Ranch Palo Verdes, CA
  90274

Manchester Baptist School
2627 West 116th St.
Inglewood, CA   90301

Bethany Baptist Elementary
  and Jr. High
10252 Mills Ave.
Whittier, CA   90604

First Baptist Christian
  School
100 North Pacific Coast Hwy.
Redondo Beach, CA   90277

Calvary Baptist School
2818 Manhattan Beach Blvd.
Manhattan Beach, CA   90266

South Bay Baptist Schools
1920 West Compton Blvd.
Gardena, CA   90249

Faith Presbyterian Alternative School
2057 West Century Blvd.
Los Angeles, CA   90047

Sycamore Grove School
  Pillar of Fire
4900 North Figueroa St.
Los Angeles, CA   90042

Los Angeles Academy
  Seventh Day Adventist
846 East El Segundo Blvd.
Los Angeles, CA   90059

Lynwood Adventist School
11011 Harris Ave.
Lynwood, CA   90262

Lutheran High School
2941 West 70th St.
Los Angeles, CA   90042

First Lutheran School
3119 West 6th St.
Los Angeles, CA   90020

Our Savior's Lutheran School
4270 West 6th St.
Los Angeles, CA   90005

Good Shepherd Lutheran
  Christian School
6338 North Figueroa St.
Los Angeles, CA   90042

Bethany Lutheran Day School
1518 North Alexandria Ave.
Los Angeles, CA   90027

Westchester Lutheran School
7831 South Sepulveda St.
Los Angeles, CA   90045

Chapel Lutheran School
1009 North Market St.
Inglewood, CA   90301

Trinity Lutheran School
4783 West 130th St.
Hawthorne, CA   90250

Pilgrim Lutheran School
1730 Wilshire Blvd.
Santa Monica, CA   90403

Saint James Episcopal School
615 South Gramercy Pl.
Los Angeles, CA   90005

Holy Nativity Episcopal School
260 North Locust St.
Inglewood, CA   90301

Saint Augustine-by-the-Sea
  Episcopal School
1227 4th St.
Santa Monica, CA   90401

Our Lady of Victory School
P.O. Box 5181
Mission Hills, CA   91345

Cathedral High School
1253 Stadium Way
Los Angeles, CA   90012

Daniel Murphy Catholic High
  School
241 South Detroit St.
Los Angeles, CA   90036

Mount Carmel Catholic High
  School
7011 South Hoover St.
Los Angeles, CA   90044

Salesian Catholic High School
960 South Soto St.
Los Angeles, CA   90023

Saint Monica's Catholic High
  School
7th & California Sts.
Santa Monica, CA   90403

Junipero Serra Catholic High
  School
14830 South Van Ness Ave.
Gardena, CA   90249

Pius X Catholic High School
7851 East Gardendale
Downey, CA   90242

Saint James Catholic School
122 North Pacific Coast Hwy.
Redondo Beach, CA   90277

Berkeley Hall Christian
  Science School Foundation
300 North Swall Dr.
Beverly Hills, CA   90211

SAN DIEGO AREA:

Christian High School of San
  Diego
2100 Greenfield Dr.
El Cajon, CA   92021

Linfield Christian High School
31950 Pauba Rd.
Temecula, CA   92390

Western Baptist Christian
  School
555 North Western Ave.
Brawley, CA   92227

Midway Christian Schools
2460 Palm Ave.
San Diego, CA   92154

Lighthouse Christian
Academy
7024 Amherst St.
San Diego, CA   92115

Calvin Christian School
1868 North Broadway
Escondido, CA   92026

Christian Elementary School
6747 Amherst
San Diego, CA   92105

Lakeside Christian School
13739 El Monte Rd.
Lakeside, CA   92040

Covenant Christian School
505 East Naples St.
Chula Vista, CA   92011

El Cajon Valley Christian
School
728 Pepper Dr.
El Cajon, CA   92021

Keystone Christian Schools
2151 Greenfield Dr.
El Cajon, CA   92021

South Bay Christian Academy
1905 East 18th St.
National City, CA   92050

Escondido Christian School
919 Idaho St., Box 715
Escondido, CA   92025

Heartland Christian School
2115 Imperial Ave.
Lemon Grove, CA   92045

Lemon Grove Christian
School
3150 Main St.
Lemon Grove, CA   92045

Hope Christian School
1307 East Brockton
Redlands, CA   92373

Light & Life Christian Day
School
120 North Ash St.
Escondido, CA   92027

Fundamental Baptist
Christian School
1111 North Ash St.
Escondido, CA   92027

Clairemont Christian School
Assembly of God
3811 Mt. Acadia Blvd.
San Diego, CA   92111

Saint Stephen's Christian
School
5825 Imperial Ave.
San Diego, CA   92114

Living Word Evangelical
Lutheran School
23561 Alicia Pkwy.
Mission Viejo, CA   92675

San Diego Academy
Seventh Day Adventist
2700 East Fourth St.
National City, CA   92050

San Miguel Episcopal School
6501 Linda Vista Rd.
San Diego, CA   92111

Southland Christian School
284 Zenith St., Box 3695
Chula Vista, CA   92011

SAN FRANCISCO AREA:

San Francisco Christian High
School
25 Whittier St.
San Francisco, CA   94112

San Francisco Christian
School
65 Dorland St.
San Francisco, CA   94110

Valley Christian School of
Marin
3 North San Pedro Rd.
San Rafael, CA   94903

Sunnyvale Christian School
1196 Lime Ave.
Sunnyvale, CA   94087

Valley Christian Jr. High
School
877 Pippin Dr.
Sunnyvale, CA   94087

Bridgemont Christian High
School
765 California St.
San Francisco, CA   94112

Highlands Academy
1900 Monterey Dr.
San Bruno, CA   94066

Contra Costa Christian High
2721 Larkey Ln.
Walnut Creek, CA   94596

Woodlands Christian Schools
2721 Larkey Ln.
Walnut Creek, CA   94596

Roger William School
Magnolia & Grand
San Francisco, CA   94123

San Francisco Jr. Academy
Seventh Day Adventist
66 Geneva Ave.
San Francisco, CA   94112

Saint John's Episcopal School
760 First Ave.
Chula Vista, CA   92010

Saint John's Lutheran School
1050 South Van Ness Ave.
San Francisco, CA   94109

Zion Lutheran School
495 Ninth Ave.
San Francisco, CA   94118

Saint Paul's Lutheran School
888 Turk St.
San Francisco, CA   94102

Lutheran Latino Ministries
School
1050 San Fernando Way
San Francisco, CA   94127

Saint Matthew's Episcopal
School
Baldwin & El Camino Real
San Mateo, CA   94401

Episcopal Cathedral School
 for Boys
1275 Sacramento St.
San Francisco, CA 94108

Saint Paul's High School
217 29th St.
San Francisco, CA 94110

Saint Paul's Intermediate
 School
1660 Church St.
San Francisco, CA 94131

Lutheran School of Saint
 Mark
East Arques Ave. & North
 Sunnyvale Ave.
Sunnyvale, CA 94086

Saint Francis Catholic High
 School
1885 Miramonte Ave.
Mountain View, CA 94040

Saint Ignatius Catholic High
 School
Stanyon & Turk Blvd.
San Francisco, CA 94118

Saint Vincent Catholic High
 School
1301 Geary Blvd.
San Francisco, CA 94109

Presentation Catholic High
 School
2350 Turk Blvd.
San Francisco, CA 94118

Mercy Catholic High School
3250 19th Ave.
San Francisco, CA 94110

Mercy Catholic High School
2750 Adeline Dr.
Burlingame, CA 94010

Most Holy Redeemer
 Catholic School
117 Diamond St.
San Francisco, CA 94114

SACRAMENTO AREA:

Sacramento Christian School
7361 24th St.
Sacramento, CA 95822

Sacramento Christian
 Education Center
641 Howe Ave.
Sacramento, CA 95825

American Heritage Christian
 Academy
6446 Lang Ave.
Sacramento, CA 95823

Trinity Christian School
4141 Madison Ave.
Sacramento, CA 95842

Woodland Christian School
1616 South West St.
Woodland, CA 95695

Victory Christian Schools
P.O. Box Q
Carmichael, CA 95608

Christian School
11525 Dillard Rd.
Wilton, CA 95693

Bible Baptist Christian School
1820 Bell St.
Sacramento, CA 95825

Temple Baptist Christian
 Academy
5540 Date Ave.
Sacramento, CA 95842

Colonial Baptist Christian
 Academy
4865 63rd St.
Sacramento, CA 95820

Sierra Christian Academy
Box 307
Durham, CA 95938

Main Avenue Christian
 Academy
5915 Main Ave.
Orangevale, CA 95662

Highlands Baptist School
3501 Q St., Box 1138
North Highlands, CA 95660

Forest Lake Christian School
12512 Combie Rd.
Auburn, CA 95603

Sacramento Friends School
4791 Franklin Blvd.
Sacramento, CA 95824

John Woolman Friends
 School
Route 1, Box J-26
Nevada City, CA 95959

Our Savior Lutheran School
5461 44th St.
Sacramento, CA 95820

Gloria Dei Lutheran School
4910 Lemon Hill Ave.
Sacramento, CA 95824

Saint Mark's Lutheran
 School
5747 Sunrise Blvd.
Citrus Heights, CA 95610

Christian Brothers Catholic
 High School
4315 Sacramento Blvd.
Sacramento, CA 95820

Saint Francis Catholic High
 School
6051 M St.
Sacramento, CA 95819

Oak Haven Academy
3600 37th St.
Sacramento, CA 95817

FREMONT AREA:

Fremont Christian School
4350 Hansen Ave.
Fremont, CA 94537

Prince of Peace Lutheran
 School
38451 Fremont Blvd.
Fremont, CA 94536

SAN JOSE AREA:

San Jose Christian Schools
1 West Campbell Ave.
Campbell, CA   95008

Valley Christian High School
15775 Sanborn Rd.
Saratoga, CA   95070

Valley Christian Jr. High
  School
3275 Williams Rd.
San Jose, CA   95117

Liberty Christian School
2790 South King Rd.
San Jose, CA   95122

Foothill Christian School
200 Abbott Ave.
Milpitas, CA   95035

Calvary Community
  Christian School
1175 Hillsdale Ave.
San Jose, CA   95118

North Valley Baptist
  Schools
941 Clyde Valley Rd.
Santa Clara, CA   95050

West Valley School
  Seventh Day Adventist
95 Dot Ave.
Campbell, CA   95008

Santa Clara Valley
  Lutheran School
5825 Bollinger Rd.
San Jose, CA   95129

Apostles Lutheran School
6085 Blossom Ave.
San Jose, CA   95123

Peace Lutheran School
885 Pomeroy Ave.
San Jose, CA   95121

Monte Vista Christian
  School
2 School Way
Watsonville, CA   95076

Archbishop Mitty Catholic
  High School
5000 Mitty Ave.
San Jose, CA   95129

Notre Dame Catholic High
  School
596 South Second St.
San Jose, CA   95112

OAKLAND AREA:

Patten Academy of Christian
  Education
2433 Coolidge Ave.
Oakland, CA   94601

American Heritage Christian
  Schools
31322 Medinah St.
Hayward, CA   94544

Christian Heritage Schools
24 Orinda Way
Orinda, CA   94563

Redwood Christian School
19300 Redwood Rd.
Castro Valley, CA   94546

Eastmont Christian Academy
2814 Havenscourt Blvd.
Oakland, CA   94605

Concord Christian School
2120 Olivera Ct.
Concord, CA   94520

Costa Christian School
1871 Arnold Dr.
Martinez, CA   94553

Berkeley Christian School
Dana & Haste Sts.
Berkeley, CA   94704

North Hills Christian School
200 Admiral Callaghan Ln.
Vallejo, CA   94590

Hilltop Christian School
210 Locust Dr.
Vallejo, CA   94590

Contra Costa Christian High
  School
2721 Larkey Ln.
Walnut Creek, CA   94598

Berean Christian High School
68 Morello Ave.
Martinez, CA   94553

Christian Center Schools
7997 Vomac Rd.
Dublin, CA   94566

Higher Heights Christian
  School
c/o John Muir Elementary
  School
205 Vista Way
Martinez, CA   94553

Alameda Christian School
2226 Pacific Ave.
Alameda, CA   94501

Manor Baptist Christian
  School
1845 Lewelling Blvd.
San Leandro, CA   94579

Pentecostal Way of Truth
  School Academy
1727 Grove St.
Oakland, CA   94612

Golden Gate Academy
  Seventh Day Adventist
3800 Mountain Blvd.
Oakland, CA   94619

Concordia Lutheran High
  School
4660 Harbor Dr.
Oakland, CA   94618

Redeemer Lutheran School
61st Ave. & Brann St.
Oakland, CA   94605

Zion Lutheran School
5201 Park Blvd.
Piedmont, CA   94611

Bethlehem Lutheran School
3100 Telegraph Ave.
Berkeley, CA   94705

Saint Peter's Lutheran
  School
294 Broadmoor Blvd.
San Leandro, CA 94577

Saint Paul's Episcopal
  School
116 Montecito Ave.
Oakland, CA 94610

Holy Names Catholic High
  School
4660 Harbor Dr.
Oakland, CA 94618

Saint Joseph's Catholic
  High School for Boys
1119 Lafayette St.
Alameda, CA 94501

Saint Patrick's Catholic
  High School
1500 Benicia Rd.
Vallejo, CA 94590

LONG BEACH AREA:

Artesia Christian School
17721 Norwalk Blvd.
Artesia, CA 90701

Light & Life Christian
  School
5951 Downy Ave.
Long Beach, CA 90805

Nazarene Christian School
  of Long Beach
5253 East Los Coyotes
  Diagonal
Long Beach, CA 90815

Community Christian
  Academy
6465 Cherry Ave.
Long Beach, CA 90805

Norwalk Christian School
11129 Pioneer Blvd.
Norwalk, CA 90650

Pioneer Christian School
15333 South Pioneer Blvd.
Norwalk, CA 90650

Nazarene Christian School
  of Norwalk
15014 South Studebaker Rd.
Norwalk, CA 90650

Bellflower Christian Schools
10818 Artesia Blvd.
Cerritos, CA 90701

Calvary Church Christian
  School
1010 North Tustin Ave.
Santa Ana, CA 92705

Vista Christian School
2966 18th St.
San Pablo, CA 94806

Brethren Jr.-Sr. High School
15733 South Orange Ave.
Paramount, CA 90723

Bethany Baptist Jr. High
  School
2244 Clark Ave.
Long Beach, CA 90815

First Baptist School
14000 San Antonio Dr.
Norwalk, CA 90650

Temple Baptist Schools
12722 Woods Ave.
Norwalk, CA 90650

Brethren School
11005 Foster Rd.
Norwalk, CA 90650

Long Beach Brethren School
3601 Linden Ave.
Long Beach, CA 90807

Seventh Day Adventist Schools
4951 Oregon Ave.
Long Beach, CA 90805

Saint John's Lutheran School
6650 Orange Ave.
Long Beach, CA 90805

First Lutheran School
946 Linden Ave.
Long Beach, CA 90813

Bethany Lutheran School
5100 East Arbor Rd.
Long Beach, CA 90808

Saint Thomas of Canterbury
  Episcopal School
5306 East Arbor Rd.
Long Beach, CA 90808

Saint Anthony's Catholic High
  School
650 Olive Ave.
Long Beach, CA 90812

PALO ALTO AREA:

New Covenant Christian High
  School
655 Arastradero St.
Palo Alto, CA 94306

Los Altos Christian School
625 Magdalene Ave.
Los Altos, CA 94022

Canterbury Christian School
101 North El Monte
Los Altos, CA 94022

Trinity Christian Academy
38325 Cedar Blvd.
Newark, CA 94560

Our Lady of the Rosary
  Catholic School
3290 Middlefield Rd.
Palo Alto, CA 94306

ANAHEIM AREA:

Anaheim Baptist Christian
  School
305 East Broadway
Anaheim, CA 92805

Bethany Christian Academy
14782 Eden St.
Midway City, CA 92655

Knott Avenue Christian
  School
315 South Knott Ave.
Anaheim, CA 92804

First Southern Baptist
Christian School
10350 Ellsworth Ave.
Anaheim, CA 92805

Dominion Christian School
925 East North St.
Anaheim, CA 92805

Community Christian School
400 West Vermont Ave.
Anaheim, CA 92805

Santa Ana Christian School
917 South Newhope St.
Santa Ana, CA 92704

Christian Life Academy
512 East Santa Ana Blvd.
Santa Ana, CA 92706

Bethel Christian Schools
901 South Euclid St.
Santa Ana, CA 92704

First Christian Church
School
1720 West 17th St.
Santa Ana, CA 92706

Trinity Lutheran Christian
Day School
4101 East Nohl Ranch Rd.
Anaheim, CA 92806

Grace Lutheran Christian
School
700 West South St.
Anaheim, CA 92805

Prince of Peace Lutheran
Christian Day School
1421 West Ball Rd.
Anaheim, CA 92802

Heritage Baptist Jr. High
School
227 North Magnolia Ave.
Anaheim, CA 92801

Grand Avenue United
Methodist School
2121 North Grand Ave.
Santa Ana, CA 92701

Zion Lutheran School
205 North East St.
Anaheim, CA 92805

Peace Lutheran School
18542 Vanderlip Ave.
Tustin, CA 92680

Trinity Lutheran School
906 South Broadway
Santa Ana, CA 92701

Saint Catherine's Catholic
Military School
215 North Harbor
Anaheim, CA 92805

Mater Dei Catholic High
School
1202 West Edinger Ave.
Santa Ana, CA 92707

Saint John the Baptist
Catholic School
1021 West Baker St.
Costa Mesa, CA 92626

FRESNO AREA:

Fresno Christian Schools
606 West Dakota St.
Fresno, CA 93705

West Fresno Christian
Academy
544 Trinity St.
Fresno, CA 93706

Ashlan Park Christian School
3740 East Ashlan Ave.
Fresno, CA 93726

Central Valley Christian
School
11948 Flint Ave.
Hanford, CA 93230

Immanuel Christian Mennonite
High School
1128 South Reed St.
Reedley, CA 93654

Mountain View Christian
School
1284 East Bullard Ave.
Fresno, CA 93710

Riverdale Christian Academy
2813 West Mt. Whitney St.
Fresno, CA 93725

Jesus Name Christian
Academy
252 East Glenn Ave.
Coalinga, CA 93210

Madera Baptist Christian
Academy
27315 Stanford Ave.
Madera, CA 93637

Christian Academy
Box 276
Kerman, CA 93630

Fresno Apostolic Christian
School
145 F St.
Fresno, CA 93706

New Life Jr.-Sr. High
School
255 West Bullard Ave.
Fresno, CA 93704

Chestnut Avenue Baptist
Academy
1461 North Chestnut St.
Fresno, CA 93703

Valley Baptist Academy
101 Barstow Ave.
Clovis, CA 93612

Fresno Adventist Academy
5397 East Olive Ave.
Fresno, CA 93727

Emmanuel Lutheran School
2822 East Floradora Ave.
Fresno, CA 93703

Armenian Community School
537 M St.
Fresno, CA 93718

Episcopal School Center
4147 East Dakota Ave.
Fresno, CA 93726

San Joaquin Memorial
Catholic High School
1406 North Fresno St.
Fresno, CA 93703

RIVERSIDE AREA:

Riverside Christian High
  School
3532 Monroe St.
Riverside, CA 92504

Newport Christian High
  School
883 West 15th St.
Newport Beach, CA 92660

Grace Christian School
25800 Pacific St.
San Bernardino, CA 92404

Garden Grove Christian
  School
13201 Century Blvd.
Garden Grove, CA 92640

Fullerton Christian School
1425 South Brookhurst Rd.
Fullerton, CA 92633

Orange Christian School
2830 North Glassell St.
Orange, CA 92667

Costa Mesa Christian School
740 West Wilson St.
Costa Mesa, CA 92627

Glen Avon Christian School
9021 Hastings Blvd.
Riverside, CA 92509

Liberty Christian School
7661 Warner Ave.
Huntington Beach, CA 92647

St. Luke's Christian School
13552 Golden W.
Westminster, CA 92683

Temple Christian School
P.O. Box 657
745 North Perris Blvd.
Perris, CA 92370

Inland Christian School
1024 North "G"
San Bernardino, CA 92410

Hope Christian School
1309 East Brockton
Redlands, CA 92373

Redlands Christian School
1145 Church St.
Redlands, CA 92373

Hesperia Christian School
P.O. Box 1122
16775 Olive St.
Hesperia, CA 92345

Baptist Christian School
26089 Girard St.
Hemet, CA 92343

Temple Baptist School
615 East Cypress St.
Redlands, CA 92373

Crystal Cathedral Academy
4201 West Chapman Ave.
Orange, CA 92668

Bethel Baptist Christian
  School
10750 Lampson Ave.
Garden Grove, CA 92640

Whittier Christian School
1601 West Malvern Ave.
Fullerton, CA 92633

Friends Christian School
5211 Lakeview Ave.
Yorba Linda, CA 92686

Eastside Christian School
2505 East Yorba Linda Blvd.
Fullerton, CA 92631

Independence Christian
  School
1820 East Meats Ave.
Orange, CA 92667

American Christian School
2591 Irvine Ave.
Costa Mesa, CA 92627

Riverside Adventist School
4850 Jurupa Ave.
Riverside, CA 92504

Orangewood Academy
  Adventist High School
13732 Clinton Ave.
Garden Grove, CA 92640

Lutheran High School of
  Orange County
2222 North Santiago Blvd.
Orange, CA 92667

Saint Paul's Lutheran School
5939 Magnolia St.
Riverside, CA 92506

Immanuel Lutheran School
5545 Alessandro Blvd.
Riverside, CA 92506

King of Kings Lutheran Day
  School
13431 Newhope St.
Garden Grove, CA 92640

Saint Paul's Lutheran School
13082 Bowen St.
Garden Grove, CA 92640

Saint John's Lutheran School
154 South Shaffer St.
Orange, CA 92666

Immanuel Lutheran School
147 South Pine St.
Orange, CA 92667

Notre Dame Catholic High
  School
7085 Brockton St.
Riverside, CA 92506

Rosary Catholic High School
1340 North Acacia Ave.
Fullerton, CA 92631

Whittier Christian Jr. High
  School
4221 Rose Dr.
Yorba Linda, CA 92686

TORRANCE AREA:

Coast Christian School
25600 Crenshaw Blvd. at
  Pacific Coast Hwy.
Torrance, CA 90505

Vermont Avenue Baptist
  Christian School
23325 South Vermont Ave.
Torrance, CA 90502

Harbor City Christian High
  School
840 255th St.
Harbor City, CA   90710

Whittier Christian High
  School
8221 South College Ave.
Whittier, CA   90605

Whittier Christian Schools
6548 South Newlin Ave.
Whittier, CA   90601

Valley Christian Jr. High
  School
18100 Dumont St.
Cerritos, CA   90701

Bellflower Christian
  Elementary School
17408 South Grand Ave.
Bellflower, CA   90706

Woodruff Christian School
16400 South Woodruff St.
Bellflower, CA   90706

Wilmington Christian School
931 Frigate Ave.
Wilmington, CA   90744

Peninsula Christian School
22507 South Figueroa St.
Carson, CA   90744

Harbor City Christian School
25416 South Vermont Ave.
Harbor City, CA   90710

Valley Christian High School
10818 Artesia Blvd.
Cerritos, CA   90701

First Baptist Christian School
1360 Broad Ave.
Wilmington, CA   90710

Christ Lutheran Christian
  Day School
28850 South Western St.
San Pedro, CA

Happiness Christian School
5202 Lincoln Ave.
Cypress, CA   90630

Calvary Christian Academy
7272 Cerritos Ave.
Stanton, CA   90680

South Bay Jr. Academy
  Seventh Day Adventist
4400 Del Amo Blvd.
Torrance, CA   90503

Seventh Day Adventist
  School
15548 South Santa Ana Ave.
Bellflower, CA   90706

First Lutheran School of
  Torrance
1725 Flower Ave.
Torrance, CA   90503

Ascension Lutheran School
17910 Prairie Ave.
Torrance, CA   90504

Saint Peter's Episcopal Day
  School
1648 9th St.
San Pedro, CA   90732

Saint John Bosco Catholic
  High School
13640 South Bellflower Blvd.
Bellflower, CA   90706

Bishop Montgomery Catholic
  High School
5430 Torrance Blvd.
Torrance, CA   90503

GLENDALE AREA:

Westminster Presbyterian
  Academy
620 North Glendale Ave.
Glendale, CA   91206

Pasadena Christian School
1515 North Los Robles Ave.
Pasadena, CA   91104

Arcadia Christian School
9845 East Lemon Ave.
Arcadia, CA   91006

Heritage Christian School
213 South Kenwood St.
Glendale, CA   91205

Elementary School
  First Baptist Church of
  Reseda
18644 Sherman Way
Reseda, CA   91335

Christian Heritage School
26534 Oak Crossing Rd.
Newhall, CA   91321

Calvary Christian School
610 North Glendale Ave.
Glendale, CA   91206

Faith Center Christian School
1615 South Glendale Ave.
Glendale, CA   91205

First Baptist Christian Day
  School
P.O. Box 177
Newhall, CA   91321

Panorama Baptist Elementary
  School
8755 Woodman Ave.
Pacoma, CA   91331

First Church of Christ
  Day School
727 Kewen St.
San Fernando, CA   91340

Salem Lutheran School
1201 North Brand Blvd.
Glendale, CA   91202

Zion Lutheran School
301 North Isabel St.
Glendale, CA   91206

Glendale Armenian School
1200 Carlton Dr.
Glendale, CA   91205

Saint Francis Catholic High
  School
4440 La Canada-Verdugo Rd.
Pasadena, CA   91101

Holy Family Catholic High
  School
400 East Lomita Ave.
Glendale, CA   91205

La Salle Catholic High
School
3880 East Sierra Madre
Blvd.
Pasadena, CA 91107

STOCKTON AREA:

Stockton Christian High
School
1981 East Cherokee Rd.
Stockton, CA 95205

Nazarene Christian School
915 Rose Marie Ln.
Stockton, CA 95207

Evangelical Methodist
School
2295 East Fremont St.
Stockton, CA 95205

Sierra Christian School
4386 North Sutter St.
Stockton, CA 95204

Walnut Creek Christian
Academy
2336 Buena Vista Ave.
Walnut Creek, CA 94596

Christian Life School
3950 Clayton Rd.
Concord, CA 94521

Evangel Christian School
Assembly of God
3040 East Fremont St.
Stockton, CA 95205

Ygnacio Valley Christian
School
5440 Michigan Blvd.
Concord, CA 94521

Tabernacle Baptist School
4380 Concord Blvd.
Concord, CA 94521

Calvary Baptist School
703 East Swain Rd.
Stockton, CA 95207

Seventh Day Adventist
School
3849 North Alvarado Ave.
Stockton, CA 95204

Trinity Lutheran School
444 North American St.
Stockton, CA 95202

Saint Mary's Catholic High
School
5648 North El Dorado St.
Stockton, CA 95207

Annunciation Catholic
School
1110 North Lincoln St.
Stockton, CA 95203

POMONA AREA:

Pomona Valley Christian
School
845 East Arrow Hwy.
Pomona, CA 91767

Western Christian High
School
490 East La Verne Ave.
Pomona, CA 91767

Ontario Christian High
School
931 West Philadelphia St.
Ontario, CA 91761

Ontario Elementary School
1907 South Euclid Ave.
Ontario, CA 91761

American Christian Academy
397 San Bernardino Ave.
Pomona, CA 91767

Bible Missionary Christian
Day School
788 East Grand Ave.
Pomona, CA 91766

First Baptist Church School
621 North Garey Ave.
Pomona, CA 91767

Pathway Christian School
1024 East Phillips Blvd.
Pomona, CA 91766

Laurel Hall School
11919 Oxnard St., N.
Hollywood, CA 91606

South Hills Academy
17250 East Francisquito Ave.
West Covina, CA 91791

Campbell Hall Argyll School
4533 Laurel Canyon Blvd.
North Hollywood, CA 91344

First Christian Disciple
School
1751 North Park Ave.
Pomona, CA 91767

Salem Christian School for the
Handicapped
1056 East Philadelphia St.
Ontario, CA 91761

San Gabriel Christian School
117 North Pine St.
San Gabriel, CA 91775

West Covina Christian School
763 North Sunset
West Covina, CA 91790

Santa Fe Springs Christian
School
11457 Florence Ave.
Santa Fe Springs, CA 90670

Western Christian School
1115 East Puente St.
Covina, CA 91724

Via Vera Christian School
7615 Lankershim Blvd.
North Hollywood, CA 91605

Lutheran High School
7500 Glenoaks Blvd.
Burbank, CA 91504

Lutheran School of Foothills
3561 Foothill Blvd.
La Crescenta, CA 91214

Alhambra First Lutheran
School
840 South Almansor St.
Alhambra, CA 91801

Pacific Ackworth Friends
School
6210 Temple City Blvd.
Temple City, CA 91780

Harvard Episcopal School
3700 Coldwater Canyon Rd.
North Hollywood, CA 91604

Saint Paul Catholic High
  School
9635 Greenleaf Ave.
Santa Fe Springs, CA 90670

All Souls Catholic School
29 South Electric Ave.
Alhambra, CA 91801

Saint Joseph Catholic School
1200 West Holt Ave.
Pomona, CA 91766

BAKERSFIELD AREA:

Bakersfield Baptist Christian
  School
714 Columbus St.
Bakersfield, CA 93305

Christian School of Santa
  Barbara
935 San Andres St.
Santa Barbara, CA 93101

Hanford Christian Elementary
  School
11948 Flint Ave.
Hanford, CA 93230

Ridgecrest Christian School
731 North Sanders
Ridgecrest, CA 93555

Pilgrim Christian School
c/o Paul W. Neipp
209 South Goss St.
Ridgecrest, CA 93555

Christian School of Santa
  Barbara
2028 Alameda Parde Serra
Santa Barbara, CA 93103

Central Valley Elementary
  School
1030 South Linwood
Visalia, CA 93277

Bethel Apostolic Pentecostal
  Academy
1418 West Columbus St.
Bakersfield, CA 93301

Bakersfield Academy
  Seventh Day Adventist
3333 Bernard St.
Bakersfield, CA 93306

Midland Episcopal School
Los Olivos, CA 93441

Cate Episcopal School
Carpinteria, CA 93013

SALINAS AREA:

Salinas Christian Schools
345 East Alvin Dr.
Salinas, CA 93906

Faith Landmark Missionary
  Baptist School
111 Prado St.
Salinas, CA 93906

Faith Christian School
1354 Cherokee Dr.
Salinas, CA 93906

Prunedale Christian Academy
8145 Prunedale Rd., N.
Salinas, CA 93907

Winham Street Christian
  Academy
526 California St.
Salinas, CA 93901

Valley Christian Academy
1949 Waring St.
Seaside, CA 93955

Seventh Day Adventist
  School
1025 Mescal St.
Seaside, CA 93955

Seventh Day Adventist
  School
2020 Santa Ana Rd.
Hollister, CA 95023

The York Episcopal School
9501 Salinas Hwy.
Salinas, CA 93901

The York Episcopal School
Laguna Seca, Box 529
Monterey, CA 93940

All Saints Episcopal Day
  School
Route 2, Box 763
Salinas, CA 93901

Palma Catholic High School
  for Boys
919 Iverson St.
Salinas, CA 93901

Notre Dame Catholic High
  School
455 Palma Dr.
Salinas, CA 93901

SANTA BARBARA AREA:

Santa Ynez Valley Christian
  School
2199 Creekside Dr.
Solvang, CA 93463

BARSTOW AREA:

A Lane Christian School
412 A Lane
Barstow, CA 92311

MODESTO AREA:

Modesto Christian School
3200 Tulley Rd.
Modesto, CA 95350

Pacific Christian Academy
  Church of Christ
Box 300
Graton, CA 95444

Ripon Christian School
217 North Maple St.
Ripon, CA 95366

Ripon Christian High School
435 North Maple
Ripon, CA 95366

Mariposa Christian School
P.O. Box 724
Mariposa, CA 95338

Turlock Christian School
1360 North Johnson Rd.
Turlock, CA 95380

Merced Christian School
3312 North G St.
Merced, CA 95340

Atwater Christian School
5809 North Winton Way
Atwater, CA 95301

Grace Mennonite School
7200 North Central Ave.
Winton, CA 95388

Calvary Christian School
1900 Highland Dr.
Hollister, CA 95023

Seventh Day Adventist
  School
3351 M St.
Merced, CA 95340

Modesto Union Academy
  Seventh Day Adventist
Hatch & North Central Sts.
Modesto, CA 95351

Redwood Empire Jr. Academy
  Seventh Day Adventist
950 Wright Rd.
Santa Rosa, CA 95401

EUREKA AREA:

Shepherd's Staff Christian
  School
625 15th St.
Eureka, CA 95501

The Christian School
1700 Union St.
Arcata, CA 95521

Redwood Valley Christian
  School
8555 Uva Dr.
Redwood Valley, CA 95470

The Four R School
R.F.D. Box 597
Fortuna, CA 95540

Hazel Avenue Baptist
  Christian School
5010 Hazel Ave.
Fair Oaks, CA 95628

Faith Lutheran School
9133 Fair Oaks Blvd.
Fair Oaks, CA 95628

Fortuna Jr. Academy
  Seventh Day Adventist
1200 Ross Hill Rd.
Rohnerville, CA 95540

Saint Bernard's Catholic High
  School
222 Dollison St.
Eureka, CA 95501

HUNTINGTON BEACH AREA:

Liberty Christian School
7661 Warner Ave.
Huntington Beach, CA 92647

HAYWARD AREA:

Hayward Christian School
354 B St.
Hayward, CA 94541

Landmark Baptist School
573 Bartlett Ave.
Hayward, CA 94541

SANTA ROSA AREA:

Rincon Valley Christian
  School
697 Benicia Dr.
Santa Rosa, CA 95405

FAIRFIELD AREA:

Vaca Valley Christian School
185 Chandler St.
Vacaville, CA 95688

Solanos Christian Academy
P.O. Box 2409
Fairfield, CA 94533

SANTA MARIA AREA:

Baptist School
Box 586
Santa Maria, CA 93454

LANCASTER AREA:

Lancaster Christian School
44339 North Beech Ave.
Lancaster, CA 93534

PALM SPRINGS AREA:

Christian School of the
  Desert
P.O. Box 31
Palm Desert, CA 92260

PITTSBURG AREA:

Christian Center School
1210 Stoneman Ave.
Pittsburg, CA 94565

CHICO AREA:

Independence Christian School
P.O. Box 1778
Chico, CA 95927

SAN CLEMENTE AREA:

Del Ray Christian School
221 South Ala Vista
Suite 203
San Clemente, CA 92672

REDDING AREA:

Northstate Schools
1195 North Balls Ferry Rd.
Anderson, CA 96007

Intermountain Christian
  School
P.O. Box 595
Burney, CA 96013

Grace Baptist Schools
3782 Churn Creek Rd.
Redding, CA 96001

CARLSBAD AREA:

Victory Christian High School
3175 Harding
Carlsbad, CA 92008

VICTORVILLE AREA:

Victor Valley Christian
  School
14411 La Paz
Victorville, CA   92392

ATASCADERO AREA:

North County Christian
  School
P.O. Box 1089
Atascadero, CA   93422

EL SOBRANTE AREA:

Bethel Christian Academy
431 Rincon Ln.
El Sobrante, CA   94803

El Sobrante Christian
  School
5100 Argyle Rd.
El Sobrante, CA   94803

TUOLUMNE AREA:

Mother Lode Christian
  School
P.O. Box 401
Tuolumne, CA   95379

COLORADO

DENVER AREA:

Denver Christian High School
2135 South Pearl St.
Denver, CO   80210

Denver Intermediate
  Christian School
735 East Florida Ave.
Denver, CO   80210

Colorado Christian Schools
2480 East Alameda Ave.
Denver, CO   80209

Tilden Day School
202 Plateau Pkwy.
Golden, CO   80401

Calvary Temple Day School
200 South University Blvd.
Denver, CO   80209

Van Dellen Christian School
4200 East Warren Ave.
Denver, CO   80222

Mountain States Baptist
  Academy
8333 Acoma Way
Denver, CO   80221

East Denver Christian
  School
1151 Xenia St.
Denver, CO   80220

Mile High Baptist School
8100 West Hampden Ave.
Denver, CO   80227

Silver State Baptist School
875 South Sheridan Blvd.
Denver, CO   80226

Christian Schools of
  Lakewood
3241 West 44th Ave.
Lakewood, CO   80215

Montbello Christian School
12505 Elmendorf Pl.
Denver, CO   80239

Beth Eden Baptist Schools
2600 Wadsworth Blvd.
Denver, CO   80215

Center of Hope Christian
  School
8400 West 94th Ave. at
  Wadsworth Hwy. 121
Denver, CO   80221

Cherry Creek Christian
  Academy
62100 South Yosemite St.
Denver, CO   80237

Liberty Christian School
5450 West 120th Ave.
Denver, CO   80234

Temple Baptist Academy
2727 South Sheridan Blvd.
Denver, CO   80227

Abundant Life Christian
  Center
6980 Pierce St.
Denver, CO   80214

Adams City Baptist School
6951 Dexter St.
Denver, CO   80022

I AM School, Inc.
777 Ogden St.
Denver, CO   80218

Lutheran High School
3201 West Arizona Ave.
Denver, CO   80219

Christ-University Hills
  Lutheran School
4949 East Eastman Ave.
Denver, CO   80222

Emmaus Lutheran School
3120 Irving St.
Denver, CO   80211

Redeemer Lutheran School
3400 West Nevada Pl.
Denver, CO   80219

Faith Lutheran School
4780 Eliot St.
Denver, CO   80211

Gethsemane Lutheran School
10675 North Washington St.
Denver, CO   80233

Grace Lutheran School
875 Forest St.
Denver, CO   80220

Belleview Preparatory School
1845 Champa St.
Denver, CO   80202

Seventh Day Adventist Schools
711 East Yale Ave.
Denver, CO   80210

Saint Anne's Episcopal
  School
2701 South York St.
Denver, CO 80210

Central Catholic High
  School
1836 Logan St.
Denver, CO 80203

Colorado Catholic Academy
3227 Chase St.
Denver, CO 80212

Saint Andrew High School
1050 South Birch St.
Denver, CO 80222

J. K. Mullen Catholic High
  School
3601 South Lowell Blvd.
Denver, CO 80211

Regis Catholic High School
West 50th Ave. & Lowell
  Blvd.
Denver, CO 80221

Saint Mary's Catholic Sr.
  High School
4545 South University Blvd.
Denver, CO 80210

Saint Mary's of Littleton
  Catholic Jr. High School
6833 South Prince St.
Littleton, CO 80120

Christ the King Catholic
  School
860 Elm St.
Denver, CO 80220

Academy Saint Scholastica
615 Pike Ave.
Canon City, CO 91212

COLORADO SPRINGS AREA:

Colorado Springs Christian
  School
301 Austin Bluffs Pkwy.
Colorado Springs, CO 80907

Evangelical Alliance
  Christian Academy
2511 North Logan Ave.
Colorado Springs, CO 80907

American Heritage Christian
  School
1218 Prairie Rd.
Colorado Springs, CO 80909

Security Christian Academy
208 Cunningham Dr.
Colorado Springs, CO 80911

Dunamis Christian Charis-
  matic Schools of Colorado
505 Castle Rd.
Colorado Springs, CO 80904

Seventh Day Adventist
  School
5410 Palmer Park Blvd.
Colorado Springs, CO 80915

Immanuel Lutheran Jr. &
  Sr. High School
838 East Pikes Peak
Colorado Springs, CO 80903

Mount Olive Evangelical
  Lutheran Christian Day
  School
918 East Cache La Poudre
Colorado Springs, CO 80903

Redeemer Lutheran School
2221 North Wahsatch Ave.
Colorado Springs, CO 80907

Saint Mary's Catholic High
  School
15 North Sierra Madre Ave.
Colorado Springs, CO 80902

Divine Redeemer Catholic
  School
901 North Logan Ave.
Colorado Springs, CO 80909

Pauline Memorial Catholic
  School
1601 Mesa Ave.
Colorado Springs, CO 80906

Holy Trinity Catholic School
3115 Larkspur Dr.
Colorado Springs, CO 80907

AURORA AREA:

Aurora Christian Academy
11001 East Alameda Ave.
Aurora, CO 80012

Rocky Mountain Christian
  Academy
1294 Fraser St.
Aurora, CO 80011

Arvada Christian Academy
5690 Yukon St.
Arvada, CO 80002

Arvada Christian School
11706 West 82nd Ave.
Arvada, CO 80005

Seventh Day Adventist Day
  Schools
7050 West 64th Ave.
Arvada, CO 80003

PUEBLO AREA:

Park Hill Christian Academy
1302 East Fifth St.
Pueblo, CO 81001

John Neumann Catholic School
800 East Routt St.
Pueblo, CO 81005

ALAMOSA AREA:

Valley Christian School
P. O. Box 1263
Alamosa, CO 81101

BOULDER AREA:

Highland Baptist School
3910 Table Mesa Dr.
Boulder, CO 80303

Seventh Day Adventist
  School
2641 4th St.
Boulder, CO 80302

Sacred Heart Catholic Jr.
  High School
1315 Mapleton Ave.
Boulder, CO 80302

FORT COLLINS AREA:

Heritage Christian School
1500 Ellis St.
Fort Collins, CO   80524

Loveland Christian School
4032 Boxelder Dr.
Loveland, CO   80537

Protestant Reformed
  Christian School
809 East 57th St.
Loveland, CO   80537

Seventh Day Adventist School
821 West Lake St.
Fort Collins, CO   80521

St. Joseph's Catholic School
127 North Howes St.
Fort Collins, CO   80521

BRIGHTON AREA:

Elmwood Baptist School
13100 East 144th Ave.
Brighton, CO   80601

Seventh Day Adventist Day
  Schools
820 South 5th Ave.
Brighton, CO   80601

Zion Lutheran School
1400 Skeel
Brighton, CO   80601

GREELEY AREA:

Dayspring Christian Schools
3451 23rd Ave.
Greeley, CO   80631

Greeley Catholic School
1112 9th Ave.
Greeley, CO   80631

LONGMONT AREA:

Faith Baptist School
833 15th Ave.
Longmont, CO   80501

SNYDER AREA:

Riverview Christian School
29269 4th St.
Snyder, CO   80850

ENGLEWOOD AREA:

Cherry Creek Christian
  Academy
9020 East Fair Ave.
Englewood, CO   80110

DURANGO AREA:

Durango Christian School
2201 Forest Ave.
P.O. Box 3212
Durango, CO   81301

CONNECTICUT

HARTFORD AREA:

Hartford Christian Academy
212 King Philip Dr.
West Hartford, CT   06007

Watkinson School
180 Bloomfield Ave.
Hartford, CT   06105

Westminster Presbyterian
  School
995 Hopmeadow
Hartford, CT

The Master's School
P.O. Box 143
West Simsbury, CT   06092

Emmanuel Christian
  Academy
Newington, CT   06111

Northwest Catholic High
  School
29 Wampanoag Dr.
West Hartford, CT   06007

South Catholic High School
215 South St.
Hartford, CT   06114

Cathedral of Saint Joseph
  Catholic School
809 Asylum Ave.
Hartford, CT   06105

Saint Michael's Ukrainian
  Catholic School
125 Wethersfield Ave.
Hartford, CT   06114

BRIDGEPORT AREA:

Christian Heritage School
575 White Plains Rd.
Bridgeport, CT   06611

Brooklawn Intermediate
  School
230 Brooklawn Ave.
Bridgeport, CT   06604

Zion Lutheran School
612 Grand St.
Bridgeport, CT   06604

Abbie Loveland Tuller
  Episcopal School
144 Tuller Rd.
Fairfield, CT   06430

Notre Dame Catholic High
  School of Bridgeport
Jefferson St.
Fairfield, CT   06430

Holy Name of Jesus
  Catholic School
1950 Barnum Ave.
Stratford, CT   06497

WATERBURY AREA:

Waterbury Christian Day
  School
359 Cooke St.
Waterbury, CT   06710

Waterbury Baptist Christian
  Academy
300 North Main St.
Waterbury, CT   06702

The Gunnery Congregational
  School
Washington, CT   06793

Canterbury Episcopal School
Aspetuck Ave.
New Milford, CT   06776

South Kent Episcopal School
South Kent, CT   06785

Kent Episcopal School
Kent, CT   06757

Waterbury Catholic High
  School
130 South Elm St.
Waterbury, CT   06702

Holy Cross Catholic High
  School
587 Oronoke Rd.
Waterbury, CT   06708

Sacred Heart Catholic High
  School
142 South Elm St.
Waterbury, CT   06710

Saints Peter & Paul Catholic
  School
116 Beecher Ave.
Waterbury, CT   06705

NORWALK AREA:

Parkway Christian Academy
260 New Canaan Ave.
Norwalk, CT   06850

The Colonial Christian
  School
34 Whipple Rd.
Wilton, CT   06897

Ridgefield Christian School
325 Danbury Rd.
Ridgefield, CT   06877

Saint Luke's High School
377 North Wilton Rd.
New Canaan, CT   06840

Central Catholic High
  School
West Rocks Rd.
Norwalk, CT   06851

NEW BRITAIN AREA:

Saint Matthews Lutheran
  School
87 Franklin Sq.
New Britain, CT   06051

Salisbury Episcopal School
Salisbury, CT   06068

Saint Thomas Aquinas
  Catholic High School
30 Pendleton Rd.
New Britain, CT   06053

DANBURY AREA:

Immanuel Lutheran School
35 Foster St.
Danbury, CT   06810

Wooster Episcopal School
Ridgebury Rd.
Danbury, CT   06810

Immaculate Catholic High
  School
Southern Blvd.
Danbury, CT   06810

St. Peter's Catholic School
98 Main St.
Danbury, CT   06810

MANCHESTER AREA:

Messiah Lutheran School
1075 Tolland Turnpike
Manchester, CT   06040

East Catholic High School
115 New State Rd.
Manchester, CT   06040

WINDSOR AREA:

Loomis School
  Interdenominational
Windsor, CT   06095

Connecticut Valley
  Adventist School
Foster Rd. S.
Windsor, CT   06095

HAMDEN AREA:

Laurel Oaks Adventist
  School
14 West Shephard Ave.
Hamden, CT   06514

Sacred Heart Catholic
  Academy
265 Benham St.
Hamden, CT   06514

NEW HAVEN AREA:

Saint Mary's Catholic High
  School
444 Orange St.
New Haven, CT   06053

Notre Dame Catholic High
  School
24 Ricardo St.
West Haven, CT   06516

Saint Joseph's Catholic High
  School
Huntington Turnpike
Trumbell, CT   06611

STAMFORD AREA:

Holy Spirit Catholic School
403 Scofield Town Rd.
Stamford, CT   06903

GREENWICH AREA:

Daycroft Christian Science
  School
Rock Ridge
Greenwich, CT   06830

BRISTOL AREA:

Immanuel Lutheran School
154 Meadow St.
Bristol, CT   06010

DELAWARE

WILMINGTON AREA:

Wilmington Christian School,
  Inc.
2414 Pennsylvania Ave.
Wilmington, DE   19806

Faith City Christian School
P.O. Box 372
Wilmington, DE 19899

Wilmington Seventh Day
  Adventist School
3001 Mill Creek Rd.
Wilmington, DE 19808

The Highland Mennonite
  School
1621 North Lincoln St.
Wilmington, DE 19806

Friends School
101 School Rd.
Wilmington, DE 19803

Saint Edmond's Academy for
  Boys
2120 Veale Rd.
Wilmington, DE 19803

Saint Anthony's Catholic
  School
9th & Scott Sts.
Wilmington, DE 19805

NEWARK AREA:

Temple Christian School
199 Polly Drummond Hill Rd.
Newark, DE 19711

Red Lion Christian Academy
P.O. Box 176
Bear, DE 19701

Saint Andrew's Episcopal
  School
Middletown, DE 19709

Saint Mark's High School
Henderson Rd.
Newark, DE 19711

Archmere Catholic Academy
Claymont, DE 19703

Saint Peter's Catholic School
6th & Harmony Sts.
New Castle, DE 19720

MILFORD AREA:

Milford Christian School
301 Old Shawnee Rd.
Milford, DE 19963

Christian Tabernacle
  Academy
Box 148
Lincoln, DE 19960

Pathway Christian Academy
  Church of God
500 North Walnut St.
Milford, DE 19963

Kent Sussex Christian
  School
Milford-Harrington Rd.
Milford, DE 19963

GEORGETOWN AREA:

Georgetown Christian School
P.O. Box 471
Georgetown, DE 19947

DOVER AREA:

Dover Christian Elementary
  School
401 Kesselring Ave.
Dover, DE 19901

Kent Christian Academy
1790 North Du Pont Hwy.
Dover, DE 19901

Holy Cross Catholic School
631 South State St.
Dover, DE 19901

SEAFORD AREA:

Seaford Christian Academy
110 Holly St.
Seaford, DE 19973

David G. Fleagle School
  Seventh Day Adventist
Route 4, Box 703
Seaford, DE 19973

LEWES AREA:

Lewes Christian Academy
P.O. Box 25
Lewes, DE 19947

LAUREL AREA:

Greenwood Mennonite School
Route 1, P.O. Box 620
Greenwood, DE 19950

DISTRICT OF COLUMBIA

National Presbyterian School
4101 Nebraska Ave., N.W.
Washington, D.C. 20016

Rev. Thomas Daniels School
4115 16th St., N.W.
Washington, D.C. 20011

Sidewell Friends School
3825 Wisconsin Ave., N.W.
Washington, D.C. 20016

Woodward School for Boys
  Young Men's Christian
  Association
1736 G St., N.W.
Washington, D.C. 20006

Seventh Day Adventist School
3985 Massachusetts Ave., S.E.
Washington, D.C. 20019

National Episcopal Cathedral
  School for Boys
Mount St. Albans
Washington, D.C. 20016

Saint Patrick Episcopal Day
  School
4700 Whitehaven Pkwy., S.E.
Washington, D.C. 20007

Saint John's Catholic High
  School
2607 Military Rd., N.W.
Washington, D.C. 20015

Saint Anthony's Catholic High
  School
12th & Lawrence Sts., N.W.
Washington, D.C. 20017

Mackin Catholic High School
1421 V St., N.W.
Washington, D.C.   20009

Archbishop Carroll Catholic
  High School
4300 Harewood Rd., N.E.
Washington, D.C.   20017

Gonzaga Catholic High School
27 Eye St., N.W.
Washington, D.C.   20001

FLORIDA

JACKSONVILLE AREA:

Greater Jacksonville
  Christian School, Inc.
5223 Wesconnett Blvd.
Jacksonville, FL   32210

Greater Jacksonville
  Christian School, Inc.
6233 San Jose Blvd.
Jacksonville, FL   32217

Central Christian School
1011 Peninsular Pl.
Jacksonville, FL   32204

Christian Heritage Academy
3930 University Blvd., S.
Jacksonville, FL   32216

Regency Baptist Schools
1211 Lee Rd.
Jacksonville, FL   32218

Saint Johns Christian Country
  Day School
Orange Park, FL   32073

University Christian Schools
5520 University Blvd., W.
Jacksonville, FL   32216

Grace Christian Bible
  Academy
6118 Bowden Rd.
Jacksonville, FL   32216

Lake Forrest Baptist
  Christian School
925 West Edgewood Ave.
Jacksonville, FL   32208

Our Savior Lutheran
  Christian Day School
2140 St. John's Bluff Rd.
South Jacksonville, FL
  32207

Victory Christian Academy
10613 Lem Turner Rd.
Jacksonville, FL   32218

Temple Baptist Schools
2591 West Beaver St.
Jacksonville, FL   32205

Anniston Road Baptist School
2016 Anniston Rd.
Jacksonville, FL   32216

Trinity Baptist Christian
  Academy
800 Hammond Blvd.
Jacksonville, FL   32221

Riverside Baptist Day School
2650 Park St.
Jacksonville, FL   32204

Cedar Hills Baptist Christian
  School
4200 Jammes Rd.
Jacksonville, FL   32210

Hendrick's Memorial
  Methodist Day School
4000 Spring Park Rd.
Jacksonville, FL   32207

Riverside Presbyterian Day
  School
830 Oak St.
Jacksonville, FL   32204

Independent Christian Private
  School
Box 145
Interlachen, FL   32048

North Jacksonville Academy
1656 Edgewood Ave., W.
Jacksonville, FL   32208

Almadale Christian Day
  School
145 Clark Rd.
Jacksonville, FL   32218

Jacksonville Jr. Academy
  Seventh Day Adventist
11009 Old St. Augustine Rd.
Jacksonville, FL   32223

Adventists Jr. Academy
2760 West Edgewood Ave.
Jacksonville, FL   32209

Jacksonville Episcopal High
  School
4455 Atlantic Blvd.
Jacksonville, FL   32207

Saint Andrew's Episcopal Day
  School
7801 Lone Star Rd.
Jacksonville, FL   32211

Saint Mark's Episcopal Day
  School
4050 Ortega Blvd.
Jacksonville, FL   32210

Saint Paul's-by-the-Sea
  Episcopal Day School
1150 North 5th St.
Jacksonville, FL   32250

Bishop Kenny Catholic High
  School
1055 Kingman Ave.
Jacksonville Beach, FL   33207

MIAMI AREA:

Miami Christian School
200 N.W. 109th Ave.
Miami, FL   33168

Westwood Christian High
  School
5801 S.W. 120th Ave.
Miami, FL   33165

Northwest Christian Academy
951 N.W. 136th St.
Miami, FL   33168

Florida Christian Bible School
101 North Ocean Dr.
Hollywood, FL   33030

Florida Christian School
4200 S.W. 89th Ave.
Miami, FL   33165

Central Christian School
1300 S.W. 87th Ave.
Miami, FL 33144

Atlantic Christian Schools,
 Inc.
12975 S.W. 6th Ave.
Miami, FL 33129

Westminster Christian School
15000 S.W. 67th Ave.
Miami, FL 33158

Grace Christian School
19301 S.W. 127th Ave.
South Miami, FL 33143

Interamerican Christian
 School
1500 N.W. 29th St.
Miami, FL 33142

North Dade Christian School
1121 N.E. 205 Terr.
Miami, FL 33162

Dade Christian Schools
6601 N.W. 167th St.
Hialeah, FL 33015

Colonial Christian School
Box 1589
Homestead, FL 33030

Cutler Ridge Christian
 Academy
10301 Caribbean Blvd.
Miami, FL 33157

Kendall Christian School
8485 S.W. 112th St.
Miami, FL 33156

The King's Christian School
8951 S.W. 44th St.
Miami, FL 33165

North Dade Christian School
1121 N.E. 205 Terr.
North Miami Beach, FL
 33179

Westview Christian Schools
13301 N.W. 24th Ave.
Miami, FL 33167

Mueller Christian Schools
3300 N.W. 17th Ave.
Miami, FL 33142

North Gate Christian School
1401 N.W. 183rd St.
Miami, FL 33169

Westwood Christian Day
 Schools
4301 S.W. 107th Ave.
Miami, FL 33165

Southern Cross Christian
 School
8025 N.W. Miami Ct.
Miami, FL 33150

Quail Roost Christian School
10950 Quail Roost Dr.
Miami, FL 33157

Coral Springs Christian
 School
2251 Riverside Dr.
Coral Springs, FL 33060

Pembroke Christian Academy
7130 Pembroke Rd.
Miramar, FL 33023

Carol City Christian Academy
5005 N.W. 173rd Dr.
Carol City, FL 33054

Princeton Christian School
Box 299
Princeton, FL 33171

Perrine Baptist Academy
16905 S.W. 90th Ave.
Miami, FL 33157

First Baptist School
140 East 7th St.
Hialeah, FL 33010

Northwest Baptist Academy
951 Northwest 136th St.
Miami, FL 33168

Lutheran Christian Day School
 of St. James & St. Matthew
110 Phoenetia Ave.
Coral Gables, FL 33134

Greater Miami Academy
 Seventh Day Adventist
3100 N.W. 18th Ave.
Miami, FL 33142

Union Academy
 Seventh Day Adventist
8001 N.W. 25th Ave.
Miami, FL 33147

Holy Cross Lutheran School
650 N.E. 135th St.
Miami, FL 33161

Saint Stephen's Episcopal
 School
3439 Main Hwy.
(Coconut Grove)
Miami, FL 33133

Saint Thomas Episcopal
 School
5690 S.W. 88th Ave.
Miami, FL 33165

First Baptist School
140 East 7th St.
Hialeah, FL 33015

TAMPA AREA:

Tampa Christian Academy
6923 North Dale Mabry Hwy.
Tampa, FL 33614

West Gate Christian Schools
5121 Kelly Rd.
Tampa, FL 33615

Temple Heights Christian
 School
8406 46th St.
Tampa, FL 33617

Bayshore Methodist Christian
 School
3909 South MacDill Ave.
Tampa, FL 33611

Providence Christian School
5416 Providence Rd.
Riverview, FL 33569

Riverhills Christian School
8718 North 46th St.
Tampa, FL 33610

Grace Christian School
1300 North Valrico Rd.
(Tampa)
Valrico, FL 33594

Good Shepherd Christian
  School
8119 East Buffalo Ave.
Tampa, FL 33619

Harvest Time Christian
  School
1511 U.S. 301 S.
Tampa, FL 33619

Ruskin Christian School
820 College Ave., W.
Ruskin, FL 33570

Gospel Assembly Christian
  School
5014 East Busch Blvd.
Tampa, FL 33610

New Orleans Baptist School
1109 East Osborne Ave.
Tampa, FL 33603

Mango Baptist School
Hwy. 574
Mango, FL 33550

Northgate Baptist School
1301 West Linebaugh Ave.
Tampa, FL 33612

Spencer Memorial Baptist
  School, Inc.
6914 North Dixon Ave.
Tampa, FL 33604

West Hillsborough Baptist
  School
2717 West Hillsborough Ave.
Tampa, FL 33614

Seminole Presbyterian School
6101 North Habana Ave.
Tampa, FL 33614

Saint Paul United Methodist
  School
3304 Sanchez St.
Tampa, FL 33605

Tampa Jr. Academy
3205 North Blvd.
Tampa, FL 33603

Mount Calvary School
  Seventh Day Adventist
3111 East Wilder Ave.
Tampa, FL 33610

First Seventh Day Adventist
  School
822 West Linebaugh Ave.
Tampa, FL 33612

Holy Trinity Lutheran
  School
3712 El Prado Blvd.
Tampa, FL 33609

Saint John's Episcopal School
902 South Orleans Ave.
Tampa, FL 33606

Mary Help School
6400 East Chelsea Ave.
Tampa, FL 33610

Tampa Catholic High School
4630 North Rome Ave.
Tampa, FL 33603

Jesuit Catholic High School
4701 North Himes Ave.
Tampa, FL 33614

Saint John Orthodox Day
  School
2418 Swann Ave.
Tampa, FL 33609

Most Holy Redeemer Catholic
  School
302 East Linebaugh Ave.
Tampa, FL 33612

Christ the King Catholic
  School
3809 Morrison Ave.
Tampa, FL 33609

Church of the Incarnation
  Catholic School
5111 Webb Rd.
Tampa, FL 33615

ST. PETERSBURG AREA:

St. Petersburg Christian
  School
2021 62nd Ave., N.
St. Petersburg, FL 33702

Northside Christian School
6000 38th Ave., N.
St. Petersburg, FL 33710

Keswick Christian School
10101 54th Ave., N.
St. Petersburg, FL 33708

Weber Christian School
1315 9th Ave., N.
St. Petersburg, FL 33705

Lake Seminole Christian
  School
8401 Magnolia Dr., N.
St. Petersburg, FL 33703

Community Christian Schools
6262 62nd Ave., N.
St. Petersburg, FL 33702

Irving Park Baptist Academy
5001 71st St., N.
St. Petersburg, FL 33709

Wesleyan Academy
4400 70th Ave., N.
Pinellas Park, FL 33565

Gulfcoast School
  Seventh Day Adventist
6001 7th Ave., S.
St. Petersburg, FL 33707

Grace Lutheran School
4301 16th St., N.
St. Petersburg, FL 33703

Bay Pines Lutheran School
7589 113th Ln., N.
Seminole, FL 33540

Saint Paul's Catholic Jr. High
  School
1358 20th Ave., N.
St. Petersburg, FL 33704

Saint John's Catholic School
84th Ave. & Blind Pass Rd.
St. Petersburg, FL 33706

FORT LAUDERDALE AREA:

Fort Lauderdale Christian
  School
6330 N.W. 31st St.
Fort Lauderdale, FL 33309

Gold Coast Christian School
2800 West Prospect School
(Tamarac)
Fort Lauderdale, FL   33308

Atlantic Christian School,
  Inc.
1153 South Andrews Ave.
Fort Lauderdale, FL   33316

Broward Christian School
1237 N.W. Flamingo Rd.
Fort Lauderdale, FL   33313

Faith Christian School
6950 Royal Palm Blvd.
Margate, FL   33063

Boca Raton Christian School
600 N.W. 4th Ave.
P.O. Box A
Boca Raton, FL   33432

Hollywood Christian High
  School
1708 North 60th Ave.
Hollywood, FL   33021

Sheridan Hills Christian
  School
3751 Sheridan St.
Hollywood, FL   33021

Covenant Teaching Fellowship
4918 Roosevelt St.
Hollywood, FL   33021

All American Christian
  School
9250 Stirling Rd.
Hollywood, FL   33024

Highland Christian Academy
P.O. Box 5990
Pompano Beach, FL   33064

Christ Church School
4845 N.E. 25th Ave.
Fort Lauderdale, FL   33308

Westminster Academy
5620 N.E. 22nd Ave.
Fort Lauderdale, FL   33308

Lutheran High School of
  South Florida
3801 S.W. 76th Ave.
Davie, FL   33314

Lutheran Central School
20 S.W. 11th St.
Fort Lauderdale, FL   33315

Peace Lutheran School
1901 East Commercial Blvd.
Fort Lauderdale, FL   33308

Faith Lutheran School
1161 S.W. 30th Ave.
Fort Lauderdale, FL   33315

Saint Andrew's Episcopal
  School
University Pk.
Boca Raton, FL   33432

Saint Mark's Episcopal School
1750 East Oakland Park Blvd.
Fort Lauderdale, FL   33334

Saint Ambrose Episcopal Day
  School
2250 S.W. 31st Ave.
Fort Lauderdale, FL   33312

Central Catholic High School
S.W. 28th Ave. & 11th Ct.
Fort Lauderdale, FL   33315

Cardinal Gibbons Catholic
  High School
4601 Bayview Dr.
Fort Lauderdale, FL   33308

Saint Thomas Aquinas
  Catholic High School
2801 S.W. 12th St.
Fort Lauderdale, FL   33312

ORLANDO AREA:

Orlando Christian School
4161 North Powers Dr.
Orlando, FL   32808

West Orlando Christian
  School
2332 North Hiawassee Rd.
Orlando, FL   32808

Orange Christian School
500 South Semoran Blvd.
Orlando, FL   32807

Covenant Presbyterian
  Christian School
4800 Howell Branch Rd.
Goldenrod, FL   32733

Central Florida Christian
  School
P.O. Box 785
Maitland, FL   32751

Northside Christian School
175 Floridahaven Dr.
Maitland, FL   32751

Lake Christian School
1327 Marshall Dr.
Leesburg, FL   32748

Casselberry Christian School
P.O. Box 395
Casselberry, FL   32707

Liberty Christian School
P.O. Box 781
Sanford, FL   32771

Heritage Prep Schools
6000 West Colonial Dr.
Orlando, FL   32802

Edgewood Christian Academy
P.O. Box 16001
Orlando, FL   32811

Calvary Baptist Christian
  School
P.O. Box 191
Winter Garden, FL   32787

Baptist Temple School
4470 West Colonial Dr.
Orlando, FL   32808

Altamont Christian School
601 Palm Springs Dr.
Altamont, FL   32701

Forrest Lake Academy
  Seventh Day Adventist
P.O. Box 157
Maitland, FL   32751

Luther High School
1515 South Semoran Blvd.
Orlando, FL   32807

Cathedral Episcopal School
228 East Central Blvd.
Orlando, FL   32801

Bishop Moore Catholic High
  School
3901 Edgewater Dr.
Orlando, FL   32804

WEST PALM BEACH AREA:

Palm Beach Christian
  Academy
854 Conniston Rd.
West Palm Beach, FL   33405

King's Academy
4215 Cherry Rd.
West Palm Beach, FL   33401

West Side Christian School
2015 Parker Ave.
West Palm Beach, FL   33401

Berean Christian School
4200 North Australian Ave.
West Palm Beach, FL   33407

Garden Grove Christian
  School
883 South Military Trail
West Palm Beach, FL   33406

Summit Christian Schools
4900 Summit Blvd.
West Palm Beach, FL   33406

Jupiter Christian School
P.O. Box 967
Jupiter, FL   33458

Christian Day Elementary
  School
17 N.W. Ave. B
Belle Glade, FL   33430

First Baptist Christian School
200 West Ocean Blvd.
Stuart, FL   33494

First Baptist Day School
1010 South Olive Ave.
West Palm Beach, FL   33401

Lake Park Baptist School
625 Park Ave.
Lake Park, FL   33403

Haverhill Baptist Day School
671 North Haverhill Rd.
West Palm Beach, FL   33406

Cardinal Newman Catholic
  High School
512 Spencer Dr.
West Palm Beach, FL   33409

Saint Francis Assisi Catholic
  School
326 Pine Terr.
West Palm Beach, FL   33405

MERRITT ISLAND AREA:

Merritt Island Christian
  School
140 Magnolia Ave.
Merritt Island, FL   32952

CLEARWATER AREA:

Clearwater Largo Christian
  School
1739 South Greenwood Ave.
Clearwater, FL   33516

Central Pinellas Christian
  School
2050 South Belcher Rd.
Clearwater, FL   33516

Skycrest Christian School
1835 Drew St.
Clearwater, FL   33515

Bradenton Christian School
3304 43rd St., W.
Bradenton, FL   33505

Lakeside Christian School
1893 Sunset Point Rd.
Clearwater, FL   33515

Harvest Temple Christian
  School
1330 Walsingham St.
Clearwater, FL

Community Christian Schools
P.O. Box 968
1804 53rd Ave., E.
Oneco, FL   33558

Weber Christian School
8542 Iris Ave., N.
Seminole, FL   33543

First Evangelical Lutheran
  Christian Day School
1644 Nursery Rd.
Clearwater, FL   33516

Seventh Day Adventist
  Jr. Academy
1439 Lakeview Rd.
Clearwater, FL   33516

Saint Paul's Episcopal Middle
  School
1600 Saint Paul's Dr.
Clearwater, FL   33516

Saint Stephen's Episcopal
  School
4030 Manatee Ave., W.
Bradenton, FL   33505

Saint Patrick's Catholic
  School
1507 Trotter Rd.
Largo, FL   33540

TALLAHASSEE AREA:

Tallahassee Christian Schools
412 Sara Lee St.
Tallahassee, FL   32312

North Florida Christian
  Schools
3000 North Meridian St.
Tallahassee, FL   32303

Aucilla Christian Academy
Route 1, Box 142-A
Monticello, FL   32344

Gadsden Christian Academy
Route 1, P.O. Box 93
Havana, FL   32333

PENSACOLA AREA:

Pensacola Christian School
125 East Saint John St.
Pensacola, FL   32503

Escambia Christian School
3311 West Moreno St.
P.O. Box 17449
Pensacola, FL   32522

East Hill Christian School
1600 East Moreno St.
Pensacola, FL   32501

Pensacola Mennonite Christian
 Day School
3928 Hollywood Ave.
Pensacola, FL   32505

Fort Walton Christian School
P.O. Box 608
Fort Walton Beach, FL
 32548

Liberty Christian School
P.O. Box 3138
Pensacola, FL   32506

Santa Rosa Christian School
P.O. Box 643
Milton, FL   32570

Rocky Bayou Christian School
2101 North Partin Dr.
Niceville, FL   32578

Redeemer Lutheran Middle
 School
333 Commerce St.
Pensacola, FL   32507

Jehovah Lutheran School
2801 North 9th Ave.
Pensacola, FL   32503

GAINESVILLE AREA:

Heritage Christian School
3401 N.W. 34th St.
Gainesville, FL   32601

Southside Christian School
516 S.W. 2nd Terr.
Gainesville, FL   32601

Cross and Sword Christian
 Academy
Route 2, Box 378A
Williston, FL   32696

SARASOTA AREA:

Sarasota Christian School
5414 Bahia Vista St.
Sarasota, FL   33580

Meadowood Christian Academy
3400 Tyne Ln.
Sarasota, FL   33582

Faith Christian School
2105 Worrington St.
Sarasota, FL   33581

Cardinal Mooney Catholic
 High School
4171 Fruitville Rd.
Sarasota, FL   33580

LAKELAND AREA:

Lakeland Christian School
1111 Forest Pk.
Lakeland, FL   33803

Lakeland Baptist Academy
1010 West Olive St.
Lakeland, FL   33802

Landmark Christian School
2020 East Hinson St.
Haines City, FL   33844

Lake Wales Christian Schools
2601 Highway 60E
Lake Wales, FL   33853

Florida Baptist Schools
1030 West Olive St.
Lakeland, FL   33801

Lake Wales Christian School
Route 4, Box 618
Lake Wales, FL   33853

Temple Christian School
4210 Lakeland Highlands Rd.
Lakeland, FL   33803

Pathway Christian Academy
2035 West Parker St.
Lakeland, FL   33801

Evangel Christian School
 Assemblies of God
1350 East Main St.
Lakeland, FL   33801

Lakeland Jr. Academy
 Seventh Day Adventist
1443 North Gilmore St.
Lakeland, FL   33801

Saint Paul Lutheran School
3020 South Florida Ave.
Lakeland, FL   33803

Immanuel Lutheran School
1449 34th St., N.W.
Winter Haven, FL   33880

FORT PIERCE AREA:

Maranatha Christian Institute
Emerson Ave.
Fort Pierce, FL   33452

Immanuel Christian School
South 25th St.
Fort Pierce, FL   33450

Palm Vista Christian School
700 South 33rd St.
Fort Pierce, FL   33450

Faith Baptist School
3607 Oleander Ave.
Fort Pierce, FL   33450

Saint Andrews Episcopal
 School
210 South Indian River Dr.
Fort Pierce, FL   33450

James E. Sampson Memorial
 Seventh Day Adventist
 School
3105 Memory Ln.
Fort Pierce, FL   33450

DAYTONA BEACH AREA:

Daytona Beach Christian
 School
910 Beville Rd.
Daytona Beach, FL   32019

Warner Christian Academy
1730 South Ridgewood Ave.
South Daytona, FL 32021

Holly Hill Christian Academy
1127 Derbyshire Rd.
Holly Hill, FL 32017

First Baptist Christian
  Academy
P.O. Box 118
Hollister, FL 32047

Masters' Memorial School
  Seventh Day Adventist
719 Walker St.
Holly Hill, FL 32017

Saint James Episcopal Day
  School
44 South Halifax Dr.
Ormond Beach, FL 32074

Father Lopez Catholic High
  School
960 Madison Ave.
Daytona Beach, FL 32014

Saint Paul's Catholic School
314 First Ave.
Daytona Beach, FL 32014

MELBOURNE AREA:

Brevard Christian School
2840 Dorchester Ave., W.
Melbourne, FL 32901

Tabernacle Baptist School
276 S.W. 6th Ave.
Vero Beach, FL 32960

Seventh Day Adventist School
210 West New Haven Ave.
Melbourne, FL 32901

Holy Trinity Episcopal School
50 Strawbridge Ave.
Melbourne, FL 32901

Saint Edward's Upper School
246 South Alabama St.
Vero Beach, FL 32960

Central Catholic High School
100 East Florida Ave.
Melbourne, FL 32901

LAKE CITY AREA:

Golden State Christian
  Academy
121 South Montrose Ave.
Lake City, FL 32055

Westwood Christian School
920 11th St., S.W.
Live Oak, FL 32060

FORT MYERS AREA:

Evangelical Christian School
2367 McGregor Blvd., S.E.
Fort Myers, FL 33901

Academy of Christian
  Education
1691 Pacific Ave.
Fort Myers, FL 33901

Sonshine Christian Academy
881 Nuna Ave.
Fort Myers, FL 33905

Saint Michael Lutheran
  School
3595 Broadway
Fort Myers, FL 33901

Bishop Verot Catholic High
  School
5598 Sunrise Dr.
Fort Myers, FL 33901

NAPLES AREA:

Naples Christian Academy
3050 Santa Barbara Blvd.
Naples, FL 33999

Seagate Christian School
750 Seagate Dr.
Naples, FL 33940

Lake Trafford Christian
  Academy
Carson Rd.
Naples, FL 33940

Faith Christian School
2132 Shadowlawn Dr.
Naples, FL 33942

Alva Christian Education
  Center
Joel Blvd.
Alva, FL 33920

POMPANO BEACH AREA:

North Pompano Christian
  School
1101 N.E. 33rd St.
Pompano Beach, FL 33064

Heritage Baptist Christian
  School
3700 N.E. 19th Terr.
Pompano, FL 33064

Coral Springs Christian
  School
2251 Riverside Dr.
Coral Springs, FL 33065

Ocean Drive Lutheran
  School
220 S.E. 9th Ave.
Pompano, FL 33060

Hope Lutheran School
1840 N.E. 41st St.
Pompano, FL 33064

LAKE WORTH AREA:

Lake Worth Elementary
  School
1325 North A St.
Lake Worth, FL 33460

Lake Worth Christian Jr. &
  Sr. High School
7592 High Ridge Rd.
Lantana, FL 33462

Jupiter Christian School
P.O. Box 967
Jupiter, FL 33458

Beacon Christian School
P.O. Box 1308
Jupiter, FL 33458

Southwide Christian Academy
517 Folson Rd.
Loxahatchee, FL 33470

Our Savior Lutheran School
1615 Lake Ave.
Lake Worth, FL 33460

Saint Luke's School
2090 South Congress Ave.
Lake Worth, FL 33460

KEY WEST AREA:

Monroe Christian School
Stock Island
Key West, FL 33040

Grace Lutheran School
2713 Flagler Ave.
Key West, FL 33040

Mary Immaculate Catholic
  High School
Truman Ave.
Key West, FL 33040

ST. AUGUSTINE AREA:

Greater Jacksonville Christian
  School, Inc.
260 Lewis Speedway
St. Augustine, FL 32084

Saint Joseph's Catholic
  Academy
241 Saint George St.
St. Augustine, FL 32084

PANAMA CITY AREA:

Panama City Christian School
1104 Balboa Ave.
Panama City, FL 32401

WABASSO AREA:

Wabasso Christian School
P. O. Box 115
Wabasso, FL 32970

GEORGIA

ATLANTA AREA:

Atlanta Christian Academy
  High School
4649 Glenwood Rd.
Decatur, GA 30032

Atlanta Christian Academy
  Elementary School
2207 Candler Rd.
Decatur, GA 30032

DeKalb Alliance Christian
  Academy
1985 La Vista Rd., N. E.
Atlanta, GA 30329

Central Christian Schools
2560 Sylvan Rd.
East Point, GA 30344

Forrest Hills Christian
  School
923 Valley Brook Rd.
Decatur, GA 30033

Forest Park Christian School
5881 Phillips Dr.
Forest Park, GA 30050

Maranatha Christian School
925 East Conley Rd.
Forest Park, GA 30315

Stone Mountain Christian
  Schools
5931 Shadow Rock Dr.
Stone Mountain, GA 30083

Marietta Christian School
1700 Allgood Rd., N. E.
Marietta, GA 30062

Crestwood Christian Academy
Highway 74
Tyrone, GA 30290

Fayette Christian Academy
Longview Rd.
Fayetteville, GA 30214

Mount Vernon Christian
  Schools
Fairview Rd.
Stockbridge, GA 30281

Perimeter South Christian
  Academy
4121 Thurmond Rd.
Conley, GA 30027

Faith Christian School
4851 River Rd.
Ellenwood, GA 30049

Old National Christian
  Academy
2500 Burdett Rd.
College Park, GA 30327

Heiskell School
3260 Northside Dr., N. W.
Atlanta, GA 30305

Mount Vernon Christian
  School
Route 1
Stockbridge, GA 30281

Bible Apostolic Christian
  School
4730 Elam Rd.
Stone Mountain, GA 30072

Colonial Hills Christian
  School
2134 Newnan St.
East Point, GA 30344

Tabernacle Christian School
1380 Blvd., S. E.
Atlanta, GA 30315

Killian Hill Christian School
151 Arcado Rd.
Lilburn, GA 30247

Mount Vernon Christian
  Academy
4449 Northside Dr., W.
Atlanta, GA 30327

Lighthouse Christian School
P. O. Box 265
Temple, GA 30179

Smyrna Christian Academy
3269 Old Concord Rd., S. E.
Smyrna, GA 30080

Mount Carmel Christian
  School
3250 Rainbow Dr.
Decatur, GA 30034

The Lovett School
4075 Paces Ferry Rd., N. W.
Atlanta, GA 30327

Woodward Academy
P. O. Box 180
College Park, GA 30327

Peace Lutheran School
1679 Columbia Dr.
Decatur, GA   30030

Saint Pius X Catholic High
  School
2674 Johnson Rd., N.E.
Atlanta, GA   30345

Marist Catholic School
3790 Ashford-Dunwoody Rd.
Atlanta, GA   30319

Saints Peter & Paul Catholic
  School
2560 Tilson Rd.
Decatur, GA   30032

MACON AREA:

Macon Christian Academy
1931 Rocky Creek Rd.
Macon, GA   31206

Tattnall Square Academy
760 Lakecrest Dr.
Macon, GA   31204

Macedonia Christian Academy
5687 Houston Rd.
Macon, GA   31206

Cross Keys Baptist School
2049 Jeffersonville Rd.
Macon, GA   31201

First Presbyterian Day School
P.O. Box 6237
5671 Calvin Dr.
Macon, GA   31208

Seventh Day Adventist School
640 Wimbish Rd.
Macon, GA   31204

Mount de Sales Catholic High
  School
851 Orange St.
Macon, GA   31201

Saint Joseph Catholic School
905 High St.
Macon, GA   31201

COLUMBUS AREA:

Columbus Christian Academy
420 38th St.
Columbus, GA   31904

Edgewood Christian Schools
1909 Morris Rd.
Columbus, GA   31907

Calvary Christian School
7556 Moon Rd.
Columbus, GA   31904

Grace Christian School
2915 14th Ave.
Columbus, GA   31904

Calvary Baptist School
3301 13th Ave.
Columbus, GA   31904

First United Pentecostal
  Christian Academy
3614 Morris Rd.
Columbus, GA   31907

First Seventh Day Adventist
  School
3700 Macon Rd.
Columbus, GA   31907

Gate Fellowship Community
  School
2323 Double Churches Rd.
Columbus, GA   31904

Pacelli Catholic High School
Trinity Dr.
Columbus, GA   31907

WARNER ROBINS AREA:

Christian Academy
2601 Watson Blvd.
Warner Robins, GA   31093

Cochran Field Christian
  Academy
8460 Hawkinsville Rd.
Warner Robins, GA   31093

Seventh Day Adventist School
Moody Rd.
Warner Robins, GA   31093

Sacred Heart Catholic School
250 South Davis St.
Warner Robins, GA   31093

DUBLIN AREA:

Trinity Christian School
Highway 441
P.O. Box 1052
Dublin, GA   31021

SAVANNAH AREA:

Savannah Christian Prepara-
  tory School
Telfair Rd.
Savannah, GA   31401

DeRenne Christian Academy
2001 East DeRenne Ave.
Savannah, GA   31406

Temple Christian Academy
Box 256
Rincon, GA   31326

Rothwell Street Christian
  School
P.O. Box 14
Pooler, GA   31322

Savannah Country Day School
P.O. Box 6208, Station C
Savannah, GA   31405

Pathway Day School
2208 East DeRenne Ave.
Savannah, GA   31406

Bible Baptist School
4700 Skidaway Rd.
Savannah, GA   31404

Calvary Baptist Day School
4625 Waters Ave.
Savannah, GA   31404

Saint Paul's Lutheran Day
  School
10 West 31st St.
Savannah, GA   31401

Cathedral of Saint John the
  Baptist School
324 Abercorn St.
Savannah, GA   31401

Saint Vincent's Catholic High
School
207 East Liberty St.
Savannah, GA   31401

Benedictine Catholic Military
School
34th & Bull St.
Savannah, GA   31401

ATHENS AREA:

Athens Christian School
Highway 29 N.
Athens, GA   30601

Saint Joseph's Catholic School
134 Prince Ave.
Athens, GA   30601

AUGUSTA AREA:

Augusta Christian Schools
313 Baston Rd.
Martinez, GA   30907

Augusta Christian Academy
1920 Tubman Home Rd.
Augusta, GA   30906

Westminster Christian School
3067 Wheeler Rd.
Augusta, GA   30909

Westside Elementary School
P.O. Box 2621
Augusta, GA   30904

Bible Baptist School
3237 Dean's Bridge Rd.
Augusta, GA   30906

Curtis Baptist School
7326 Broad St.
Augusta, GA   30901

One Way Christian School
4220 Frontage Rd.
Augusta, GA

Hillcrest Baptist School
3045 Dean's Bridge Rd.
Augusta, GA   30906

Southgate Baptist School
P.O. Box 5130
Augusta, GA   30906

Hephzibah Mennonite School
c/o Timothy Myers
Route 1, Box 392 D
Augusta, GA   31707

Boggs Presbyterian Academy
Keysville, GA   30816

Seventh Day Adventist School
2514 Richmond Hill Rd.
Augusta, GA   30906

Episcopal Day School
2248 Walton Way
Augusta, GA   30904

Aquinas Catholic High School
1920 Highlands Ave.
Augusta, GA   30904

DALTON AREA:

Pathway Christian School
1007 Underwood Ave.
Dalton, GA   30720

Chatsworth Christian Academy
Highway 225 S., Route 4
Chatsworth, GA   30705

Dogwood Christian Academy
1296 Dogwood Valley Rd.
Tunnel Hill, GA   30755

Unity Christian Schools
2010 Mack Smith Rd.
Rossville, GA   30741

Dalton Christian School
P.O. Box 1792
Dalton, GA   30720

Seventh Day Adventist School
Tibbs Rd.
Dalton, GA   30720

ALBANY AREA:

Albany Alliance Academy
2200 Stuart Ave.
Albany, GA   31705

Dougherty Christian Academy
725 East Albany Expressway
Albany, GA   31705

South Georgia Christian
Academy
1731 Beattie Rd.
Albany, GA   31701

Circle Baptist Academy
3400 Dawson Rd.
Albany, GA

Saint Teresa's Catholic School
420 Edgewood Ln.
Albany, GA   31705

GAINESVILLE AREA:

Christian Education Center,
Inc.
Gainesville, GA   30501

Toccoa Falls Alliance
Academy
P.O. Box 36
Toccoa Falls, GA   30577

Rabun Gap-Nacoochee
Presbyterian School
Rabun Gap, GA   30568

Emmanuel Pentecostal
Holiness Academy
Franklin Springs, GA   30639

Tabernacle Christian Academy
Route 13
Skelton Rd. & Whiting Dr.
Gainesville, GA   30501

WAYCROSS AREA:

Ware Christian Academy
Wadley Rd.
Waycross, GA   31501

Grace Baptist School
204 Lisbon Dr.
Waycross, GA   31501

Faith Temple Christian
Academy
600 Riverside Ave.
Waycross, GA   31501

BRUNSWICK AREA:

Brunswick Christian Academy,
   Inc.
   Junior High School
Darien Hwy.
Brunswick, GA   31501

THOMASVILLE AREA:

Rose City Christian School
North Pinetree Blvd.
Thomasville, GA   31792

Vashti Methodist School
Thomasville, GA   31792

AMERICUS AREA:

Americus Baptist Temple
   School
Southland Dr.
Americus, GA   31709

Brooklyn Heights Christian
   School
1502 Washington St.
Americus, GA   31709

GRIFFIN AREA:

Griffin Christian School
1417 Atlanta Rd.
Griffin, GA   30226

McDonough Christian Academy
P.O. Box 657
McDonough, GA   30253

ROME AREA:

Berry Academy
Mount Berry, GA   30149

Saint Mary's Catholic School
401 East 7th St.
Rome, GA   30161

VALDOSTA AREA:

Georgia Christian School
Route 2
Valdosta, GA   31601

Lawndes Christian Academy
P.O. Box 3166
3901 Bemis Rd.
Valdosta, GA   31601

LA GRANGE AREA:

Oakside Christian School
1921 Hamilton Rd.
La Grange, GA   30240

BAINBRIDGE AREA:

Bainbridge Christian School
P.O. Box 995
Bainbridge, GA   31717

BRUNSWICK AREA:

Brunswick Christian Academy
159 D Darien Hwy.
Brunswick, GA   31520

NEWNAN AREA:

Newnan Christian School
U.S. 29, P.O. Box 829
Newnan, GA   30264

HAWAII

HONOLULU AREA:

Hawaii Baptist Academy
1234 Heulu St.
Honolulu, HI   96822

Hawaii Baptist Academy
2429 Pali Hwy.
Honolulu, HI   96817

Pacific Baptist Academy
135 North Kukui St.
Honolulu, HI   96817

Kaimuki Christian School
1117 Koko Head Ave.
Honolulu, HI   96816

Grace Bible Christian School
1052 Ilima Dr.
Honolulu, HI   96817

Mid Pacific Institute
   Congregational
2445 Kaala St.
Honolulu, HI   96822

Kamehameha Schools
   Congregational
Honolulu, HI   96817

Honolulu Jr. Academy
   Seventh Day Adventist
2345 Nuuanu Ave.
Honolulu, HI   96817

Our Redeemer Lutheran
   Schools
1404 University Ave.
(Waikiki)
Honolulu, HI   96815

Our Savior Lutheran School
98-1098 Moanalua Rd.
Honolulu, HI   96819

Saint Mark Lutheran School
45-725 Kam Hwy.
Honolulu, HI   96819

Iolani Episcopal School
Honolulu, HI   96814

Saint Andrew's Priory
   Episcopal School
224 Queen Emma Sq.
Honolulu, HI   96813

Epiphany Episcopal School
1041 10th Ave.
Honolulu, HI   96816

Holy Nativity Episcopal School
5286 Kalanianaole Hwy.
Honolulu, HI   96821

Hawaiian Mission Academy
1438 Pensacola St.
Honolulu, HI   96809

Saint Francis Catholic High
   School
2707 Pamoa Rd.
Honolulu, HI   96822

Star of the Sea Catholic High
   School
4469 Malia St.
Honolulu, HI   96821

Sacred Heart Catholic Academy
   High School
3253 Waialae Ave.
Honolulu, HI   96816

Cathedral School
1728 Nuuanu Ave.
Honolulu, HI 96817

Holy Trinity Catholic School
5919 Kalanianaole Hwy.
Honolulu, HI 96821

KAHULUI,
MAUI ISLAND AREA:

Doris Todd Memorial
  Christian School
Baldwin Ave.
Paia, HI 96779

Immanuel Lutheran Schools
Kahului, HI 96732

Seabury Hall Episcopal
  Preparatory School
Makawao, HI 96768

Christ the King Catholic
  School
Kahului, HI 96732

Saint Joseph Catholic School
Makawao, HI 96768

Saint Anthony School
Wailuku, HI 96793

WAHIAWA,
OAHU ISLAND AREA:

King's Schools
300 Wilikina Dr.
Wahiawa, HI 96786

Trinity Lutheran School
1611 California Ave.
Wahiawa, HI 96786

Leeward Mission Adventist
  School
1313 California Ave.
Wahiawa, HI 96786

KAILUA,
OAHU ISLAND AREA:

Kailua Christian School
201 North Kainalu Dr.
Kailua, HI 96734

Good Shepherd School
355 North Kainalu Dr.
Kailua, HI 96734

KANEOHE,
OAHU ISLAND:

Koolau Baptist Academy
45-633 Keneke St.
Kaneohe, HI 96744

Hawaii Episcopal
  Preparatory Academy
Kamuela, HI 96743

WAIPAHU,
OAHU ISLAND:

Lanakila Baptist Schools
94-1250 Waipahu St.
Waipahu, HI 96797

Lanakila Baptist High School
91-1219 Renton
Ewa Beach, HI 96706

HALEIWA,
OAHU ISLAND:

Sunset Beach Christian
  School
59-578 Kam Hwy.
Haleiwa, HI 96712

LIHUE,
KAUAI ISLAND:

Kauai Christian Academy
Anahola, HI 96763

Kauai Adventist School
Omao, HI 96766

Saint Catherine's Catholic
  School
Kapaa, HI 96746

HILO,
HAWAII ISLAND:

Saint Joseph Catholic High
  School
Ululani & Hualalai Sts.
Hilo, HI 96720

KAUNAKAKAI,
MOLOKAI ISLAND:

Seventh Day Adventist School
Kalamaula, HI 96748

IDAHO

BOISE AREA:

Boise Christian School
219 North Roosevelt St.
Boise, ID 83702

Maranatha Christian School
12000 Fairview Ave.
Boise, ID 83707

Cole Christian School
1400 North Cole Rd.
Boise, ID 83704

Boise Valley School
  Seventh Day Adventist
1800 Eldorado St.
Boise, ID 83704

Bishop Kelly Catholic High
  School
7009 Franklin Rd.
Boise, ID 83705

Saint Mark's Catholic School
7503 Northview St.
Boise, ID 83704

Saint Joseph's Catholic
  School
825 Fort St.
Boise, ID 83702

IDAHO FALLS AREA:

Gethsemane Christian School
2345 Broadway
Idaho Falls, ID 83401

Hope Lutheran School
1300 East 17th St.
Idaho Falls, ID 83401

Holy Rosary Catholic School
161 9th St.
Idaho Falls, ID 83401

TWIN FALLS AREA:

Twin Falls Christian Academy
798 Eastland Dr., N.
Twin Falls, ID 83301

Immanuel Lutheran School of
  Twin Falls
272 Shoup Ave., W.
Twin Falls, ID 83301

Clover Trinity Lutheran
  School
Route 1
Buhl, ID 83316

Magic Valley Jr. High School
  Seventh Day Adventist
Grandview Dr., Route 2
Twin Falls, ID 83301

NAMPA AREA:

Nampa Nazarene Christian
  High School
439 Orchard Ave.
Nampa, ID 83651

Greenleaf Friends Academy
P.O. Box 368
Greenleaf, ID 83626

Eagle Seventh Day Adventist
  School
P.O. Box 186
Eagle, ID 83616

Saint Paul's School
1515 8th St., S.
Nampa, ID 83651

Zion Lutheran School
1012 12th Ave.
Nampa, ID 83651

LEWISTON AREA:

Bible Way Christian School
3312 9th St.
Lewiston, ID 83501

Valley Christian School
  Assembly of God
2021 11th Ave.
Lewiston, ID 83501

Beacon School
  Seventh Day Adventist
1212 19th St.
Lewiston, ID 83501

Saints Peter & Paul Catholic
  School
South B & Lake Sts.
Lewiston, ID 83501

Holy Family Catholic School
1002 Chestnut St.
Lewiston, ID 83501

CALDWELL AREA:

Boulevard Christian School
Highway 30 E.
Caldwell, ID 83605

Gem State Academy
  Seventh Day Adventist
2419 South Indiana St.
Caldwell, ID 83605

POCATELLO AREA:

Lutheran Christian Day School
1050 East Center St.
Pocatello, ID 83201

Grace Lutheran School
1250 Pershing Ave.
Pocatello, ID 83201

Saint Joseph's Catholic School
403 North Hayes Ave.
Pocatello, ID 83201

Saint Anthony Catholic School
540 North 7th Ave.
Pocatello, ID 83201

MOUNTAIN HOME AREA:

Bible Baptist School
1555 American Legion Blvd.
Mountain Home, ID 83647

MOSCOW AREA:

Seventh Day Adventist School
1015 West C St.
Moscow, ID 83843

Saint Mary's Catholic School
Polk & 1st Sts.
Moscow, ID 83843

COEUR D' ALENE AREA:

Seventh Day Adventist School
111 Locust St.
Coeur d'Alene, ID 83814

Catholic School
Coeur d'Alene, ID 83814

SALMON AREA:

Salmon Church School
500 Monroe
Salmon, ID 87467

ILLINOIS

CHICAGO AREA:

Chicago Christian High School
12001 South Oak Park Ave.
Palos Heights, IL 60463

Elim Christian School
13020 South Central Ave.
Palos Heights, IL 60463

Chicago Christian Academy
5110 West Diversey Ave.
Chicago, IL 60639

Chicago Baptist Institute
5120 South Dr. Martin Luther,
  Jr.
Chicago, IL 60615

Midwestern Christian Academy
3465 North Cicero Ave.
Chicago, IL 60641

Bible View Christian School
Normantown Rd.
Romeoville, IL 60441

The Bible Speaks
  The **Christian** Free Academy
19 West Jackson St.
Chicago, IL 60604

Evangelical Christian School
10 West 110th St.
Chicago, IL 60628

Fellowship Christian Academy
1925 East 95th St.
Chicago, IL 60617

Marguette Manor Christian
  School
Box 507
Downer's Grove, IL 60515

Roseland Christian School
314 West 108th St.
Chicago, IL 60628

Wheaton Christian High School
2N120 Prince Crossing Rd.
West Chicago, IL 60185

Emmanuel Christian School
8910 South Route 83
Hinsdale, IL 60521

Evergreen Park Christian
  School
3450 West 97th St.
Evergreen Park, IL 60642

Salem Christian School
2845 West McLean Ave.
Chicago, IL 60647

Mr. Gus Anagnost Koraes
  Elementary School
11025 45 South Roberts Rd.
Palos Hills, IL 60465

Hephzibah Christian Academy
11353 South State St.
Chicago, IL 60628

South Side Baptist School
5345 West 99th St.
Oak Lawn, IL 60453

Oak Lawn Christian Jr. High
  School
5665 West 101st St.
Oak Lawn, IL 60453

Oak Forest Christian Academy
5217 West 149th St.
Oak Forest, IL 60452

Illiana Christian High School
2261 Indiana Ave.
Lansing, IL 60438

Lansing Christian School
3660 Randolph St.
Lansing, IL 60438

West Side Christian School
1241 South Pulaski Rd.
Chicago, IL 60623

Calvin Christian School
528 East 161st Pl.
South Holland, IL 60473

Aurora Christian School
14 Blackhawk St.
Aurora, IL 60506

Fox River Valley Christian
  School
Oak St. & Randall Rd., N.
Aurora, IL 60506

Elim Christian School
13020 South Central Ave.
Palos Heights, IL 60463

Wesleyan Missionary Academy
5656 West 64th Pl.
Chicago, IL 60638

Central Y.M.C.A. High
  School
29 West Randolph St.
Chicago, IL 60601

Lake Shore School
  Seventh Day Adventist
717 North Wolcot Ave.
Chicago, IL 60622

North Shore School
  Seventh Day Adventist
5220 North California St.
Chicago, IL 60625

Pillar of Fire School
1115 West Barry Ave.
Chicago, IL 60657

St. Paul's Apostolic Academy
7201 South Western Ave.
Chicago, IL 60636

Seventh Day Adventist School
502 Westgate Terr.
Chicago, IL 60607

Grace English Evangelical
  Lutheran School
2725 North Laramie Ave.
Chicago, IL 60639

Grace Evangelical Lutheran
  School
4106 West 28th St.
Chicago, IL 60623

Saint Paul Evangelical
  Lutheran School
846 North Menard Ave.
Chicago, IL 60651

Christ English Evangelical
  Lutheran School
5335 West LeMoyn St.
Chicago, IL 60651

Emmanuel Christian School
8301 South Damen
Chicago, IL 60620

First Evangelical Lutheran
  School
Grove and Ann St.
Blue Island, IL 60406

Timothy Lutheran School
1700 West 83rd St.
Chicago, IL 60620

Christ Evangelical Lutheran
  School
2018 North Richmond Ave.
Chicago, IL 60647

First Bethlehem Evangelical
  Lutheran School
1645 West LeMoyne St.
Chicago, IL 60622

Zion Evangelical Lutheran
  School
5821 Archer Rd.
Summit, IL 60501

Saint Philip Evangelical
  Lutheran School
2454 West Bryn Mawr Ave.
Chicago, IL 60645

Messiah Lutheran School
6200 West Patterson Ave.
Chicago, IL   60634

Emmanuel Evangelical
Lutheran School
551 4th Ave.
Aurora, IL   60505

Saint Matthew Evangelical
Lutheran School
9200 Milwaukee St.
Niles, IL   60648

Our Savior Lutheran School
7151 West Cornelia Ave.
Chicago, IL   60634

Redeemer Lutheran School
23rd & 53rd Sts.
Cicero, IL   60650

Luther High School North
5700 West Berteau St.
Chicago, IL   60634

Luther High School South
3130 West 87th St.
Chicago, IL   60652

Ashburn Lutheran School
3345 West 83rd St.
Chicago, IL   60652

Bethel Lutheran School
4215 West West End
Chicago, IL   60624

Bethlehem Lutheran School
3715 East 103rd St.
Chicago, IL   60617

Saint Luke Lutheran School
1500 West Belmont
Chicago, IL   60657

Saint James Lutheran School
850 West Dickens
Chicago, IL   60614

Pilgrim Lutheran School
4300 North Winchester St.
Chicago, IL   60613

Peace Lutheran School
4307 South Mozart St.
Chicago, IL   60632

Saint Peter's Lutheran
School
310 North Broadway
Joliet, IL   60435

Saint Paul's Lutheran School
550 2nd Ave.
Aurora, IL   60505

Saint Edmund's Episcopal
School
6105 South Michigan Ave.
Chicago, IL   60637

Saint Demetrios Greek
Orthodox School
2727 West Winona St.
Chicago, IL   60625

Holy Trinity High School
1443 West Division
Chicago, IL   60622

Resurrection High School
7500 West Talcott Rd.
Chicago, IL   60631

Saint Joseph Catholic High
School
4831 South Hermitage Ave.
Chicago, IL   60609

Saint Augustine Catholic
High School
5019 South Laflin St.
Chicago, IL   60609

Mount Carmel Catholic High
School
6410 South Dante Ave.
Chicago, IL   60637

Saint Philip Basilica Catholic
High School
3141 West Jackson Blvd.
Chicago, IL   60612

The Hardey Catholic
Preparatory School for Boys
6250 North Sheridan Rd.
Chicago, IL   60626

The Aquinas Dominican
Catholic High School
2100 East 72nd St.
Chicago, IL   60649

Brother Rice High School
10001 South Pulaski Rd.
Chicago, IL   60642

Cathedral High School
751 North State St.
Chicago, IL   60602

De LaSalle Catholic High
School
3455 South Wabash Ave.
Chicago, IL   60616

Hales Franciscan Catholic
High School
4930 South Cottage Grove
Ave.
Chicago, IL   60615

Saint Gregory Catholic High
School
1677 West Bryn Mawr Ave.
Chicago, IL   60626

Saint Benedict Catholic High
School
3900 North Leavitt St.
Chicago, IL   60618

Saint Patrick Catholic High
School for Boys
5900 West Belmont Ave.
Chicago, IL   60634

Providence Catholic High
School
199 South Central Park Ave.
Chicago, IL   60624

Mendel Catholic High School
250 East 111th St.
Chicago, IL   60628

Saint Sebastian Catholic High
School
810 West Wellington St.
Chicago, IL   60657

Saint Procopius Catholic
 High School
1625 South Allport St.
Chicago, IL   60608

Lourdes Catholic High School
4034 West 56th St.
Chicago, IL   60629

Saint Barbara Catholic High
 School
2800 South Quinn St.
Chicago, IL   60608

Immaculata Catholic High
 School
640 West Irving Park Rd.
Chicago, IL   60613

Saint Rita Catholic High
 School
6310 South Claremont St.
Chicago, IL   60636

Loretto Catholic High School
6535 Stewart Ave.
Chicago, IL   60621

Joliet Catholic High School
31-33 North Broadway
Joliet, IL   60435

Trinity Catholic High School
7574 West Division St.
River Forest, IL   60405

Aurora Central Catholic High
 School
157 North Root St.
Aurora, IL   60505

Rosary Catholic High School
901 North Edgelawn
Aurora, IL   60506

Annunciation Catholic Middle
 School
Church Rd.
Aurora, IL   60505

Cathedral School of Saint
 Raymond's
713 Douglas St.
Joliet, IL   60435

Notre Dame Catholic High
 School
7655 South California St.
Niles, IL   60648

Christ the King Catholic
 School
9240 South Hoyne Ave.
Chicago, IL   60620

Transfiguration Catholic
 School
2600 West Winnemac St.
Chicago, IL   60625

Good Shepherd Catholic
 School
2733 South Kolin Ave.
Chicago, IL   60623

Saints Peter & Paul Catholic
 School
12255 South Emerald Ave.
Chicago, IL   60628

Saints Peter & Paul Catholic
 School
2938 East 91st St.
Chicago, IL   60617

Saints Peter & Paul Catholic
 School
3745 South Paulina St.
Chicago, IL   60609

Saint Barnabas Catholic
 School
10121 South Longwood
Chicago, IL   60643

Saint Bartholomew's Catholic
 School
4941 West Patterson St.
Chicago, IL   60641

Saint Timothy's Catholic
 School
6330 North Washtenaw Ave.
Chicago, IL   60645

ROCKFORD AREA:

Rockford Christian School
200 Hemlock Ln.
Rockford, IL   61107

Rockford Baptist School
Meridian & Flora Rds.
Rockford, IL   61103

North Love Christian School
5301 East Riverside Blvd.
Rockford, IL   61103

Pleasant Valley Christian
 Day School
3202 Pleasant Valley Rd.
Rockford, IL   61111

Berean Christian Schools
5626 Safford Rd.
Rockford, IL   61103

Christian Life Center Schools
5950 Spring Creek Rd.
Rockford, IL   61111

Kishwaukee Baptist School
6286 Linden Rd.
Rockford, IL   61109

Baptist Christian School
1637 7th Ave.
Belvidere, IL   61008

Open Bible Academy
8200 North 2nd St.
Rockford, IL   61111

Seventh Day Adventist School
325 North Alpine Rd.
Rockford, IL   61107

Rockford Lutheran High
 School
3411 North Alpine Rd.
Rockford, IL   61111

Immanuel Lutheran School
174 McHenry Ave.
Crystal Lake, IL   60014

Saint Paul Lutheran School
811 Locust St.
Rockford, IL   61103

Concordia Lutheran School
7424 North 2nd St.
Rockford, IL   61111

Saint Thomas High School
920 Mulberry St.
Rockford, IL   61103

Boylan Central Catholic High
  School
Campus Hills Blvd.
Rockford, IL   61103

DECATUR AREA:

Decatur Christian Schools
3770 North Water St.
Decatur, IL   62526

Glad Tidings Christian
  Academy
1050 South 44th St.
Decatur, IL   62521

West Mound Christian School
530 West Mound Rd.
Decatur, IL   62526

East Park Baptist Academy
1762 East Prairie St.
Decatur, IL   62521

Bethel Education Academy
Union School Rd.
Harristown, IL   62537

Seventh Day Adventist School
540 North Sunnyside Rd.
Decatur, IL   62522

Lutheran Middle School of
  Decatur
340 West Wood St.
Decatur, IL   62522

Saint Teresa Catholic High
  School
2700 North Water St.
Decatur, IL   62526

SPRINGFIELD AREA:

Christian Faith Academy
  High School
New Berlin, IL   62670

West Side Christian School
  Church of Christ
900 West Edwards St.
Springfield, IL   62704

Harvard Park Christian
  School
2401 South 9th St.
Springfield, IL   62703

Berean Baptist Academy
612 Flora St.
Springfield, IL   62703

Grace Baptist Academy
2812 South Walnut St.
Springfield, IL   62704

Oak Hill Christian School
Route 1
Springfield, IL   62707

Calvary Academy
1730 West Jefferson St.
Springfield, IL   62702

Third Presbyterian School
515 South MacArthur St.
Springfield, IL   62704

Our Savior's Lutheran School
Old Jacksonville Rd.
Springfield, IL   62704

Immanuel Lutheran School
2750 Sangamon Ave.
Springfield, IL   62702

Trinity Lutheran School
515 South MacArthur St.
Springfield, IL   62704

Concordia Lutheran School
2300 Wilshire Rd.
Springfield, IL   62703

Saint James Catholic Trade
  and High School
Route 1
Springfield, IL   62707

Cathedral School of the
  Immaculate Conception
815 South 6th St.
Springfield, IL   62703

Christ the King Catholic
  School
1920 Barberry Ln.
Springfield, IL   62704

EVANSTON AREA:

Wheaton Christian High School
2 North 120 Prince Crossing
  Rd.
West Chicago, IL   60185

Villa Christian School
2111 South 17th Ave.
Broadview, IL   60153

Wheaton Christian School
530 East Harrison St.
Wheaton, IL   60187

Grace Evangelical Lutheran
  School
7300 West Division St.
River Forest, IL   60305

Walther Lutheran High School
900 Chicago Ave.
Melrose Park, IL   60160

Saint Paul Lutheran School
1000 Superior St.
Melrose Park, IL   60160

Saint John's Lutheran School
125 East Seminary St.
Wheaton, IL   60187

Bethlehem Lutheran School
1510 Lake St.
Evanston, IL   60201

Christ Lutheran School
607 Harvard St.
Oak Park, IL   60304

Fenwick Catholic High School
  for Boys
505 Washington Blvd.
Oak Park, IL   60302

Saint Francis Catholic High
  School
2130 West Roosevelt St.
Wheaton, IL   60187

Saint George Catholic High
  School
350 Sherman Ave.
Evanston, IL   60202

CARBONDALE AREA:

Covenant Christian School
P.O. Box 143
Carbondale, IL   62901

WAUKEGON AREA:

Waukegon Christian School
2200 Bethesda Blvd.
Zion, IL 60099

Christian Liberty Academy
203 East Camp McDonald Rd.
Prospect Heights, IL 60070

Lake County Baptist School
1550 Vorkhouse Rd.
Waukegon, IL 60085

Des Plaines Christian School
1485 Whitcomb Ave.
Des Plaines, IL 60016

River Trail Christian School
2980 Milwaukee Ave.
Northbrook, IL 60062

First Baptist Church School
1266 North Northwest Hwy.
Park Ridge, IL 60068

Brentwood Baptist Christian
 Academy
588 Dara James
Des Plaines, IL 60016

Immanuel Evangelical
 Lutheran School
1310 North Frolic Ave.
Waukegon, IL 60085

Our Savior's Evangelical
 Lutheran School
1800 23rd St.
Zion, IL 60099

Saint Paul Evangelical
 Lutheran School
105 Army Trail
Addison, IL 60101

Waukegon Seventh Day
 Adventist Academy
2170 North Fuller Rd.
Gurnee, IL 60031

Immanuel Lutheran School
832 Lee St.
Des Plaines, IL 60016

Saint Paul Lutheran School
7870 Niles Center
Skokie, IL 60076

Saint John's Lutheran School
215 South Lincoln St.
Lombard, IL 60148

Trinity Lutheran School
Roosevelt Rd. & Meyers Rd.
Lombard, IL 60148

Saint Andrews Lutheran
 School
260 Northwest Hwy.
Park Ridge, IL 60068

Resurrection Catholic
 Christian High School
7500 West Talcott Ave.
Park Ridge, IL 60068

Christ the King Catholic
 School
115 East 15th St.
Lombard, IL 60148

Saint Philip the Apostle
 Catholic School
1223 Holtz St.
Addison, IL 60101

Saint Bartholomew Catholic
 School
914 Eighth St.
Waukegon, IL 60085

EAST ST. LOUIS AREA:

Berean Christian Schools
P.O. Box 806
Edgemont Station
East St. Louis, IL 62203

Bethel Christian Academy
1417 Herbert Ave.
P.O. Box 535
South Roxana, IL 62087

Zion Lutheran School
1810 McClintock St.
Belleville, IL 62221

Assumption Catholic High
 School
950 Kingshighway
East St. Louis, IL 62203

Althoff Catholic High School
5401 West Main St.
Belleville, IL 62223

Holy Family Catholic School
116 East 1st St.
Cahokia, IL 62206

Saint Augustine of Canterbury
 School
1900 West Belle St.
Belleville, IL 62221

Saint John's School
2620 Lebanon Rd.
East St. Louis, IL 62203

PEORIA AREA:

Peoria Christian School
423 East Tripp Ave.
Peoria, IL 61603

Lincoln Christian School
Route 2
Roanoke, IL 61561

Roanoke Valley Christian
 Schools
6520 Williamson Rd., N.W.
Roanoke, IL 24019

Faith Baptist Christian School
1501 Howard Ct.
Pekin, IL 61554

Christ Lutheran School
1311 South Faraday
Peoria, IL 61605

Concordia Lutheran School
2000 West Glen St.
Peoria, IL 61611

Catholic Academy of Our Lady
404 N.E. Madison
Peoria, IL 61603

ELGIN AREA:

Westminster Christian
  School
991 Deborah St.
Elgin, IL 60120

Timothy Christian High
  School
1061 South Prospect St.
Elmhurst, IL 60126

Timothy Christian Jr. High
  School
188 West Butterfield St.
Elmhurst, IL 60126

Broadview Academy
  Seventh Day Adventist
La Fox, IL 60147

Immanuel Lutheran School
148 East 3rd St.
Elmhurst, IL 60126

Good Shepherd Lutheran
  School
1111 Van St.
Elgin, IL 60120

Saint John's Lutheran School
109 North Spring St.
Elgin, IL 60120

Saint Edward High School
335 Locust St.
Elgin, IL 60120

Immaculate Conception
  Catholic High School
217 Cottage Hill St.
Elmhurst, IL 60126

Visitation Catholic Jr. High
  School
851 South York Rd.
Elmhurst, IL 60126

Chicago Jr. School
  Christian Science
1600 Dundee Ave.
Elgin, IL 60120

MOLINE AREA:

Quad Cities Baptist Academy
5102 47th Ave.
Moline, IL 61265

Bible Missionary Institute
3501 46th Ave.
Rock Island, IL 61201

Temple Christian Academy
2305 7th Ave.
Moline, IL 61265

Quad Cities Christian
  Academy
5323 180th St.
East Moline, IL 61244

Victory Baptist Christian
  School
900 46th Ave.
East Moline, IL 61244

Faith Christian Schools
1901 12th St.
Moline, IL 61265

Riverside Christian School
309 East Third St.
Andalusia, IL 61232

Community Christian School
711 10th St.
Fulton, IL 61252

Seventh Day Adventist School
36th Ave. & 53rd St.
Moline, IL 61265

Immanuel Lutheran School
3300 24th St.
Rock Island, IL 61201

Alleman Catholic High School
1103 40th St.
Rock Island, IL 61201

Jordan Catholic Middle
  School
214 15th St.
Rock Island, IL 61201

DANVILLE AREA:

Danville Baptist School
1211 North Vermilion St.
Danville, IL 61832

Heritage Christian Schools
911 West Bradley St.
Champaign, IL 61820

Wescove Christian High
  School
Route 2, Box 317
Potomac, IL 61865

Hope Christian School
914 Fowler St.
Danville, IL 61832

Community Christian School
2502 South Race St.
Urbana, IL 61801

Community Christian School
310 West Church
Savoy, IL 61874

Immanuel Lutheran School
1930 Bowman Avenue Rd.
Danville, IL 61832

Trinity Lutheran School
826 East Main St.
Danville, IL 61832

Schlarman Catholic High
  School
2112 North Vermilion St.
Danville, IL 61832

Saint Patrick Catholic School
5 Park St.
Danville, IL 61832

QUINCY AREA:

American Christian School
300 North 30th St.
Quincy, IL 62301

Columbus Road Baptist
  School
36th & Columbus Rd.
Quincy, IL 62301

Chaddock Methodist Boys'
School
205 South 24th St.
Quincy, IL 62301

Saint James Lutheran School
17th & Madison Sts.
Quincy, IL 62301

Quincy Notre Dame Catholic
High School
1400 South 11th St.
Quincy, IL 62301

BLOOMINGTON AREA:

Calvary Baptist Academy
1017 North School St.
Normal, IL 61761

Trinity Lutheran School
701 South Madison St.
Bloomington, IL 61701

Central Catholic High School
710 North Center St.
Bloomington, IL 61701

GALESBURG AREA:

Bethany Christian Academy
590 South Academy St.
Galesburg, IL 61401

Grace Episcopal Day School
151 East Carl Sandburg Dr.
Galesburg, IL 61401

Costa Catholic School
2726 Costa St.
Galesburg, IL 61401

BELLEVILLE AREA:

Twin Oaks Christian School
Route 1, P.O. Box 299-A
McBride Ave.
Dupo, IL 62239

ALTON AREA:

Mississippi Valley Christian
School
2009 Seminary St.
Alton, IL 62002

Marquette Catholic High
School
219 East Fourth St.
Alton, IL 62002

GRANITE CITY AREA:

Zion Lutheran School
625 Church Dr.
Bethalto, IL 62010

KANKAKEE AREA:

Unity Christian School
P.O. Box 406
Momence, IL 60954

STERLING AREA:

Faith Baptist Christian School
2005 Freeport Rd.
Sterling, IL 61081

KEENSBURG AREA:

Wabash Christian Academy
P.O. Box 120
Keensburg, IL 62852

SPARTA AREA:

Faith Christian School
406 West Monroe St.
Sparta, IL 62286

INDIANA

INDIANAPOLIS AREA:

Indianapolis Christian Schools,
Inc.
429 East Vermont St.
Indianapolis, IN 46202

Indianapolis Baptist High
School
2711 South East St.
Indianapolis, IN 46225

Capitol City Christian Academy
3743 East Pleasant Run Pkwy.
South Dr.
Indianapolis, IN 46201

Heritage Christian School
6401 East 75th St.
Indianapolis, IN 46250

Southside Christian School
3830 East Southport Rd.
Indianapolis, IN 46227

Broadway Christian School
7676 East 38th St.
Indianapolis, IN 46226

Westside Nazarene Christian
Schools
8610 West 10th St.
Indianapolis, IN 46234

Bethesda Jr. & Sr. Christian
High Schools
Richwine Rd.
Brownsburg, IN 46112

Tabernacle Christian Academy
2599 East 98th St.
Indianapolis, IN 46280

Colonial Christian School
8140 Union Chapel Rd.
Indianapolis, IN 46240

Greenfield Christian Academy
Highway 40
Charlottesville, IN 46117

Lakeview Christian Academy
47 Beachway Dr.
Indianapolis, IN 46224

Mooresville Christian School
State Road 67
Mooresville, IN 46158

West Newton Christian Academy
7860 Mooresville Rd.
Indianapolis, IN 46241

Calvary Christian School
902 Fletcher Ave.
Indianapolis, IN 46203

Nazarene Christian School
P.O. Box 59
Beech Grove, IN 46107

Bethesda Christian School
Route 1
Brownsburg, IN   46112

Whitefield Presbyterian
 Academy
7900 Allisonville Rd.
Indianapolis, IN   46250

Suburban Baptist Schools
722 East South County Line
 Rd.
Indianapolis, IN   46227

Southside Baptist School
1401 East Pleasant Run Pkwy.
South Dr.
Indianapolis, IN   46203

Eagledale Baptist School
4950 West 34th St.
Indianapolis, IN   46224

Gateway Wesleyan School
170 & 267 Plainfield Ave.
Indianapolis, IN   46241

Southwood Christian Assembly
 School
8700 South Meridian St.
Indianapolis, IN   46217

Westside Christian Academy
 Assembly of God
1460 South Belmont Ave.
Indianapolis, IN   46221

Trinity Lutheran School
8540 East 16th St.
Indianapolis, IN   46219

Saint Peter Lutheran School
2525 East 11th St.
Indianapolis, IN   46201

Saint Richard's Episcopal
 School
3243 North Meridian St.
Indianapolis, IN   46208

All Saints Catholic School
337 North Warman Ave.
Indianapolis, IN   46222

ANDERSON AREA:

Indiana Christian Academy
52 West Hartman Rd.
Anderson, IN   46012

Liberty Christian School
2129 McKinley St.
Anderson, IN   46014

Christian Academy
P.O. Box 263
Clermont, IN   46119

Indiana Academy
 Seventh Day Adventist
Route 1
Cicero, IN   46034

FORT WAYNE AREA:

Fort Wayne Christian School
1800 Laverne Ave.
Fort Wayne, IN   46805

Blackhawk Christian School
7321 East State Blvd.
Fort Wayne, IN   46815

Calvary Christian School
2901 North Clinton St.
Fort Wayne, IN   46805

Colonial Christian School
3200 Hillegas Rd.
Fort Wayne, IN   46808

Victory Bible School, Inc.
Route 3
Decatur, IN   46733

Cedar Creek Amish Parochial
 School
Route 2, Page Rd.
Grabill, IN   46741

Concordia Evangelical
 Lutheran School
4245 Lake Ave.
Fort Wayne, IN   46805

Concordia Lutheran High
 School
1601 St. Joe River Dr.
Fort Wayne, IN   46805

Saint Paul's Lutheran School
1126 South Barr St.
Fort Wayne, IN   46802

Saint John's Lutheran School
725 West Washington Blvd.
Fort Wayne, IN   46804

Suburban Bethlehem Lutheran
 Schools
6318 West California Rd.
Fort Wayne, IN   46808

Canterbury Episcopal School
611 West Berry St.
Fort Wayne, IN   46802

Central Catholic High School
130 East Lewis St.
Fort Wayne, IN   46802

Bishop Luers Catholic High
 School
333 East Paulding Rd.
Fort Wayne, IN   46806

Bishop Dwenger Catholic High
 School
1300 East Washington Center
Fort Wayne, IN   46805

HAMMOND AREA:

Portage Nazarene Christian
 Jr. & Sr. High School
3134 Swanson Rd.
Portage, IN   46368

Landmark Christian High
 School
7224 West 400 N.
Michigan City, IN   46360

Le Mans Christian Academy
 for Boys
5901 North 500 East Rolling
 Prairie Rd.
Valparaiso, IN   46383

New Horizon Christian
 Academy
2801 Central Ave.
Hobart, IN   46342

Calumet Baptist School
3910 West 47th St.
Gary, IN   46408

Hammond Baptist Schools
P.O. Box 1007
Schererville, IN   46375

Pentecostal Christian School
619 Sibley St.
Hammond, IN   46320

Highland Christian School
3040 Ridge Rd.
Highland, IN   46322

Michigan City Christian
Schools
1314 South Woodland Ave.
Michigan City, IN   46360

Hobart Baptist School
1 North Pennsylvania St.
Hobart, IN   46342

Saint Paul Christian Day
School
114 East 9th St.
Michigan City, IN   46360

Fairhaven Christian Academy
East Oak Hill Rd.
Chesterton, IN   46304

Westville Christian School
U.S. Highway 2
Westville, IN   46391

Mizpah Seventh Day Adventist
School
2350 Jefferson St.
Gary, IN   46407

Seventh Day Adventist School
1621 Roberts St.
La Porte, IN   46350

Immanuel Lutheran School
1700 North Monticello Park
Dr.
Valparaiso, IN   46383

Saint John's Lutheran School
111 Kingsbury Ave.
La Porte, IN   46350

Trinity Lutheran School
900 Luther Dr.
Hobart, IN   46342

Saints Peter & Paul Catholic
School
5885 Harrison St.
Gary, IN   46408

Saint Michael Catholic School
15 East Wilhelm St.
Schererville, IN   46375

Saint Mary Catholic School
525 North Broad St.
Griffith, IN   46319

Our Lady of Grace Catholic
School
3025 Hwy.
Highland, IN   46322

Marquette Catholic High
School
306 West 10th St.
Michigan City, IN   46360

Saint Joseph Catholic School
101 C St.
La Porte, IN   46350

EVANSVILLE AREA:

Evansville Christian Schools
4400 Lincoln Ave.
Evansville, IN   47715

Mill Road Baptist Schools
80 West Mill Rd.
Evansville, IN   47710

Mill Road Baptist Schools
5720 Division St.
Evansville, IN   47715

Evansville Lutheran School
1000 West Illinois St.
Evansville, IN   47710

Trinity Lutheran School
Boonville-New Harmony Rd.
Evansville, IN   47711

Reitz Memorial High School
1500 Lincoln Ave.
Evansville, IN   47714

Mater Dei Catholic High
School
1300 Harmony Way
Evansville, IN   47712

Christ the King Catholic
School
3101 Bayard Park Dr.
Evansville, IN   47714

Resurrection Catholic School
5301 New Harmony Rd.
Evansville, IN   47712

SOUTH BEND AREA:

Michiana Christian School
22987 Edison Rd.
South Bend, IN   46615

Brethren Christian Schools
201 Oregon St.
Osceola, IN   46561

Grace Baptist School
19637 Dubois Ave.
South Bend, IN   46637

Calvary Temple Academy
3717 South Michigan St.
South Bend, IN   46614

Seventh Day Adventist School
1910 East Altgeld St.
South Bend, IN   46614

Howe Episcopal Military
School
Howe, IN   46746

Saint Joseph Catholic High
School
1441 North Michigan St.
South Bend, IN   46601

Christ the King Catholic
School
52473 U.S. 31 N.
South Bend, IN   46637

LAFAYETTE AREA:

Lafayette Christian School
525 North 26th St.
Lafayette, IN   47904

Lafayette Baptist School
2901 Kossuth St.
Lafayette, IN   47904

WARSAW AREA:

Warsaw Christian School
909 South Buffalo St.
Warsaw, IN   46580

RICHMOND AREA:

Richmond Christian Schools
315 West National Rd.
Richmond, IN   47374

Hillcrest Jr. & Sr. Christian
  High School
3469 State Road 38
Route 1, Box 388A
Richmond, IN   47374

New Creations Christian
  School
6400 East National Rd.
Richmond, IN   47374

Temple Christian Day School
Box 667
New Castle, IN   47362

North Seton Catholic School
720 North A St.
Richmond, IN   47374

South Seton Catholic School
233 South 5th St.
Richmond, IN   47374

NEW ALBANY AREA:

Graceland Baptist Christian
  Jr. High School
3600 Kamer Miller Rd.
New Albany, IN   47150

River Falls Christian Academy
State Road 62
New Albany, IN   47150

Clearfork Wesleyan Christian
  Academy
Budd Rd.
New Albany, IN   47150

Jeffersonville Baptist Schools
5015 Highway 62
Jeffersonville, IN   47130

East Columbus Christian
  School
3170 Indiana Ave.
Columbus, IN   47201

Southeastern Jr. Academy
  Seventh Day Adventists
1805 Olive St.
New Albany, IN   47150

Our Lady of Providence
  Catholic High School
707 West Hwy. 131
New Albany, IN   47150

LAGRANGE AREA:

Hebron Fellowship School
Route 4, P.O. Box 141
Lagrange, IN   46741

ELKHART AREA:

Elkhart Baptist Christian
  School
2626 Prairie St.
Elkhart, IN   46514

Clinton Christian School
61763 CR 35
Goshen, IN   46526

Syracuse Christian Schools
Route 2, Box 44
Syracuse, IN   46567

Trinity Lutheran School
425 Massachusetts Ave.
Elkhart, IN   46514

Wawassee Catholic
  Preparatory School
Route 1
Syracuse, IN   46567

Saint Thomas the Apostle
  Catholic School
1331 North Main St.
Elkhart, IN   46514

TERRE HAUTE AREA:

Terre Haute Baptist School
2500 Margaret Ave.
Terre Haute, IN   47802

Schulte Catholic High School
2901 Ohio St.
Terre Haute, IN   47807

Saint Patrick's Catholic School
449 South 19th St.
Terre Haute, IN   47803

LOGANSPORT AREA:

Church of the Bible Covenant
  Christian School
2510 George St.
Logansport, IN   46947

Calvary Bible
  Landmark Christian School
3925 U.S. Hwy. 24 E.
Logansport, IN   46947

Saint Joseph's Catholic
  School
121 Eel River Ave.
Logansport, IN   46947

MUNCIE AREA:

Heritage Hall Christian School
5801 River Rd.
Muncie, IN   47304

Wesleyan Day School
1818 East 18th St.
Muncie, IN   47302

Saint Lawrence Catholic School
920 East Charles St.
Muncie, IN   47305

BLOOMINGTON AREA:

Grace Baptist Academy
2320 Smith Pike
Bloomington, IN   47401

Saint Charles Catholic School
2224 East Third St.
Bloomington, IN   47401

MISHAWAKA AREA:

First Baptist School
724 North Main St.
Mishawaka, IN 46544

Marion Catholic High School
1311 South Logan St.
Mishawaka, IN 46544

VINCENNES AREA:

Saint John's Lutheran School
707 North 8th St.
Vincennes, IN 47591

Saint Peter's Lutheran School
Old Decker Rd.
Vincennes, IN 47591

Rivet Catholic High School
210 Barnett St.
Vincennes, IN 47591

KOKOMO AREA:

Kokomo Christian School
2635 South Dixon Rd.
Kokomo, IN 46901

Temple Christian Academy
1700 South Goyer Rd.
Kokomo, IN 46901

Saint Patrick Catholic School
1230 North Armstrong St.
Kokomo, IN 46901

Saint Joan of Arc
  Catholic School
824 South Purdum St.
Kokomo, IN 46901

BEDFORD AREA:

Lawrence County Christian
  School
c/o William J. Taton
Route 16, Box 46
Bedford, IN 47421

WASHINGTON AREA:

Trinity Holiness Academy
Route 3
Washington, IN 47501

HEBRON AREA:

Demotte Christian School
P.O. Box 430
Demotte, IN 46310

IOWA

DES MOINES AREA:

Des Moines Christian School
4801 Franklin Ave.
Des Moines, IA 50310

Grandview Park Baptist
  School
1701 East 33rd St.
Des Moines, IA 50317

Kingsway Christian Academy
1000 College St.
Des Moines, IA 50314

Mount Olive Lutheran School
5625 Franklin Ave.
Des Moines, IA 50310

Saint Pius X Catholic High
  School
3601 66th St.
Des Moines, IA 50322

Christ the King Catholic
  School
701 Wall Ave.
Des Moines, IA 50315

Holy Trinity School
2922 Beaver Ave.
Des Moines, IA 50310

Saint John's School
1915 University Ave.
Des Moines, IA 50314

Saint Peter's School
618 East 18th St.
Des Moines, IA 50316

Saint Anthony's School
16 Columbus Ave.
Des Moines, IA 50315

All Saints' School
3rd & Ovid Sts.
Des Moines, IA 50313

SIOUX CITY AREA:

Morningside Christian School
6100 Morningside Ave.
Sioux City, IA 51106

Saint Paul's Lutheran School
614 Jennings St.
Sioux City, IA 51105

Heelan Catholic High School
1021 Douglas St.
Sioux City, IA 51105

ALGONA AREA:

Saint Paul Immanuel
  Lutheran School
P.O. Box 248
Whittemore, IA 50598

DAVENPORT AREA:

Westside Christian Education
  Center
1523 South Fairmount Ave.
Davenport, IA 52802

Tipton Christian Day School
Second & Spruce Sts.
Tipton, IA 52772

Seventh Day Adventist School
4444 West Kimberly Rd.
Davenport, IA 52806

Trinity Lutheran School
1122 West Central Park Ave.
Davenport, IA 52804

Assumption Catholic High
  School
1020 West Central Park Ave.
Davenport, IA 52804

Holy Trinity Catholic
  Intermediate School
1116 West 6th St.
Davenport, IA 52802

Sacred Heart Cathedral School
408 East 11th St.
Davenport, IA 52803

Saint Paul the Apostle School
1007 East Rusholme St.
Davenport, IA 52803

WATERLOO AREA:

Walnut Ridge Baptist Academy
1307 West Ridgeway
Waterloo, IA 50701

Timothy Christian School
Wellsburg, IA 50680

Seventh Day Adventist
 School
560 West Airline Hwy.
Waterloo, IA 50701

Immanuel Lutheran School
130 Walnut St.
Waterloo, IA 50703

Waterloo Catholic High School
320 Mulberry St.
Waterloo, IA 50703

DUBUQUE AREA:

Wahlert Catholic High School
2005 Kane St.
Dubuque, IA 52001

KNOXVILLE AREA:

Regular Baptist School
210 North Iowa
Knoxville, IA 50138

ORANGE CITY-HULL AREA:

Western Christian High
 School
927 Fifth St.
Hull, IA 51239

Hull Christian School
1301 5th St.
Hull, IA 51239

Unity Christian High School
216 Michigan Ave., S.W.
Orange City, IA 51041

Orange City Christian
 School
604 Third St., S.W.
Orange City, IA 51041

Rock Valley Christian School
1405 17th St.
Rock Valley, IA 51247

Rock Rapids Christian School
311 South Bradley St.
Rock Rapids, IA 51246

Lebanon Christian School
Route 1
Sioux Center, IA 51250

Sheldon Christian School
1425 East 9th St.
Sheldon, IA 51201

Sanborn Christian School
405 2nd St., Drawer H
Sanborn, IA 51248

Hospers Christian School
104 North 6th Ave.
Hospers, IA 51238

Inwood Christian School
302 East Madison
Drawer C
Inwood, IA 51240

Ireton Christian School
104 5th St., Box 127
Ireton, IA 51027

Ocheyedan Christian School
Box 7, Route 2
Ocheyedan, IA 51354

Sibley Christian School
736 Poplar Dr.
Sibley, IA 51249

Northwest Iowa Protestant
 Reformed School
P.O. Box 67
Doon, IA 51235

Doon Christian School
P.O. Box 8, Route 2
Doon, IA 51235

Hull Protestant Reformed
 School
306 2nd St.
Hull, IA 51239

Netherlands Reformed
 Christian School
Route 1, P.O. Box 269K
Rock Valley, IA 51247

AMES AREA:

Baptist Christian School
Ames, IA 50010

Saint Cecilia Catholic School
Ames, IA 50010

FORT MADISON AREA:

Aquinas Catholic High School
Fort Madison, IA 52627

CEDAR RAPIDS AREA:

Cedar Rapids Christian
 School
1203 Third Ave., S.W.
Cedar Rapids, IA 52404

Iowa Christian School
Route 2
Central City, IA 52214

Trinity Lutheran School
1361 7th Ave., S.W.
Cedar Rapids, IA 52405

La Salle Catholic High School
3700 1st Ave., N.W.
Cedar Rapids, IA 52405

Regis Catholic High School
Prairie Dr. & K Ave., N.E.
Cedar Rapids, IA 52405

IOWA CITY AREA:

Iowa Mennonite School
Route 2
Kalona, IA 52247

Cono Bible Presbyterian
 Christian School
Walker, IA 52352

Scattergood Friends School
West Branch, IA 52358

Regina Catholic High School
Rochester Ave.
Iowa City, IA 52240

Iowa City Catholic School
229 East Court St.
Iowa City, IA 52240

MUSCATINE AREA:

Academy of the Living Water
3120 Park Ave., W.
Muscatine, IA 52761

Saint Katherine's - Saint
  Mark's Interdenominational
  School
1821 Sunset Dr.
Bettendorf, IA 52722

Seventh Day Adventist School
2904 Mulberry St.
Muscatine, IA 52761

Hayes Catholic School
2407 Cedar St.
Muscatine, IA 52761

COUNCIL BLUFFS AREA:

Sioux Center Christian School
630 1st Ave., S. E.
Sioux Center, IA 51250

Saint Albert Catholic High
  School
400 Gleason St.
Council Bluffs, IA 51501

FORT DODGE AREA:

Community Christian School
3058 Tenth Ave., N.
Fort Dodge, IA 50501

Saint Paul's Lutheran School
1225 Fourth Ave., S.
Fort Dodge, IA 50501

Trinity Lutheran School
Route 3
Fort Dodge, IA 50501

Saint Edmond Catholic High
  School
501 North 22nd St.
Fort Dodge, IA 50501

MASON CITY AREA:

Kanawha Christian School
470 East Fifth St.
Route 1
Kanawha, IA 50447

Mason City Christian School
340 20th St., S.W.
Mason City, IA 50401

Seventh Day Adventist School
811 North Kentucky St.
Mason City, IA 50401

Newman Catholic High School
106 West St.
Mason City, IA 50401

OTTUMWA AREA:

Bible Baptist Christian Day
  School
944 West Williams St.
Ottumwa, IA 52501

Oskaloosa Christian School
810 North E St.
Oskaloosa, IA 52577

Faith Christian Academy
1209 South Sixth
Fairfield, IA 52556

Trinity Lutheran School
295 Shaul Ave.
Ottumwa, IA 52501

Seton Catholic School
117 East Fourth St.
Ottumwa, IA 52501

MARSHALLTOWN AREA:

Central Iowa Christian
  Academy
1008 East Olive St.
Marshalltown, IA 50158

Saint Henry's Catholic School
Columbus Dr.
Marshalltown, IA 50158

Saint Mary's Catholic School
10 West Linn St.
Marshalltown, IA 50158

CEDAR FALLS AREA:

Christian Heritage School
14th & Main Sts.
Cedar Falls, IA 50613

Excelsior Christian School
901 Grand St.
Parkersburg, IA 50665

Timothy Christian School
Box N
Wellsburg, IA 50680

Saint Patrick Catholic School
7th & Washington Sts.
Cedar Falls, IA 50613

MARION AREA:

Grace Christian School
440 South 15th St.
Marion, IA 52302

Seventh Day Adventist School
Route 1
Marion, IA 52302

Saint Joseph's Catholic School
1430 14th St.
Marion, IA 52302

BOONE AREA:

Christian Boarding School
924 West Second St.
Boone, IA 50036

Trinity Lutheran School
Boone, IA 50036

Roman Catholic School
Boone, IA 50036

NEWTON AREA:

Newton Christian School
703 East 11th St., N.
Newton, IA 50208

Pella Christian High School
604 Jefferson St.
Pella, IA 50219

Pella Christian School
216 Liberty St.
Pella, IA 50219

Peoria Christian School
Route 2
Pella, IA   50219

Sully Christian School
Box 326
Sully, IA   50251

Prairie City Christian
  School
Box 308, Route 1
Prairie City, IA   50228

Oak Park Academy
  Seventh Day Adventist
Nevada, IA   50201

KEOKUK AREA:

Calvary Baptist Christian
  High School
Keokuk, IA   52632

Cardinal Stritch Catholic
  High School
Keokuk, IA   52632

LIDDERDALE AREA:

Immanuel Lutheran School
Lidderdale, IA   51452

CRESTON AREA:

Stanzel Christian High
  School
Route 2
Greenfield, IA   50849

CHEROKEE AREA:

Zion Lutheran School
103 West Bertha St.
Paullina, IA   51046

CENTERVILLE AREA:

Heritage Christian School
North Park Ave.
P.O. Box 868
Centerville, IA   52544

KANSAS

WICHITA AREA:

Wichita Collegiate Upper
  School
9115 East Thirteenth St.
Wichita, KS   67206

Christian Challenge School
300 Ohio St.
Wichita, KS   67214

Christian Challenge Elementary School
24 North Athenian
Wichita, KS   67203

Christian Center Academy
2900 West Kellogg Dr.
Wichita, KS   67213

Bethel Life School
  Interdenominational
2801 South Seneca St.
Wichita, KS   67217

Wichita Christian School
201 North West St.
Wichita, KS   67203

Wichita Heights Baptist
  School
6400 North Hydraulic
Wichita, KS   67219

Baptist Tabernacle School
405 Cleveland St.
Wichita, KS   67214

Gospel Lighthouse Christian
  School
2356 Arkansas St.
Wichita, KS   67204

Messiah Evangelical Lutheran
  School
1241 North Ridge Rd.
Wichita, KS   67212

Berean Mennonite Academy
Elbing, KS   67041

Wichita Jr. Academy
  Seventh Day Adventist
2725 South Osage St.
Wichita, KS   67217

Saint John's Lutheran
  Academy
Seventh & College Sts.
Winfield, KS   67156

Bethany Lutheran School
1000 West 26th St., S.
Wichita, KS   67217

Holy Cross Lutheran School
1018 North Dellrose St.
Wichita, KS   67208

Christ the King Catholic
  School
4501 Maple St.
Wichita, KS   67209

Holy Savior Catholic School
1432 North Erie St.
Wichita, KS   67214

Saint Thomas Aquinas
  Catholic School
1215 North Stratford St.
Wichita, KS   67206

KANSAS CITY AREA:

Kansas City Christian High
  School
5701 Merriam Ln.
Merriam, KS   66203

Kansas City Central Christian
  School
4645 Booth St.
Kansas City, KS   66103

Open Door Baptist Jr. & Sr.
  High School
824 State Ave.
Kansas City, KS   66101

Muncie Christian Schools
230 South 65th St.
Kansas City, KS   66111

Oak Grove Baptist School
5500 Woodend St.
Kansas City, KS   66106

Bible Baptist School
426 Emerson
Bonner Springs, KS   66012

Maranatha Academy
2737 South 42nd St.
Kansas City, KS 66106

Midland Adventist School
6601 West 88th Terr.
Kansas City, KS 66109

Grace Lutheran School
3333 Wood Ave.
Kansas City, KS 66102

Saint Joseph Catholic High
  School
5900 Bond St.
Kansas City, KS

Saint John the Evangelist
  Catholic School
1340 South 30th St.
Kansas City, KS 66106

Christ the King Kansas
  Catholic School
3027 North 54th St.
Kansas City, KS 66104

FORT SCOTT AREA:

Fort Scott Christian School
12th & Margrave
Fort Scott, KS 66701

TOPEKA AREA:

Topeka Lutheran Schools
701 Roosevelt St.
Topeka, KS 66606

Topeka Seventh Day
  Adventist School
2301 Wanamaker Rd.
Topeka, KS 66614

Saint Matthew's Catholic
  School
1000 East 28th St.
Topeka, KS 66605

SHAWNEE AREA:

Shawnee Mission Christian
  School
4901 Mission Rd.
Shawnee Mission, KS 66216

Kansas City Christian School
5701 Merriam Dr.
Shawnee Mission, KS 66203

Trinity Baptist School
15000 West 63rd St.
Shawnee Mission, KS 66216

Hope Lutheran Christian
  School
63rd & Quivira Rd.
Shawnee, KS 66216

HUTCHINSON AREA:

Central Christian High School
1910 East 30th St.
Hutchinson, KS 67501

Berean Christian School
6th & Patton Sts.
Great Bend, KS 67530

Trinity Catholic High School
1400 East 17th St.
Hutchinson, KS 67501

COFFEYVILLE AREA:

Heritage Christian Academy
9th & Sunflower Sts.
Coffeyville, KS 67337

Holy Name Catholic School
406 Willow St.
Coffeyville, KS 67337

ATCHISON AREA:

Maur Hill Catholic Prep
  School
10th & Green Sts.
Atchison, KS 66002

LAWRENCE AREA:

Sunshine Acres Methodist
  School
2141 Maple Ln.
Lawrence, KS 66044

Saint John's School
1208 Kentucky St.
Lawrence, KS 66044

DODGE CITY AREA:

Meade Mennonite Bible
  Academy
Meade, KS 67864

Sacred Heart Catholic School
905 Central St.
Dodge City, KS 67801

JUNCTION CITY AREA:

Lutheran School
700 West 7th St.
Junction City, KS 66441

Saint Xavier's Catholic High
  School
2nd & Washington Sts.
Junction City, KS 66441

Luckey Catholic High School
220 South Juliette St.
Manhattan, KS 66502

NEWTON AREA:

Bible Church School of
  Newton
900 Old Main St.
Newton, KS 67114

Saint Mary Catholic School
100 East 8th St.
Newton, KS 67114

PITTSBURG AREA:

Seventh Day Adventist School
Route 4
Pittsburg, KS 66762

Colgan Catholic High School
213 East 9th St.
Pittsburg, KS 66762

Saint Mary's – Our Lady of
  Lourdes Catholic School
213 East 9th St.
Pittsburg, KS 66762

SALINA AREA:

Saint John's Episcopal
  Military School
End of North Santa Fe St.
Salina, KS 67401

Sacred Heart Catholic High
  School
230 East Cloud St.
Salina, KS 67401

OVERLAND PARK AREA:

Faith Christian School
Route 2, Box 347
Olathe, KS 66061

Berean Christian School
Box 806
15021 51st St.
Olathe, KS 66061

KENTUCKY

LOUISVILLE AREA:

Metropolitan Christian School
5100 Preston Hwy.
Louisville, KY 40213

Christian Academy of
  Louisville
Box 22226
Louisville, KY 40222

Buechel Alliance Christian
  School
3726 Bardstown Rd.
Louisville, KY 40218

Beth Haven Baptist Christian
  School
5515 Johnsontown Rd.
Valley Station, KY 40272

Northside Christian School
2214 Bank St.
Louisville, KY 40212

South Louisville Christian
  School
1105 New Grade Ln.
Louisville, KY 40213

Shively Christian School
1848 Kendall Ln.
Louisville, KY 40216

Ninth & 0 Christian School
2921 Taylor Blvd.
Louisville, KY 40208

Highview Baptist Christian
  Academy
7711 Fegenbush Ln.
Louisville, KY 40228

Farmdale Christian School
6501 Vandre Ave.
Louisville, KY 40228

Gethsemane Christian School
10400 Blue Lick Rd.
Louisville, KY 40229

Evangel High School
3701 Fern Valley Rd.
Louisville, KY 40219

Evangel Jr. High School
5400 Minors Ln.
Louisville, KY 40219

Faith Temple Schools
5627 New Cut Rd.
Louisville, KY 40214

Portland Christian School
  Church of Christ
2500 Portland Ave.
Louisville, KY 40212

Greater Louisville Jr.
  Academy
7315 Southside Dr.
Louisville, KY 40214

Immanuel Lutheran High
  School
124 South Galt Ave.
Louisville, KY 40206

Martin Luther School
1335 Gardiner Ln.
Louisville, KY 40213

Saint Francis Catholic High
  School
3rd & Broadway
Louisville, KY 40202

Saint Xavier Catholic High
  School
1609 Poplar Level Rd.
Louisville, KY 40217

Loretto Catholic High School
723 South 45th St.
Louisville, KY 40211

Good Shepherd School
8012 Vaughn Mill Rd.
Louisville, KY 40228

Saint Andrew's Catholic
  School
334 South Chiles St.
Harrodsburg, KY 40330

LEXINGTON AREA:

Blue Grass Baptist School
1330 Red River Dr.
Lexington, KY 40502

Sayre Presbyterian School
194 North Limestone St.
Lexington, KY 40507

Gardenside Christian School
940 Holly Springs Dr.
Lexington, KY 40504

Lexington Catholic High
  School
2250 Clay's Mill Rd.
Lexington, KY 40503

Christ the King Catholic
  School
412 Cochran Rd.
Lexington, KY 40502

COVINGTON AREA:

Calvary Christian School
5955 Taylor Mill Rd.
Taylor Mill, KY 41015

Covington Catholic High School
1600 Dixie Hwy.
Covington, KY 41011

Newport Catholic High School
Caruthers Rd.
Newport, KY 41071

Bishop Brossart Catholic
High School
Grove & North Jefferson Sts.
Alexandria, KY 41001

OWENSBORO AREA:

Owensboro Christian Academy
4430 Old Calhoun Rd.
Owensboro, KY 42301

Trinity High School
Whitesville, KY 42378

Owensboro Catholic High
School
1525 Parrish Ave.
Owensboro, KY 42301

Saint Stephen's School
600 Locust St.
Owensboro, KY 42301

BOWLING GREEN AREA:

Anchored Christian Schools
1000 Roselawn Way
Bowling Green, KY 42101

Potter Christian School
2600 Nashville Rd.
Bowling Green, KY 42101

Faith Evangelical Christian
Schools
West Porter St.
P.O. Drawer 609
Morgantown, KY 42261

Bible Baptist Christian
School
Radcliffe, KY 40160

Seventh Day Adventist School
1155 Lee St.
Bowling Green, KY 42101

Saint Joseph Catholic School
416 Church St.
Bowling Green, KY 42101

Saint James Catholic School
114 North Miles St.
Elizabethtown, KY 42701

PADUCAH AREA:

Paducah Christian Schools
1915 North 10th St.
Paducah, KY 42001

Southland Christian Schools
Box 277
Paducah, KY 42001

Concord United Methodist
School
Hinkleville Rd.
Paducah, KY 42001

Saint Mary's Catholic High
School
Lone Oak Rd. & Kennedy Rd.
Paducah, KY 42001

Saint Joseph Catholic School
South 14th St.
Mayfield, KY 42066

MIDDLESBORO – CORBIN
AREA:

Oneida Baptist Institute
Oneida, KY 40972

Annville Institute
Reformed Church
Annville, KY 40402

Saint Julian Catholic School
116 East Chester Ave.
Middlesboro, KY 40965

Saint Camillus Catholic
Academy
East Center St.
Corbin, KY 40701

JACKSON AREA:

Oakdale Christian High School
Free Methodist
Route 1, Box 288
Jackson, KY 41339

Riverside Christian School
Brethren
(Breathitt County)
Haddix, KY 41331

Hazelgreen Academy
Disciples of Christ
Hazel Green, KY 41332

Our Lady of the Mountain
Catholic School
300 Third St.
Paintsville, KY 41240

HAZARD AREA:

The Hazard Christian
Academy
Highway 15 N.
Hazard, KY 41701

Calvary Day School
Letcher, KY 41832

FRANKFORT AREA:

Tabernacle Christian Schools
Highway 421 S.
Frankfort, KY 40601

Good Shepherd School
320 Wapping St.
Frankfort, KY 40601

MADISONVILLE AREA:

Madisonville Christian
School
Princeton Rd.
Madisonville, KY 42431

Christ the King Catholic
School
U.S. Highway 41 N.
Madisonville, KY 42431

Holy Name Catholic School
628 Second St.
Henderson, KY 42420

BEREA AREA:

Christian Schools, Inc.
Box 447
Berea, KY 40403

Margaret Hall Episcopal
School
Versailles, KY 40383

Sisters of Divine Providence
  Catholic School
244 Main St.
Winchester, KY   40391

HOPKINSVILLE AREA:

University Heights Academy
North Dr.
Hopkinsville, KY   42240

Saints Peter & Paul Catholic
  School
902 East 9th St.
Hopkinsville, KY   42240

ASHLAND AREA:

Southland Bible Institute
Meade Station, Route 6
Box 20
Ashland, KY   41101

Holy Family Catholic High
  School
932 Winchester Ave.
Ashland, KY   41101

SOMERSET AREA:

Science Hill Baptist
  Christian Academy
Science Hill, KY   42533

PIKEVILLE AREA:

East Kentucky Bible Institute
Route 3, Box 385
Pikeville, KY   41501

LOUISIANA

NEW ORLEANS AREA:

Crescent City Baptist School
4828 Utica St.
Metairie, LA   70003

John Curtis Christian School
10125 Jefferson Hwy.
River Ridge
New Orleans, LA   70123

Lake Forest Christian
  School
8358 Lake Forest Blvd.
New Orleans, LA   70126

First Assembly Academy
8825 Airline Hwy.
New Orleans, LA   70118

Carrollton Presbyterian
  School
2032 South Carrollton Ave.
New Orleans, LA   70118

Crescent City Adventist
  School
3711 Franklin Ave.
New Orleans, LA   70122

Ephesus Jr. Academy
  Seventh Day Adventist
1019 Caffin Ave.
New Orleans, LA   70117

Jefferson Heights Jr.
  Academy
625 Newman Ave.
New Orleans, LA   70121

Lutheran High School
1201 Washington Ave.
New Orleans, LA   70130

First English Lutheran
  School
2521 Marais St.
New Orleans, LA   70117

Saint Paul First English
  Lutheran School
2624 Burgundy St.
New Orleans, LA   70117

Christ Lutheran School
714 Caffin Ave.
New Orleans, LA   70117

Our Savior Lutheran School
6054 Vermillion Blvd.
New Orleans, LA   70122

Saint John Lutheran School
136 North Pierce St.
New Orleans, LA   70119

A Faith Lutheran School
300 Colonial Club Dr.
Harahan, LA   70123

Mount Olive Lutheran School
315 Ridgelake Dr.
Metairie, LA   70001

Saint Stephen Lutheran
  School
6700 Westbank Expressway
Marrero, LA   70114

Salem Lutheran School
418 Fourth St.
Gretna, LA   70053

Trinity Episcopal School
2111 Chestnut St.
New Orleans, LA   70130

Saint Paul's Episcopal School
6249 Canal Blvd.
New Orleans, LA   70124

Saint Andrew's Episcopal
  School
8012 Oak St.
New Orleans, LA   70118

Saint George's Episcopal
  School
923 Napoleon Ave.
New Orleans, LA   70115

Saint Martin's Protestant
  Episcopal School
5309 Airline Hwy.
Metairie, LA   70003

Jesuit Catholic High School
4533 South Carrollton Ave.
New Orleans, LA   70119

Jesuit Catholic High School
4133 Banks St.
New Orleans, LA   70119

Brother Martin Catholic High
  School
4401 Elysian Fields Ave.
New Orleans, LA   70122

Saint Augustine Catholic High
  School
2600 London Ave.
New Orleans, LA   70119

Saint James Major Catholic
High School
3774 Gentilly Blvd.
New Orleans, LA 70122

De La Salle Catholic High
School
5300 St. Charles Ave.
New Orleans, LA 70115

Christian Brothers Catholic
School
City Park Ave.
New Orleans, LA 70119

Archbishop Shaw Catholic
High School
Avenue J
Marrero, LA 70072

Holy Cross Catholic High
School
4950 Dauphine St.
New Orleans, LA 70117

Saint Mary's Dominican
Catholic High School
7701 Walmsley Ave.
New Orleans, LA 70125

Saint Louis Cathedral
Catholic School
820 Dauphine St.
New Orleans, LA 70116

SHREVEPORT AREA:

Shreve Christian School
7425 Broadacres Rd.
Shreveport, LA 71109

Cross Roads Academy
445 Meriwether Rd.
Shreveport, LA 71109

Westview Christian Elementary
School
3401 Greenwood Rd.
Shreveport, LA 71109

First Baptist High School in
Shreveport
543 Ockley Dr.
Shreveport, LA 71106

Baptist Christian Academy
3031 Hollywood Ave.
Shreveport, LA 71108

Spring Hill Christian Academy
Box 123
Springhill, LA 71075

Central Free Methodist
School
2755 Ashton St.
Shreveport, LA 71103

Grawood Christian Schools
Colquitt Rd.
Keithville, LA 71047

Trinity Heights Christian
School
38200 Old Mooringsport Rd.
Shreveport, LA 71107

Southside Baptist School
6500 Fairfield Ave.
Shreveport, LA 71106

Calvary Baptist Academy
9333 Linwood Ave.
Shreveport, LA 71106

Trinity Baptist School
Doyline, LA 71023

Shreveport Jr. Academy
Seventh Day Adventist
Route 6, Box 777
Shreveport, LA 71109

Philadelphia School
Seventh Day Adventist
1143 Madison Ave.
Shreveport, LA 71103

Seventh Day Adventist School
106 Magnolia St.
Minden, LA 71055

Jesuit Catholic High School
921 Jordan St.
Shreveport, LA 71101

BATON ROUGE AREA:

Central Baptist Christian
School
5050 Greenwell St.
Baton Rouge, LA 70805

Temple Christian Schools
7513 Prescott Rd.
Baton Rouge, LA 70812

Calvary Christian School
9611 Siegan Ln.
Baton Rouge, LA 70810

First Lutheran School
321 North 16th
Baton Rouge, LA 70802

First Lutheran Christian Day
School
1553 Florida St.
Baton Rouge, LA 70802

Baton Rouge Jr. Academy
Seventh Day Adventist
3601 Prescott Rd.
Baton Rouge, LA 70805

Berean School
Seventh Day Adventist
926 South 14th St.
Baton Rouge, LA 70802

Episcopal High School
3200 Woodland Ridge Blvd.
Baton Rouge, LA 70816

Trinity Episcopal Day School
3552 Morning Glory Ave.
Baton Rouge, LA 70808

Saint Luke's Episcopal Day
School
8833 Goodwood Blvd.
Baton Rouge, LA 70806

Redemptorist Sr. Catholic
High School
5300 Wildwood Pkwy.
Baton Rouge, LA 70805

Redemptorist Catholic Jr.
High School
4000 St. Gerard Ave.
Baton Rouge, LA 70805

Catholic High School
855 Hearthstone Dr.
Baton Rouge, LA 70806

LAFAYETTE AREA:

Lafayette Christian Academy
223 Stone Ave.
Lafayette, LA 70507

Acadiana Christian School
H. Mouton Rd.
Lafayette, LA   70506

W. B. Vennard Academy
P.O. Box 2069
Lafayette, LA   70501

Acadia Baptist Academy
Eunice, LA   70535

Assembly Christian School
605 South College Rd.
Lafayette, LA   70503

Episcopal School of Acadiana
P.O. Box 4826
Lafayette, LA   70502

Cathedral Carmel Catholic
  High School
848 Saint John St.
Lafayette, LA   70501

Holy Rosary Catholic Trade
  School for Boys
421 Breaux Bridge Ave.
Lafayette, LA   70501

Father Teurlings Catholic
  High School
139 Teurlings Dr.
Lafayette, LA   70501

MONROE AREA:

Monroe Christian School
480 Garrett Rd.
Monroe, LA   71202

Quachita Christian School,
  Inc.
Highway 165 N.
Route 4, Box 197B
Monroe, LA   71201

West Monroe Christian
  Academy
Martin Ln.
West Monroe, LA   71203

Twin Cities Christian
  Academy
702 Montgomery St.
West Monroe, LA   71203

Evangel Christian Academy
777 Hadley St.
Monroe, LA   71202

American Christian Schools
  of Religion
3201 North Seventh St.
West Monroe, LA   71291

Seventh Day Adventist School
Sandel Dr.
Monroe, LA   71203

Saint Christopher's Episcopal
  Day School
1400 North 4th St.
Monroe, LA   71201

Quachita Catholic High School
Kansas Ln.
Monroe, LA   71203

Saint Frederick High School
3300 Westminster Ave.
Monroe, LA   71201

Jesus the Good Shepherd
  School
800 Good Shepherd Ln.
Monroe, LA   71201

HOUMA AREA:

Grace Christian Academy
Houma, LA   70360

Saint Matthew's Episcopal
  School
711 Belanger St.
Houma, LA   70360

Vandebilt Catholic High School
209 South Hollywood Rd.
Houma, LA   70360

Saint Francis de Sales
  Catholic School
300 Verrett St.
Houma, LA   70360

LAKE CHARLES AREA:

Glad Tidings Christian
  Academy
3400 Texas St.
Lake Charles, LA   70605

Saint Louis Catholic High
  School
1620 Bank St.
Lake Charles, LA   70601

Landry Memorial Catholic
  High School
Lake Charles, LA   70601

Saint Charles Catholic
  Academy
1536 Ryan St.
Lake Charles, LA   70601

ALEXANDRIA AREA:

Hope Baptist Schools
Leesville Hwy.
Route 1, P.O. Box 91A
Alexandria, LA   71301

Holy Savior Menard Catholic
  Central High School
4603 Gardener Hwy.
Alexandria, LA   71301

Saint Mary's Catholic School
1101 East 5th St.
Natchitoches, LA   71457

BOGALUSA AREA:

Northlake Christian School
P.O. Box 1566
Covington, LA   70433

Mount Pleasant Baptist
  Christian Academy
Mount Pleasant Rd.
Route 1
Bogalusa, LA   70427

Natalbany Baptist Christian
  School
P.O. Box 219
Natalbany, LA   70451

Saint Paul's Catholic High
  School
917 South Jahncke Ave.
Covington, LA   70433

Holy Ghost Catholic School
506 North Magnolia St.
Hammond, LA   70401

Annunciation Catholic School
511 Ave. C
Bogalusa, LA 70427

BASTROP AREA:

Bastrop Christian School
839 Van Ave.
Bastrop, LA 71220

Cherry Ridge Christian
School
1001 Cherry Ridge Rd.
Bastrop, LA 71220

Saint Joseph Catholic School
217 Harrington Ave.
Bastrop, LA 71220

OPELOUSAS AREA:

Westminster Presbyterian
Academy
146 East Cherry St.
Opelousas, LA 70570

Opelousas Catholic High
School
787 North Walnut St.
Opelousas, LA 70570

MORGAN CITY AREA:

Atkins Memorial Presbyterian
School
212 4th St.
Morgan City, LA 70380

Central Catholic Jr.-Sr.
High School
2100 Cedar St.
Morgan City, LA 70380

SLIDELL AREA:

Temple Christian Baptist
School
U.S. Highway 190 at Badon
Rd., Route 2, Box 7
Slidell, LA 70458

Trinity Presbyterian School
Route 7, P.O. Box 7283
Slidell, LA 70458

MAINE

PORTLAND AREA:

Greater Portland Christian
School
55 Pitt St.
Portland, ME 04103

North Deering Christian
School
1571 Washington Ave.
Portland, ME 04105

Greater Portland Christian
School
85 South St.
Gorham, ME 04038

Grace Baptist School
95 Florida Ave.
Portland, ME 04103

Cheverus Catholic High
School
267 Ocean Ave.
Portland, ME 04103

Saint Patrick's Catholic
School
1251 Congress St.
Portland, ME 04102

Holy Cross Catholic School
436 Broadway
South Portland, ME 04106

Saint Joseph's Catholic
School
695 Stevens Ave.
Portland, ME 04103

WATERVILLE AREA:

Kennebec Valley Christian
School
Marston Rd.
Waterville, ME 04901

Calvary Temple Academy
60 West River Rd.
Waterville, ME 04901

Canaan Christian School
Easy St.
Canaan, ME 04924

Oak Grove Friends School
Vassalboro, ME 04989

Saint John the Baptist
Catholic School
Garand St.
Winslow, ME 04901

BANGOR AREA:

Bangor Christian School
Outer Broadway
Bangor, ME 04401

Penobscot Christian School
234 French St.
Bangor, ME 04401

Glad Tidings Academy
1033 Broadway
Bangor, ME 04401

John the Baptist Catholic
High School
Broadway
Bangor, ME 04401

AUGUSTA AREA:

Central Maine Christian
Schools
North Whitefield, ME 04353

Kents Hill Methodist School
Kents Hill, ME 04349

Saint Augustine Catholic
School
Washington St.
Augusta, ME 04330

Saint Mary's Catholic School
56 Sewall St.
Augusta, ME 04330

LEWISTON AREA:

Hebron Baptist Academy
Hebron, ME 04238

Leavitt Institute
Interdenominational
Turner Center, ME 04283

Saint Dominic Regional
  Catholic High School
177 Blake St.
Lewiston, ME 04240

ROCKLAND AREA:

The Lamp Post
  Christian Schools, Inc.
Glen Cove, ME 04846

BIDDEFORD AREA:

Alfred Congregational School
Saco Rd.
Alfred, ME 04002

West Newfield School
  Congregational
Maplewood Rd.
West Newfield, ME 04095

Saint Louis Catholic High
  School
Biddeford, ME 04005

Notre Dame Catholic Institute
Waterboro Rd.
Alfred, ME 04002

Saint Joseph Catholic School
Graham St.
Biddeford, ME 04005

Saint Andre's Catholic School
39 Sullivan St.
Biddeford, ME 04005

MARYLAND

BALTIMORE AREA:

Dundalk Alliance Christian
  Academy
1731 Rita Rd.
Dundalk, MD 21222

Essex Christian Academy
200 North Marlyn Ave.
Essex, MD 21221

Elkridge Christian School
Montgomery Rd. & Timber-
  view
Elkridge, MD 21227

Christian Liberty Academy
454 East Cross St.
Baltimore, MD 21230

Grace Bible Baptist Christian
  School
1518 Rolling Rd.
Baltimore, MD 21228

Perry Hall Christian School
3919 Shroeder Ave.
Baltimore, MD 21239

Tabernacle Day School
Box 3566
Baltimore, MD 21214

Arlington Baptist School
3030 North Rolling Rd.
Baltimore, MD 21207

Bethlehem Christian Day
  School
4815 Hamilton Ave.
Baltimore, MD 21206

Calvary Christian Day School
Northern Pkwy. & Old
  Harford
Baltimore, MD 21214

Calvary Baptist Academy
407 Marley Station Rd.
Baltimore, MD 21226

Saint Paul's Evangelical
  Lutheran School
2001 Old Frederick Rd.
Catonsville, MD 21228

Baltimore Lutheran High
  School
1145 Concordia Dr.
Baltimore, MD 21204

Immanuel Lutheran School
Loch Raven Blvd. & Belvedere
Baltimore, MD 21218

Holy Comforter Lutheran
  School
York Rd. & Harwood Ave.
Baltimore, MD 21212

Saint James Lutheran Day
  School
8 West Overlea Ave.
Baltimore, MD 21206

Friends School of Baltimore
5114 North Charles St.
Baltimore, MD 21207

Open Bible Day School
5814 Harford Rd.
Baltimore, MD 21214

Saint James Academy
Monktown Rd.
Monktown, MD 21111

Saint Gabriel's School
Hilton Ave.
Baltimore, MD 21228

Saint John's Christian Day
  School
Third and Washburn Ave.
Baltimore, MD 21225

Baltimore Jr. Academy
  Seventh Day Adventist
3006 West Cold Spring Ln.
Baltimore, MD 21215

Greater Baltimore Jr.
  Academy
100 South Rock Glen Rd.
Baltimore, MD 21229

Catholic High School of
  Baltimore
2800 Edison Hwy.
Baltimore, MD 21213

Loyola Catholic High School
North Charles St. & Chestnut
Towson, MD 21204

Catholic Community School
  of South Baltimore
1530 East Fort Ave.
Baltimore, MD 21230

Saint Timothy's Episcopal
  School
200 Ingleside Ave.
Catonsville, MD 21228

Archbishop Curley Catholic
  High School
3701 Sinclair Ln.
Baltimore, MD   21213

Cardinal Gibbons Catholic
  High School for Boys
Wilkins & Caton Aves.
Baltimore, MD   21229

Archbishop Keough Catholic
  High School
1201 South Caton Ave.
Baltimore, MD   21227

Mount Saint Joseph Catholic
  High School
4403 Frederick Ave.
Baltimore, MD   21229

Church of the Redeemer Day
  School
5603 North Charles St.
Baltimore, MD   21210

Saint James & Saint John's
  School
1010 Somerset St.
Baltimore, MD   21210

CUMBERLAND AREA:

Calvary Christian Academy
14513 McMullen Hwy.
Cresaptown, MD   21502

Bishop Walsh Catholic
  High School
Cumberland, MD   21502

SILVER SPRING AREA:

Washington Christian School
1216 Arcola Ave.
Silver Spring, MD   20902

Sandy Spring Friends School
Sandy Spring, MD   20860

Forcey Christian School
2130 East Randolph
Silver Spring, MD   20904

Calvary Lutheran School
9545 Georgia Ave.
Silver Spring, MD   20910

Saint John's Lutheran School
5820 Riverdale Rd.
Riverdale, MD   20840

Grace Episcopal Day School
9115 Georgia Ave.
Silver Spring, MD   20910

Christ Episcopal Day School
109 South Washington St.
Rockville, MD   20850

Tacoma Academy
  Seventh Day Adventist
8120 Carroll Ave.
Takoma Park, MD   20012

Saint Patrick's Episcopal
  Day School
9440 Logan Dr.
Potomac, MD   20854

Good Counsel Catholic High
  School for Boys
11601 Georgia Ave.
Wheaton, MD   20902

Pallotti Catholic High School
8th St.
Laurel, MD   20810

Catholic Academy of Holy
  Names
Silver Spring, MD   20907

Saint John the Baptist
  Catholic School
12319 New Hampshire Ave.
Silver Spring, MD   20903

Georgetown Catholic
  Preparatory School
Garrett Park, MD   20766

COLUMBIA AREA:

Puritan Christian School
P.O. Box 1016
6325 Griffith Rd.
Laytonsville, MD   20879

Atholton Adventist School
Martin Rd.
Columbia, MD   21043

Saint Paul's Episcopal School
(Falls)
Brooklandville, MD   21022

Atholton Seventh Day
  Adventist School
P.O. Box 68
Simpsonville, MD   21150

FORESTVILLE AREA:

Capital Christian Academy
610 Largo Rd.
Upper Marlboro, MD   20870

Grace Brethren Christian
  Day School
5000 St. Barnabas Rd.
Temple Hills, MD   20031

Temple Christian School
P.O. Box 232B, Route 1
Hollywood, MD   20636

Riverdale Baptist School
1133 Largo Rd.
Upper Marlboro, MD   20870

Clinton Christian School
6707 Woodyard Rd.
Upper Marlboro, MD   20870

Queen Anne Episcopal School
Oak Grove Rd.
Upper Marlboro, MD   20870

Bishop McNamara Catholic
  High School
Forestville, MD   20028

HAGERSTOWN AREA:

Heritage Academy
Walnut Point Rd.
Route 2, Box 264
Hagerstown, MD   21740

Grace Academy
Route 3, P.O. Box 270
Williamsport, MD   21795

Broadfording Christian
  Academy
P.O. Box 262, Route 4
Hagerstown, MD   21740

Hagerstown Mennonite
 Fellowship School
Old Greencastle Pike
Huyett's Crossroads
Hagerstown, MD 21740

Highland View School
Route 1, P.O. Box 286
Hagerstown, MD 21740

Paradise Mennonite School
P.O. Box 32, Route 8
Hagerstown, MD 21740

Saint James Episcopal School
Saint James, MD 21781

Saint Maria Goretti Catholic
 High School
1535 Oak Hill Ave.
Hagerstown, MD 21740

Saint Joseph's Catholic High
 School
Emmitsburg, MD 21727

ANNAPOLIS AREA:

Annapolis Area Christian
 School
Ridgely Ave. & Wilson Rd.
Annapolis, MD 21401

Antioch Christian Schools
923 Windsor Ave.
Annapolis, MD 21403

Saint Martin's Evangelical
 Lutheran School
1120 Spa Rd.
Annapolis, MD 21403

Saint Paul's Lutheran School
Roscoe Rowe Blvd.
Annapolis, MD

FREDERICK AREA:

Frederick Christian Academy
6642 Carpenter Rd.
Frederick, MD 21701

Trinity Christian School
North Main St.
Frederick, MD 21701

Seventh Day Adventist
 School
New Design Rd.
Frederick, MD 21701

Saint Joseph's Catholic High
 School
DePaul St.
Frederick, MD 21701

BOWIE AREA:

Bowie Alliance Little Red
 School House
1925 Mitchellville Rd.
Bowie, MD 20715

Grace Christian School
7210 Race Track Rd.
P.O. Box 576
Bowie, MD 20715

Grace Christian School
16531 Abbey Dr.
Mitchellville, MD 20716

Puritan Christian School
12032 Scaggsville Rd.
Fulton, MD 20759

Seventh Day Adventist School
4200 Amendal Rd.
Beltsville, MD 20705

Concordia Lutheran School
3705 Longfellow St.
Hyattsville, MD 20782

Canterbury Episcopal School
Accokeek, MD 20607

De Matha Catholic High
 School
4313 Madison St.
Hyattsville, MD 20781

Regina Catholic High School
8910 Riggs Rd.
Hyattsville, MD 20783

Holy Trinity Day School
Old Defense Hwy.
Bowie, MD 20715

WESTMINSTER AREA:

Carroll Christian Academy
550 Baltimore Blvd.
Westminster, MD 21157

Harford Christian School
 Evangelical Methodist
Route 2
Street, MD 21154

Tabernacle Christian School
8855 Belair Rd.
Perry Hall, MD 21128

Perry Hall Christian Schools
3919 Schroeder Ave.
Perry Hall, MD 21128

Mountain Christian School
1824 Mountain Rd.
Joppa, MD 21085

Saint Paul's Evangelical
 Lutheran School
12022 Jerusalem Rd.
Kingsville, MD 21087

Crest Lane School
 Seventh Day Adventist
Westminster, MD 21157

Severn Christian School
Donaldson Ave.
North Anne Arundel County
Severn, MD 21144

Martin Spalding Catholic High
 School
8080 New Cut Rd.
Severn, MD 21144

Saint John the Evangelist
 School
Ritchie Hwy. & Cypress
 Creek
Severna Park, MD 21146

Trinity School
Landing Rd.
Ilchester, MD 21083

CAMBRIDGE AREA:

Golden Shore Christian
  School
201 Mill St.
Cambridge, MD   21613

Countryside Christian School
Route 50 & Austin Rd.
Cambridge, MD   21613

Open Bible Academy
1715 Race St.
Cambridge, MD   21613

SALISBURY AREA:

Christian School of Salisbury
Parker & Outten Rds.
Salisbury, MD   21801

Liberty Christian School
1313 Old Ocean City Rd.
Salisbury, MD   21801

Crisfield Christian Academy
134 Maryland Ave.
Crisfield, MD   21817

Crusaders Christian Academy
P.O. Box 986
Salisbury, MD   21801

Salisbury Seventh Day
  Adventist School
Allen, MD   21810

Saint Francis de Sales
  Catholic School
Camden Ave.
Salisbury, MD   21801

ELKTON AREA:

Elkton Christian School
P.O. Box 707
Elkton, MD   21921

Spirit & Life Christian
  Academy
Pleasant Hill
Elkton, MD   21921

West Nottingham Presby-
  terian Academy
Route 276
Colora, MD   21919

Susquehanna Jr. Academy
  Seventh Day Adventist
Old Route 222
Blythedale, MD   21921

Immaculate Conception
  Catholic School
Bow St.
Elkton, MD   21921

PRINCE FREDERICK AREA:

Calvert Christian School
P.O. Box 600
Prince Frederick, MD
20678

GLEN BURNIE AREA:

Calvary Christian Academy
407 Marley Station Rd.
Glen Burnie, MD   21061

GREENSBORO AREA:

Chesapeake Christian
  Academy
Route 1, P.O. Box 288
Greensboro, MD   21639

SUITLAND AREA:

Independent Baptist Academy
9255 Piscataway Rd.
Box 206
Clinton, MD   20735

CAMP SPRINGS AREA:

Camp Springs Christian
  School
5406 Brinkley Rd.
Camp Springs, MD   20031

Grace Brethren Christian
  Day School
5000 St. Barnabas Rd.
Temple Hills, MD   20031

MASSACHUSETTS

BOSTON AREA:

New England Baptist
  Christian Academy
30 Salem St.
Medford, MA   02155

Massachusetts Bay Christian
  School
701 Broadway
Everett, MA   02149

Lexington Christian High
  School
48 Bartlett Ave.
Lexington, MA   02173

Greater Boston Academy
  Seventh Day Adventist High
  School
20 Woodland Rd.
Stoneham, MA   02180

The Imago School
Merriam Building
Charter Rd.
Acton, MA   01720

Cambridge Friends School
5 Cadbury Rd.
Cambridge, MA   02140

Mission Church High School
67 Alleghany St.
Roxbury, MA   02120

Swedenborg School of Religion
48 Sargent St.
Newton, MA   02158

The Advent School
17 Brimmer St.
Boston, MA   02108

Greek Orthodox School
70 Corey St.
West Roxbury, MA   02132

Cathedral High School
74 Union Park St.
Boston, MA   02118

Saint Clement's Catholic High
School
Boston Ave.
Somerville, MA   02144

Arlington Catholic High School
16 Medford St.
Arlington, MA   02174

Newman Catholic Preparatory
School
245 Marlborough St.
Boston, MA   02116

Don Bosco Catholic Technical
High School
29 Warrenton St.
Boston, MA   02116

Malden Catholic High School
Crystal St.
Malden, MA   02148

Monsignor Ryan Catholic High
School
11 Mayhew St.
Dorchester, MA   02125

Archbishop Williams Catholic
High School
8 Independence Ave.
Braintree, MA   02184

Cardinal Cushing Central
Catholic High School
50 West Broadway
South Boston, MA   02127

Christopher Columbus Catholic
High School
Tileston St.
Boston, MA   02126

Saint Thomas Aquinas Catholic
High School
19 Saint Joseph St.
Jamaica Plain, MA   02130

Holy Cross Catholic Academy
575 Boyleston St.
Brookline, MA   02146

Newton Catholic High School
575 Washington St.
Newton, MA   02158

Saint Mary's Polish School
52 Boston St.
South Boston, MA   02127

Saint John the Evangelist
School
30 Oceanview
Winthrop, MA   02152

School of Saint John the
Evangelist
251 Watertown St.
Newton, MA   02158

Saint Patrick's Catholic
School
25 Chestnut St.
Watertown, MA   02172

Saint Stanislaus Catholic
School
163 Chestnut St.
Chelsea, MA   02150

Immaculate Conception
Catholic School
Revere, MA   02151

North Cambridge Catholic
High School
40 Norris St.
Cambridge, MA   02140

Saint Peter's High School
96 Concord Ave.
Cambridge, MA   02140

Pope John 23rd Catholic
High School
888 Broadway
Everett, MA   02149

Catholic Memorial High School
Baker & Gardner Sts.
West Roxbury, MA   02132

WORCESTER AREA:

Seven Hills Christian Academy
350 Stafford St.
Cherry Valley, MA   01611

Whitinsville Christian School
279 Linwood Ave.
Whitinsville, MA   01588

Saint Mark's Episcopal
School
Southborough, MA   01772

Saint John's High School
378 Main St.
Shrewsbury, MA   01545

Worcester Central Catholic
School
865 Main St.
Worcester, MA   01610

Holy Name Catholic High
School
144 Granite St.
Worcester, MA   01604

Assumption Catholic Preparatory School
670 West Boyleston St.
Worcester, MA   01606

Saint Joseph's School
759 Main St.
Leicester, MA   01524

SPRINGFIELD AREA:

East Longmeadow Christian
Day School
50 Parker St.
East Longmeadow, MA   01028

Tabernacle Baptist Christian
Schools
603 New Ludlow Rd.
Chicopee, MA   01020

Heritage Academy
302 Maple St.
Springfield, MA   01105

Springfield Y.M.C.A. Day
Preparatory School
122 Chestnut St.
Springfield, MA   01103

Cathedral High School
260 Surrey Rd.
Springfield, MA   01118

Saint Michael's Cathedral
School
70 Elliot St.
Springfield, MA   01105

Saint John the Baptist School
207 Hubro St.
Ludlow, MA   01056

NEW BEDFORD AREA:

Central Baptist School
New Bedford, MA

The Christian School of
  Greater Fall River
484 Highland Ave.
Fall River, MA   02720

New Testament Christian
  Schools
One New Taunton Ave.
Norton, MA   02766

Westport Christian Academy
1100 State Rd. on Route 6
Westport, MA   02790

Long Plains Baptist Christian
  School
1180 Main St.
Acushnet, MA   02743

Friends Academy
1088 Tucker Rd.
North Dartmouth, MA   02747

Cedar Brook School
24 Ralsie Rd.
Rehoboth, MA   02769

Saint Anthony Catholic High
  School
New Bedford, MA

Holy Family Catholic High
  School
Summer St.
New Bedford, MA   02740

Monsignor James Coyle
  Catholic High School
61 Summer St.
Taunton, MA   02780

Bishop Stang Catholic High
  School
Slocum Rd.
North Dartmouth, MA   02747

Saint George School
American Legion Hwy.
Westport, MA   02790

LOWELL AREA:

Westford Baptist Temple
  Christian Academy
Westford, MA   01886

Church of the Open Bible
  School
Winn & Wyman Sts.
Burlington, MA   01803

Christian Formation Center
River Rd.
West Andover, MA   01810

Hillside School
Robin Hill Rd.
Marlboro, MA   01752

Walnut Hill School
12 Highland St.
Natick, MA   01760

Fellowship Bible School
525 Turnpike St.
North Andover, MA   01845

Brook's Episcopal School
1160 Great Pond Rd.
North Andover, MA   01845

Holy Trinity Hellenic
  American School
41 Broadway
Lowell, MA   01854

Franco-American Catholic
  School
357 Pawtucket St.
Lowell, MA   01854

Saint Joseph's Catholic High
  School
760 Merrimack St.
Lowell, MA   01854

Central Catholic High School
99 Auburn St.
Lawrence, MA   01841

Saint Mary's Catholic High
  School
300 Haverhill St.
Lawrence, MA   01844

Presentation of Mary Catholic
  Academy
209 Lawrence St.
Methuen, MA   01844

LYNN AREA:

North Shore Christian School
26 Urban St.
Lynn, MA   01904

Immanuel Church Day School
138 Bridge St.
Beverly, MA   01915

Cardinal Cushing Catholic
  Academy
Route 113
West Newbury, MA   01985

Saint John's Catholic
  Preparatory School
72 Spring St.
Danvers, MA   01923

Saint Joseph's Catholic High
  School
20 Harbor St.
Salem, MA   01970

Austin Catholic Preparatory
  School
101 Willow St.
Reading, MA   01867

Saint Mel's Catholic Day
  School
Farrington Ave.
Gloucester, MA   01930

Saint Ann's Catholic School
70 Pleasant St.
Gloucester, MA   01930

BROCKTON AREA:

Brockton Christian School
1367 Main St.
Brockton, MA   02401

Saint Paul's Day School
80 Pleasant St.
Brockton, MA   02401

Saint Edward's Catholic
  School
North Main St.
Brockton, MA   02401

Sacred Heart Catholic School
283 Court St.
Brockton, MA   02401

PITTSFIELD AREA:

Berkshire Regional Christian
  Education Center
Lenox Ave.
Pittsfield, MA   01201

Starrett Memorial Christian
  School
24 Hale St.
Dalton, MA   01226

Saint Joseph's Central Catholic
  High School
Pittsfield, MA   01201

Notre Dame Catholic Middle
  School
41 Melville St.
Pittsfield, MA   01201

YARMOUTH AREA:
(CAPE COD)

Trinity Christian School
10 Carter Rd.
P.O. Box 388
South Yarmouth, MA   02664

ATTLEBORO AREA:

Bethany School
516 Newport Ave.
South Attleboro, MA   02703

Saint John the Evangelist
  Catholic School
North Main & Peck Sts.
Attleboro, MA   02703

Saint Joseph's Catholic School
208 South Main St.
Attleboro, MA   02703

LENOX AREA:

Stevens's Christian School
40 Kemble St.
Lenox, MA   01240

Lenox Episcopal School
Kemble St.
Lenox, MA   01240

FITCHBURG AREA:

Applewild School
120 Prospect St.
Fitchburg, MA   01420

Trinity Christian Academy
839 Ashby State Rd.
Box 3
Fitchburg, MA   01420

Groton Episcopal School
Farmers Row
Groton, MA   01450

Notre Dame Catholic High
  School
151 South St.
Fitchburg, MA   01420

FRAMINGHAM AREA:

Marian Catholic High School
273 Union Ave.
Framingham, MA   01701

Saint Bridget Catholic School
83 Worcester Rd.
Framingham, MA   01701

NORTHAMPTON AREA:

Northampton Bible Baptist
  Academy
720 Florence Rd.
Northampton, MA   01060

ATHOL AREA:

North New Salem Christian
  School
133 South Main
Orange, MA   01364

PLYMOUTH AREA:

Plymouth Christian Academy
RFD 4
Sandwich Rd., Box 1049
Plymouth, MA   02360

Plymouth Christian Academy
P.O. Box B
Duxbury, MA   02332

GREENFIELD AREA:

Charlemont Christian School
Route 2
Charlemont, MA   01339

MICHIGAN

DETROIT AREA:

Grosse Point Christian School
1444 Maryland St.
Grosse Point, MI   48230

Temple Christian School
23750 Elmira St.
Detroit, MI   48239

Temple Christian School
23800 West Chicago Blvd.
Redford, MI   48239

Greater Grace Temple School
18940 Schaefer Hwy.
Detroit, MI   48285

United Christian School
29205 Florence
Garden City, MI   48135

Victory Christian School
13220 Greenfield Ave.
Detroit, MI   48227

Bethesda Elementary School
7616 East Nevada
Detroit, MI   48234

Plymouth Christian School
43065 Joy Rd.
Canton, MI   48187

Galilean Baptist School
28875 West Seven Mile
Livonia, MI   48152

Pathway Baptist School
2020 Pachard Rd.
Ypsilanti, MI   48197

Calvary Christian Academy
1007 Ecorse Rd.
Ypsilanti, MI   48197

Ecorse Baptist Temple
  Schools
47 Joseph St.
Ecorse, MI   48229

Friends School in Detroit
1100 Saint Aubin St.
Detroit, MI   48207

Faith Way Baptist Schools
2146 Moeller Ave.
Ypsilanti, MI   48197

Light & Life Methodist
  Christian Academy
8900 Pardee St.
Taylor, MI   48180

Taylor Center Baptist
  Academy
10950 Telegraph St.
Taylor, MI   48180

Northline Baptist Schools
23695 Northline Rd.
Taylor, MI   48180

Cathedral Christian School
2727 South Inkster Rd.
Inkster, MI   48141

Dearborn Christian School
21360 Donaldson
Dearborn, MI   48124

Grace Bible Christian
  Academy
1300 South Maple Rd.
Ann Arbor, MI   48103

Inter-City Christian Schools
4700 Allen St.
Allen Park, MI   48101

Gospel Church School
2253 Baker Rd.
Dexter, MI   48130

Southfield Christian Secondary
  School
28650 Lahser St.
Southfield, MI   48034

Seventh Day Adventist Jr.
  Academy
15350 Southfield Rd.
Detroit, MI   48223

Seventh Day Adventist School
2796 Packard Rd.
Ann Arbor, MI   48104

Lutheran High School West
8181 Greenfield St.
Detroit, MI   48228

Detroit Urban Lutheran
  School
8091 Ohio St.
Detroit, MI   48204

Zion Lutheran School
4305 Military
Detroit, MI   48210

Lutheran High School East
20100 Kelly Rd.
Harper Woods, MI   48236

Emmanuel Lutheran School
22425 Morly St.
Dearborn, MI   48124

Redeemer Lutheran School
1360 Pauline Blvd.
Ann Arbor, MI   48103

Atonement Lutheran School
6961 Mead St.
Dearborn, MI   48124

Saint Paul's Lutheran School
459 Earhart Rd.
Ann Arbor, MI   48105

Saint John Lutheran School
13115 Telegraph St.
Taylor, MI   48180

Saint Thomas Lutheran School
23801 Kelly St.
East Detroit, MI   48021

Saint Peter's Lutheran School
23000 Gratiot St.
East Detroit, MI   48021

Saint Philip's Lutheran School
82 Belmont St.
Detroit, MI   48202

Saint Timothy Lutheran School
19400 Evergreen Rd.
Detroit, MI   48219

Berea Lutheran School
7047 Tireman St.
Detroit, MI   48204

Holy Cross Lutheran School
14213 Whitcomb St.
Detroit, MI   48227

Redford Lutheran School
17200 Boswith St.
Redford Township, MI   48239

Salem Lutheran School
2075 Streiter Rd.
Ann Arbor, MI   48103

East Bethlehem Lutheran
  School
3510 East Outer Dr.
Detroit, MI   48234

Evergreen Lutheran School
8680 Evergreen Ave.
Detroit, MI   48228

Greenfield Peace Lutheran
  School
7000 West Outer Dr.
Detroit, MI   48235

Mount Hope Lutheran School
5323 Southfield Rd.
Allen Park, MI   48101

Armenian Day School
19310 Ford Rd.
Dearborn, MI   48124

Messiah Episcopal School
1480 Townsend St.
Detroit, MI 48214

Salesian Catholic High School
60 Harper Ave.
Detroit, MI 48202

Detroit Cathedral High School
60 Belmont St.
Detroit, MI 48102

Catholic Central High School
6565 West Outer Dr.
Detroit, MI 48235

Austin Catholic Preparatory
  School
18300 East Warren Ave.
Detroit, MI 48224

Dominican Catholic High
  School
9740 McKinney St.
Detroit, MI 48224

De La Salle Catholic
  Collegiate School
1055 Glenfield Ave.
Detroit, MI 48213

Saint Andrew's Catholic High
  School
5690 Cecil St.
Detroit, MI 48210

Immaculate Conception
  Catholic Ukrainian High
  School
3056 Hanly St.
Hamtramck, MI 48212

Notre Dame Catholic High
  School
20254 Kelly Rd.
Harper Woods, MI 48236

WARREN AREA:

Van Dyke Christian Academy
8207 Nine Mile Rd.
Warren, MI 48089

West Highland Christian
  School
1116 South Hickory Ridge Rd.
Milford, MI 48042

Lakewood Christian School
24905 Manhattan St.
St. Clair Shores, MI 48080

Luckett Christian Academy
115 South Campbell St.
Royal Oak, MI 48067

Oakland Christian School
3075 Shinmons Rd.
Box 118
Pontiac, MI 48057

Oakland Christian School
100 Lewis St.
Pontiac, MI 48058

Southfield Christian Secondary
  School
28650 Lahser St.
Southfield, MI 48034

Calvary Christian School
17000 Eastland St.
Roseville, MI 48066

Sterling Christian School
33380 Ryan Ave. near 14 Mile
  Rd.
Sterling Heights, MI 48077

Springfield Christian Academy
8731 Dixie Hwy.
Clarkston, MI 48016

Rochester Hills Christian
  Schools
3300 Livernois
Rochester, MI 48063

Clarkston Christian Academy
8585 Dixie Hwy.
Clarkston, MI 48016

Oxford Christian Academy
150 Pontiac Rd., Box 4
Oxford, MI 48051

Indianwood Christian Academy
1100 South Baldwin Rd.
Oxford, MI 48051

Bethany Christian School
2601 John R.
Troy, MI 48094

Carmel Christian School
7847 McClellan St.
Utica, MI 48087

Novi Christian School
45301 West 11 Mile Rd.
Novi, MI 48050

Zion Christian School
1040 Grant St.
Clawson, MI 48017

Baptist Academy
18500 Martin St.
Roseville, MI 48066

Faith Temple School
  Church of God
29101 Rose St.
Madison Heights, MI 48071

Pontiac Jr. Academy
  Seventh Day Adventist
5725 Pontiac Lake Rd.
Pontiac, MI 48054

Northfield Jr. Academy
  Seventh Day Adventist
251 Morse St.
Troy, MI 48084

Lutheran High School North
16825 24-Mile Rd.
Utica, MI 48087

Lutheran High School
  Northwest
1800 West Maple St.
Birmingham, MI 48009

Christ the Master Lutheran
  School
28847 Beck Rd.
Walled Lake, MI 48088

Saint Paul's Lutheran School
20815 Middlebelt
Farmington Hills
Clarenceville, MI   48024

Saint Matthew's Lutheran
  School
2040 South Commerce Rd.
Walled Lake, MI   48088

Peace Lutheran School
11701 12-Mile Rd.
Warren, MI   48093

Saint John Lutheran School
16339 14-Mile Rd.
Fraser, MI   48026

Trinity Lutheran School
8150 Chapp St.
Warren, MI   48089

Saint Paul Lutheran School
508 Williams St.
Royal Oak, MI   48067

Bethlehem Lutheran School
29675 Gratiot St.
Roseville, MI   48066

Saint Paul Lutheran School
42681 Hayes St.
Sterling Heights, MI   48093

Saint Luke Lutheran School
21400 Nunneley St.
Mt. Clemens, MI   48043

Trinity Lutheran School
38900 Harper St.
Mt. Clemens, MI   48043

Saint John Lutheran School
1110 West University Dr.
Rochester, MI   48063

Our Shepherd Lutheran
  School
2225 East 14 Mile Rd.
Birmingham, MI   48009

Martin Luther School
28500 Alden St.
Madison Heights, MI   48071

Trinity Lutheran School
45091 Deschon St.
Utica, MI   48087

Peace Lutheran School
6580 24-Mile Rd.
Utica, MI   48087

Cranbrook Episcopal School
Lone Pine Rd.
Bloomfield Hills, MI   48013

Brother Rice High School
7101 Lahser St.
Birmingham, MI   48010

Saint Clement Catholic High
  School
8155 Ritter St.
Center Line, MI   48015

Saint Patrick's Catholic
  School
9040 Hutchins Rd.
Union Lake, MI   48085

Pontiac Catholic High School
1300 Giddings Rd.
Pontiac, MI   48055

Saint Michael Catholic School
25175 Code Rd.
Southfield, MI   48075

Saint Bede Catholic School
18300 West 12-Mile Rd.
Southfield, MI   48076

Cardinal Mooney Central
  Catholic High School
39165 Charbeneau St.
Mt. Clemens, MI   48043

Bishop Foley Catholic High
  School
32000 North Campbell Rd.
(Madison Heights)
Lamphere, MI   48071

Saint Mary's Catholic High
  School
Orchard Lake, MI   48033

Catholic Academy of the
  Sacred Heart
1250 Kensington Rd.
Bloomfield Hills, MI   48013

Our Lady of Mercy Catholic
  High School
29300 Eleven Mile Rd.
Farmington Hills, MI   48018

Saint Anne High School
6100 Arden St.
Warren, MI   48092

Saint Mary Catholic High
  School
715 South Lafayette St.
Royal Oak, MI   48067

Marian Catholic High School
7225 Lahser Rd.
Birmingham, MI   48010

GRAND RAPIDS AREA:

Grand Rapids Christian High
  School
2300 Plymouth Rd., S.E.
Grand Rapids, MI   49506

Grand Rapids Baptist
  Academy High School
3101 Leonard St., N.E.
Grand Rapids, MI   49505

Christian Schools International
3350 East Paris St., S.E.
Kentwood, MI   49508

South Christian High School
160 68th St., S.W.
Grand Rapids, MI   49508

Covenant Christian High
  School
1401 Ferndale Ave., S.W.
Grand Rapids, MI   49504

Unity Christian High School
3487 Oak St.
Hudsonville, MI   49426

Calvin Christian Jr. High
  School
2500 Newport, S.W.
Wyoming, MI   49509

Jenison Christian Jr. High
  School
366 Church St.
Jenison, MI   49428

Calvin Christian High School
3750 Ivanrest Rd., S.W.
Grandville, MI   49418

Baptist Temple School
3450 East Beltline, N.E.
Grand Rapids, MI   49505

West Side Christian School
955 Westend, N.W.
Grand Rapids, MI   49504

Godwin Christian School
601 36th St., S.W.
Wyoming, MI   49509

The Potter's House
749 Hogan, S.W.
Grand Rapids, MI   49509

Hudsonville Christian School
3435 Oak St.
Hudsonville, MI   49426

Beaverdam Christian School
5181 64th Ave.
Hudsonville, MI   49426

Jenison Christian Elementary
  School
7700 Greenfield Ave.
Jenison, MI   49428

Grandville Christian School
3934 Wilson Ave.
Grandville, MI   49418

Faith Community Christian
  School
8750 North Storey Rd.
Belding, MI   48809

Forest Hills School
c/o Laurie Martin
5739 Fulton E.
Ada, MI   49301

Mayfield Christian School
225 Mayfield St., N.E.
Grand Rapids, MI   49503

Sylvan Christian School
1630 Griggs St., S.E.
Grand Rapids, MI   49506

Millbrook Christian Schools
3662 Poinsettia St., S.E.
Grand Rapids, MI   49508

Cutlerville Christian School
6746 Interurban Ave., S.W.
Cutlerville, MI   49508

Oakdale Christian School
1050 Fisk St., S.E.
Grand Rapids, MI   49507

Cutlerville South East
  Elementary Unit
520 68th St., S.E.
Cutlerville, MI   49508

Seymour Christian School
2550 Eastern St., S.E.
Grand Rapids, MI   49507

Creston-Mayfield Christian
  School
1031 Page St., N.E.
Grand Rapids, MI   49505

Kelloggsville Christian School
624 52nd St., S.E.
Grand Rapids, MI   49508

Lamont Christian School
5260 Leonard St.
Coopersville, MI   49404

Plymouth Christian School
965 Plymouth Ave., N.E.
Grand Rapids, MI   49505

Dutton Christian School
6980 Hanna Lake Rd., S.E.
Dutton, MI   49511

Moline Christian School
1253 First St.
Moline, MI   49335

Ada Christian School
7192 Bradfield St., S.E.
Ada, MI   49301

Middleville School
9607 100th St.
Alto, MI   49304

Adams Street Protestant
  Reformed Christian School
1150 Adams St., S.E.
Grand Rapids, MI   49507

Hope Protestant Reformed
  Christian School
1545 Wilson Ave., S.W.
Grand Rapids, MI   49504

American Reformed Church
  School
3169 68th St., S.E.
Caledonia, MI   49316

Holy Trinity Evangelical
  Lutheran School
4201 Burlingame Ave., S.W.
Grand Rapids, MI   49509

Martin Luther School
1916 Ridgewood Ave., S.E.
Grand Rapids, MI   49506

Immanuel Lutheran School
338 Division Ave., N.
Grand Rapids, MI   49502

Saint James Lutheran School
2066 Oakwood St., N.E.
Grand Rapids, MI   49505

Seventh Day Adventist School
256 Alger St., S.E.
Grand Rapids, MI   49507

Catholic Central High School
319 Sheldon Ave., S.E.
Grand Rapids, MI   49502

West Catholic High School
1801 Bristol Ave., N.W.
Grand Rapids, MI   49505

Saint Andrew's Catholic
  Cathedral School
302 Sheldon Ave., S.E.
Grand Rapids, MI   49502

Saint Paul the Apostle
  Catholic School
2750 Burton St., S.E.
Grand Rapids, MI   49506

Saints Peter & Paul School
1433 Hamilton Ave., N.W.
Grand Rapids, MI 49504

Saint Stephen's Catholic
  School
740 Gladstone Dr., S.E.
Grand Rapids, MI 49506

Holy Spirit Catholic School
2222 Lake Michigan Dr.,
  N.W.
Grand Rapids, MI 49504

STURGIS AREA:

Sturgis Christian Academy
P.O. Box 340
Sturgis, MI 49091

FLINT AREA:

Flint Christian School
3488 North Jennings Rd.
Flint, MI 48504

Genesee Christian School
3178 West Ridgeway Ave.
Westwood Heights, MI 48504

Foss Avenue Christian School
1037 East York St.
Flint, MI 48505

Imlay City Christian School
7197 East Imlay Rd.
Imlay City, MI 48444

First Baptist Academy
860 North Leroy St.
Fenton, MI 48430

John R. Rice Academy
1350 South Packard St.
Burton, MI 48509

John R. Rice Baptist School
4100 West Coldwater Rd.
Westwood Heights, MI 48504

Our Savior Lutheran School
6901 North Saginaw St.
Flint, MI 48505

Redeemer Lutheran School
460 West Atherton Rd.
Flint, MI 48507

Saint Paul Lutheran School
402 South Ballenger Hwy.
Flint, MI 48504

Good Shepherd Lutheran School
5496 Lippincott Blvd.
Bentley, MI 48613

Saint Mark Lutheran School
5073 Daly Blvd.
Kearsley, MI 48506

Adelphian Academy
  Seventh Day Adventist
820 Academy Rd.
Holly, MI 48442

First Flint Seventh Day
  Adventist School
4285 Beecher Rd.
Carman, MI 48442

Linden Road School
  Seventh Day Adventist
3415 North Linden Rd.
Westwood Heights, MI 48504

Spring Vale Academy
  Seventh Day Church of God
Owosso, MI 48867

Holy Redeemer Catholic
  School
G-3468 South Grand Traverse
Carman, MI 48442

Saint Mary Catholic School
2500 North Franklin Ave.
Flint, MI 48506

SAGINAW AREA:

Sheridan Road Christian
  School
6911 Sheridan Rd.
Saginaw, MI 48601

Saginaw Valley Lutheran High
  Schools
3560 McCarty Rd.
Saginaw, MI 48603

Valley Lutheran High School
2731 Deindorfer St.
Saginaw, MI 48602

Messiah Lutheran School
4640 North Michigan St.
Saginaw, MI 48604

Redeemer Lutheran School
3830 Lamson St.
Saginaw, MI 48601

Immanuel Lutheran School
8220 East Holland St.
Saginaw, MI 48601

Good Shepherd Lutheran
  School
5335 Brockway Rd.
Saginaw, MI 48603

Saint Paul Lutheran School
2745 West Genesee St.
Saginaw, MI 48602

Bethlehem Lutheran School
2777 Hermansau St.
Saginaw, MI 48604

Saint Michael's Lutheran
  School
9444 West Saginaw St.
Richville, MI 48758

Tri-City School
  Seventh Day Adventist
7580 Sarle St.
Freeland, MI 48623

Saints Peter & Paul Area
  Catholic High School
2555 Wieneke
Saginaw, MI 48603

Saint Stephen Area High
  School
1315 Sutton St.
Saginaw, MI 48602

Saint Mary's Cathedral High
  School
621 Hoyt St.
Saginaw, MI 48607

LANSING AREA:

Lansing Christian School
5525 South Pennsylvania Ave.
Lansing, MI 48910

Capital City Christian
 School
3815 West Saint Joseph St.
Lansing, MI   48917

Capital City Baptist School
5430 South Washington
Lansing, MI   48910

Our Savior Lutheran School
1601 West Holmes Rd.
Lansing, MI   48910

Seventh Day Adventist
 School
2100 West Saint Joseph St.
Lansing, MI   48915

Lansing Central Catholic
 High School
501 Marshall St.
Lansing, MI   48912

KALAMAZOO AREA:

Kalamazoo Christian High
 School
2121 Stadium Dr.
Kalamazoo, MI   49008

Battle Creek Christian
 School
1035 Wagner Dr.
Battle Creek, MI   49017

North Christian School
1340 Cobb Ave.
Kalamazoo, MI   49007

South Christian School
3333 South Westnedge Ave.
Kalamazoo, MI   49008

Providence Christian School
100 Pratt Rd.
Kalamazoo, MI   49001

East Martin Christian
 School
1758 5th St.
Martin, MI   49070

Temple Baptist School
301 North 26th St.
Kalamazoo, MI   49004

United Mission Christian
 School
18th St.
Route 3
Vicksburg, MI   49097

Seventh Day Adventist Jr.
 Academy
1601 Nichols Rd.
Kalamazoo, MI   49007

Saint Augustine Catholic
 School
201 North Westnedge Ave.
Kalamazoo, MI   49007

Saint Monica Catholic School
530 West Kilgore Rd.
Kalamazoo, MI   49008

MUSKEGON AREA:

Western Michigan Christian
 High School
1212 Kingsley St.
Muskegon, MI   49442

Holland Christian Sr. High
 School
950 Ottawa Ave.
Holland, MI   49423

Holland Christian Middle
 School
32 West 19th St.
Holland, MI   49423

Muskegon Christian School
1220 Eastgate St.
Muskegon, MI   49442

Zeeland Christian School
334 West Central Ave.
Zeeland, MI   49464

Fremont Christian School
208 Hillcrest Dr.
Fremont, MI   49412

Allendale Christian School
6448 Lake Michigan Dr.
Allendale, MI   49401

Maplewood Christian School
913 Pine Ave.
Holland, MI   49423

Rose Park Christian School
556 Butternut Dr.
Holland, MI   49423

Beaver Dam Christian
 School
5181 64th Ave.
Holland, MI   49423

South Olive Christian
 School
6230 120th Ave.
Holland, MI   49423

West Shore Christian
 Academy
635 Lakeshore Blvd.
Muskegon, MI   49441

Borculo Christian School
Route 1
6830 96th Ave.
Zeeland, MI   49464

New Era Christian School
1901 Oak Ave.
New Era, MI   49446

Grand Haven Christian
 School
1102 Grant St.
Grand Haven, MI   49417

Grant Christian School
12931 Poplar
Grant, MI   49327

Calvary Baptist School
518 Plasman Ave.
Holland, MI   49423

Catholic Central High
 School
West Laketon Ave.
Muskegon, MI   49441

JACKSON AREA:

Lumen Christian High School
3483 Spring Arbor Rd.
Jackson, MI   49203

North Sharon Christian
  School
17999 Washburn Rd.
Grass Lake, MI 49240

Jackson Baptist Schools
575 Murphy Dr.
Jackson, MI 49202

Bible Heritage School
6497 West Michigan Ave.
Jackson, MI 49201

Trinity Lutheran School
4900 McCain Rd.
Jackson, MI 49201

Seventh Day Adventist
  School
3600 County Farm Rd.
Jackson, MI 49201

Jackson Catholic Middle
  School
915 Cooper St.
Jackson, MI 49202

TRAVERSE CITY AREA:

Traverse City Christian
  Schools
1971 Cass Rd.
Box 1074
Traverse City, MI 49684

Lutheran School
Traverse City, MI 49684

Saint Francis Catholic High
  School
123 East 11th St.
Traverse City, MI 49684

HOLT AREA:

Capital City Baptist School
5100 Willoughby St.
Holt, MI 48842

Saint Matthew Lutheran
  School
2418 North Aurelius Rd.
Holt, MI 48842

MIDLAND AREA:

Midland Christian School
4417 West Wackerly Rd.
Midland, MI 48640

Calvary Christian Academy
502 Cherry St.
Midland, MI 48640

BAY CITY AREA:

Saint Bartholomew Lutheran
  School
1033 East Beaver St.
Kawkawlin, MI 48631

Saint John the Evangelist
  School
619 Main St.
Essexville, MI 48732

CADILLAC AREA:

Northern Michigan Christian
  High School
128 Martin St.
McBain, MI 49657

BYRON CENTER AREA:

Byron Center Christian Jr.
  High School
8840 Byron Center Rd.,
  S.W.
Byron Center, MI 49315

Trinity Lutheran School
1907 Broadway
Byron Center, MI 49315

All Saints Central Catholic
  High School
North Campus
217 South Monroe St.
Byron Center, MI 49315

All Saints Central Catholic
  Jr. High School
1503 22nd St.
South Campus
Byron Center, MI 49315

PORT HURON AREA:

Sandusky Christian School
34 Gaige St.
Sandusky, MI 48471

American Heritage Christian
  School
804 South Parker St.
Marine City, MI 48039

SAULT STE. MARIE AREA:

Rudyard Christian School
P.O. Box 707
Rudyard, MI 49780

SAINT JOSEPH AREA:

Heritage Christian Academy
P.O. Box 254
New Buffalo, MI 49117

Michigan Lutheran High
  School
615 East Marquette Woods
  Rd.
Saint Joseph, MI 49085

ALMA AREA:

Rock Lake Christian Day
  School
Route 1
Vestaburg, MI 48891

CHARLOTTE AREA:

Hastings Christian School
P.O. Box 254
Hastings, MI 49058

THREE RIVERS AREA:

Locust Grove Mennonite
  School
28560 Marvin Rd.
Centreville, MI 49032

HILLSDALE AREA:

New Hope Christian School
505 West Montgomery Rd.
Camden, MI 49232

SAINT JOHNS AREA:

Grove Christian School
6900 Price Rd., Route 5
Saint Johns, MI   48879

PETOSKEY AREA:

Central Christian Academy
M-68 and McMichael Rd.
Burt Lake, MI   49717

Ebenezer Christian School
P.O. Box 87
Ellsworth, MI   49729

TAWAS CITY AREA:

Saint Joseph School
935 West Houghton Ave.
West Branch, MI   48661

Emmanuel Lutheran School
216 West North St.
Tawas City, MI   48763

MINNESOTA

MINNEAPOLIS AREA:

Minnehaha Evangelical
  Covenant Academy
3107 47th Ave., S.
Minneapolis, MN   55406

Plymouth Baptist Christian
  Schools
13030 47th Ave., N.
Minneapolis, MN   55442

Powderhorn Park Christian
  School
4259 Minnehaha Ave., S.
Minneapolis, MN   55406

Calvin Christian School
4015 Inglewood Ave., S.
Minneapolis, MN   55416

Blaine Christian Academy
1264 109th Ave., N.E.
Minneapolis, MN   55433

Brookdale Christian Center
  School
6030 Xerxes Ave., N.
Minneapolis, MN   55430

Christ Center Ministries
1020 Nicollet Ave.
Minneapolis, MN   55403

Chapel Hill Christian School
17850 Ducklake
Eden Prairie, MN   55343

Fourth Baptist Christian Day
  School
2105 Fremont Ave., N.
Minneapolis, MN   55411

Maranatha Christian Academy
2501 West 84th St.
Minneapolis, MN   55431

Maranatha Christian Academy
9600 Third Ave., S.
Minneapolis, MN   55412

North Side Christian Center
7901 N.E. Red Oak Dr.
Minneapolis, MN   55432

Immanuel Lutheran Christian
  Day School
2201 Girard Ave., N.
Minneapolis, MN   55411

Bryant Avenue Baptist School
5601 Bryant Ave., S.
Minneapolis, MN   55419

Calvary Memorial School
2420 Dunwoody Ave.
Wayzata, MN   55391

Faith Academy
4140 North East 4th St.
Minneapolis, MN   55421

New Life Academy
3115 East 42nd St.
Minneapolis, MN   55406

Lutheran High School of
  Minneapolis
4242 Wentworth Ave.
Minneapolis, MN   55409

Bloomington Lutheran School
10600 Bloom Ferry Rd.
Bloomington, MN   55420

Lutheran School of the
  Redemption
927 East Old Shakopee Rd.
Minneapolis, MN   55420

King of Grace Lutheran
  School
6000 Duluth St.
Minneapolis, MN   55422

Mount Calvary Lutheran
  School
6541 16th Ave., S.
Minneapolis, MN   55423

Saint Peter's Lutheran School
5421 France Ave., S.
Minneapolis, MN   55410

Timothy Lutheran School
7814 Minnetonka Blvd.
Minneapolis, MN   55426

Trinity First Lutheran School
1115 East 19th St.
Minneapolis, MN   55404

Prince of Peace Lutheran
  School
7700 N.E. Monroe St.
Minneapolis, MN   55432

Zion Lutheran School
P.O. Box 108
Mayer, MN   55360

Pilgrim Lutheran School
3901 First Ave., S.
Minneapolis, MN   55409

Minneapolis Jr. Academy
  Seventh Day Adventist
3500 Williston St.
Minnetonka, MN   55343

Maplewood Academy
  Seventh Day Adventist
Hutchinson, MN   55350

Breck Episcopal School
4200 West River Rd.
Minneapolis, MN   55406

Chapel Hill Academy
322 Second St.
Excelsior, MN 55331

De La Salle Catholic High
  School
25 Island Ave., W.
Minneapolis, MN 55401

Catholic Academy of the Holy
  Angels
6600 Nicollet Ave.
Minneapolis, MN 55401

Benilde – Saint Margaret's
  Catholic High School
2501 South Hwy. 100
Minneapolis, MN 55416

Most Holy Trinity Catholic
  School
3946 Wooddale Ave.
Minneapolis, MN 55416

Saint Peter's Catholic School
6720 Nicollet Ave.
Richfield, MN 55423

Saint Stephen's Catholic
  School
2123 Clinton Ave.
Minneapolis, MN 55404

Saint Thomas the Apostle
  School
2900 West 44th St.
Minneapolis, MN 55410

Saint Albert the Great
  Catholic School
2840 33rd Ave., S.
Minneapolis, MN 55406

Saint Bonaventure Catholic
  School
901 East 90th St.
Minneapolis, MN 55420

Saint Charles Borromeo
  School
2727 N.E. Stinson Blvd.
Minneapolis, MN 55418

Saint Richards Catholic
  School
7540 Penn Ave., S.
Minneapolis, MN 55423

ST. PAUL AREA:

New Life Christian School
501 6th Ave., S.
South St. Paul, MN 55075

Rosemount Baptist Schools
14400 Diamond Path W.
Rosemount, MN 55068

Temple Baptist Christian Day
  School
200 West 77th St.
St. Paul, MN 55102

Saint John Evangelical
  Lutheran School
771 Margaret St.
St. Paul, MN 55106

Heritage Christian School
  Assembly of God
1451 Stickney St.
South St. Paul, MN 55107

Saint Croix Lutheran High
  School
110 Crusader Ave.
West St. Paul, MN 55104

Concordia Lutheran Academy
2400 North Dale St.
St. Paul, MN 55113

Central Lutheran School
775 North Lexington Pkwy.
St. Paul, MN 55104

King of Kings Lutheran School
2330 North Dale St.
St. Paul, MN 55113

Emmanuel Lutheran School
Crusader Ave. & Stryker
West St. Paul, MN 55104

Rose of Sharon Lutheran
  School
7241 South 80th St.
Cottage Grove, MN 55016

East St. Paul Lutheran School
674 Johnson Pkwy.
St. Paul, MN 55106

Gethsemane Lutheran School
2410 Stillwater Rd.
St. Paul, MN 55119

Capital City Adventist School
1220 South McKnight Rd.
St. Paul, MN 55119

Cretin Catholic High School
495 South Hamline Ave.
St. Paul, MN 55118

St. Thomas Catholic Academy
949 Mendota Heights Rd.
St. Paul, MN 55118

DULUTH AREA:

Duluth Cathedral School
1215 Rice Lake Rd.
Duluth, MN 55811

Saint John's School
Chisolm St. & Woodland Ave.
Duluth, MN 55803

Saint Michael's School
4924 Pitt St.
Duluth, MN 55804

Saint Anthony's School
1028 East 8th St.
Duluth, MN 55805

Saint Margaret Mary School
8830 Idaho St.
Duluth, MN 55808

Grand Marsh Bible School
Route 7, P.O. Box 79
Meadowlands, MN 55765

ST. CLOUD AREA:

Central Minnesota Christian
  School
Box 98
Prinsburg, MN 56281

Granite City Baptist Academy
375 South 5th Ave.
St. Cloud, MN 56301

Pease Christian School
Box 68
Pease, MN 56363

Saint Luke's Lutheran School
Woodlake, MN   56297

John XXIII Cathedral
  Catholic High School
North 7th Ave. & 3rd St.
St. Cloud, MN   56301

Saints Peter & Paul Middle
  School
North 11th Ave. & 12 St.
St. Cloud, MN   56301

Saint Mary's Cathedral School
823 South First St.
St. Cloud, MN   56301

Saint John's Catholic
  Preparatory School
Collegeville, MN   56321

WINONA AREA:

Winona Christian School
1363 Homer Rd.
Winona, MN   55987

Cotter High School
101 East 7th St.
Winona, MN   55987

Cotter Jr. High School
354 Lafayette St.
Winona, MN   55987

Saint Matthew's Lutheran
  School
756 West Wabasha St.
Winona, MN   55987

Saint Martin's Lutheran
  School
253 Liberty St.
Winona, MN   55987

Cathedral of Sacred Heart
  Catholic School
352 Center St.
Winona, MN   55987

Saint Stanislaus Catholic
  School
602 East Fifth St.
Winona, MN   55987

ROCHESTER AREA:

Faith Christian School
Austin, MN   55912

Stewartville Christian School
100 5th St., S.E.
Stewartville, MN   55976

Rochester Lutheran School
2619 9th Ave., N.W.
Rochester, MN   55901

Holy Cross Lutheran School
300 N.E. 16th St.
Austin, MN   55912

Church of the Open Bible
  School
301 S.W. 4th St.
Austin, MN   55912

Lourdes Catholic High School
7th Ave. & West Center St.
Rochester, MN   55901

Saint Augustine Catholic
  School
405 N.W. 4th St.
Austin, MN   55912

Saint Francis Catholic School
11th Ave. & 4th St., S.E.
Rochester, MN   55901

Saint Edward's Catholic
  School
2000 West Oakland Ave.
Austin, MN   55912

WORTHINGTON AREA:

Worthington Christian School
1118 Johnson Ave.
Worthington, MN   56187

Southwest Minnesota
  Christian High School
550 Elizabeth
Edgerton, MN   56128

Faith Christian High School
Box 38
Bigelow, MN   56117

Christian Day School
Mountain Lake, MN   56159

Chandler Christian School
P.O. Box 125B
Chandler, MN   56122

Leota Christian School
5501 Main, P.O. Box 278
Leota, MN   56153

Free Christian School
P.O. Box 431
Edgerton, MN   56128

Edgerton Christian School
210 West Elizabeth St.
P.O. Box 236
Edgerton, MN   56128

Hills Christian School
P.O. Box 27
Hills, MN   56138

Saint Mary's Catholic School
12th St. & 8th Ave.
Worthington, MN   56187

MC KINLEY AREA:

Mc Kinley Christian Academy
2nd Ave., N. & 1st St., W.
Mc Kinley, MN   55761

MOORHEAD AREA:

Daystar Christian School
121 6th Ave., S.
Moorhead, MN   56560

Hillcrest Lutheran Academy
  Lutheran Brethren
P.O. Box 317
Fergus Falls, MN   56537

Saint Joseph Catholic School
202 South 10th St.
Moorhead, MN   56560

Saint Francis de Sales
  Catholic School
1330 8th Ave., N.
Moorhead, MN   56560

EAST GRAND FORKS AREA:

Bible Baptist Christian School
309 8th Ave., N.W.
East Grand Forks, MN   56721

Seventh Day Adventist School
1600 Fourth Ave., N.
East Grand Forks, MN   56721

Sacred Heart Catholic High
  School
126 N.W. 3rd St.
East Grand Forks, MN   56721

FARIBAULT AREA:

Trinity Lutheran School
N.W. Fourth St. & Sixth Ave.
Faribault, MN   55021

Calvary Assembly of God
  School
1685 East Hwy. 96
White Bear Lake, MN   55110

Peace Lutheran School
S.W. Sixth Ave. & Third St.
Faribault, MN   55021

Seventh Day Adventist School
5th St. & N.W. 3rd Ave.
Faribault, MN   55021

The Bishop Whipple Schools
  of Shattuck Episcopal
Faribault, MN   55021

Bethlehem Catholic Academy
105 S.W. Third Ave.
Faribault, MN   55021

Saint Mary of the Lake
  Catholic School
112 Bald Eagle Ave.
White Bear Lake, MN   55110

MANKATO AREA:

Immanuel Lutheran High
  School
2002 Third Ave.
Mankato, MN   56001

Martin Luther Academy
1634 Boettger
New Ulm, MN   56073

Saint Mark's Lutheran School
Sibley & West 7th St.
Mankato, MN   56001

Mount Olive Lutheran School
Corner of Marsh & Guenther
Mankato, MN   56001

Loyola Catholic High School
Mankato, MN   56001

Fitzgerald Catholic Middle
  School
Mankato, MN   56001

Saints Joseph & John Catholic
  School
Mankato, MN   56001

Saints Peter & Paul Catholic
  School
Mankato, MN   56001

WILLMAR AREA:

Community Christian School
P.O. Box 280
Route 3
Willmar, MN   56201

HOLLANDALE AREA:

Hollandale Christian School
P.O. Box 182
Hollandale, MN   56045

FERGUS FALLS AREA:

Hillcrest Lutheran Academy
P.O. Box 317
Fergus Falls, MN   56537

RED WING AREA:

Saint John Lutheran School
Route 3
Goodhue, MN   55027

MISSISSIPPI

JACKSON AREA:

Jackson Christian Academy
4908 Ridgewood Rd.
Jackson, MS   39211

Riverside Christian Day School
835 Riverside Dr.
Jackson, MS   39202

Capital City Christian School
3328 Oak Forest Dr.
Jackson, MS   39212

Mississippi Baptist High
  School
1635 Boling St.
Jackson, MS   39213

Hillcrest Baptist School
3102 Monticello Dr.
Jackson, MS   39212

First Presbyterian Day School
1390 North State St.
P.O. Box 4862
Jackson, MS   39216

Mount Salus Presbyterian
  Christian Day School
Box 194
Clinton, MS   39056

Saint Paul's Presbyterian
  Day School
5125 Robinson Rd.
Jackson, MS   39204

Seventh Day Adventist School
Robinson St.
Jackson, MS   39203

Saint Andrew's Episcopal Day
  School
4120 Old Canton Rd.
Jackson, MS   39216

Saint Joseph Catholic High
  School
2221 Boling St.
Jackson, MS   39213

Christ the King Catholic
School
1217 Hattiesburg Rd.
Jackson, MS   39209

GULFPORT AREA:

Bible Baptist Christian
School
1420 Dedeaux Rd.
Gulfport, MS   39503

Gautier Christian Schools
1617 Old Spanish Trail
Pascagoula, MS   39567

Ocean Springs Christian
School
Highway 90 E.
Ocean Springs, MS   39564

Apostolic Christian School
P.O. Box 853
3705 Old Mobile Hwy.
Pascagoula, MS   39567

Coast Episcopal School
Espy Ave.
Pass Christian, MS   39571

Saint John Interparochial High
School
2415 17th St.
Gulfport, MS   39501

Saint Thomas School
Highway 90
Long Beach, MS   39560

Our Lady of Victories
Catholic Central High School
Watts Ave.
Pascagoula, MS   39567

Saint Alphonsus Catholic
School
504 Jackson Ave.
Ocean Springs, MS   39564

BILOXI AREA:

Calvary Christian School
2941 Pass Rd.
Biloxi, MS   39531

Christ Episcopal Day School
912 Beach Blvd., S.
Bay St. Louis, MS   39520

Notre Dame Catholic High
School
900 Hopkins Blvd.
Biloxi, MS   39530

Saint Stanislaus Catholic
School
Bay St. Louis, MS   39520

GREENVILLE AREA:

Greenville Christian School
Highway 1 S.
P.O. Box 4398
Greenville, MS   38701

Payne Christian School
520 North Poplar St.
Greenville, MS   38701

Faith Baptist School
1876 Burning Bush Dr.
Greenville, MS   38701

Our Lady of Lourdes Catholic
School
1600 Reed Rd.
Greenville, MS   38701

COLUMBUS AREA:

Immanuel Center for
Christian Education
503 18th Ave., N.
Columbus, MS   39701

French Camp Academy
Presbyterian
French Camp, MS   39745

Heritage Academy High School
625 Magnolia Ln.
Columbus, MS   39701

Saint Mary's Catholic School
North Browder Rd.
Columbus, MS   39701

NATCHEZ AREA:

Christian Jr. & Sr. High
School
300 Chinquapin Ln.
Natchez, MS   39120

Maranatha Baptist Schools
Maranatha Dr.
Natchez, MS   39120

Trinity Episcopal Day School
Highway 61 S.
Natchez, MS   39120

Cathedral High School
North Pine St.
Natchez, MS   39120

CLARKSDALE AREA:

Clarksdale Christian School
324 Desoto St.
Clarksdale, MS   38614

Clarksdale Baptist School
401 First St.
Clarksdale, MS   38614

Riverside Baptist School
520 Hickory St.
Clarksdale, MS   38614

Presbyterian Day School
944 Catalpa
Clarksdale, MS   38614

Saint George Episcopal Day
School
West 2nd St.
Clarksdale, MS   38614

Immaculate Conception
Catholic High School
520 Ritchie St.
Clarksdale, MS   38614

VICKSBURG AREA:

Porter's Chapel Academy
Porter's Chapel Rd.
Vicksburg, MS   39180

Chamberlain Hunt Presbyterian
Academy
Port Gibson, MS   39150

All Saints Episcopal School
Confederate Ave.
Vicksburg, MS   39180

OXFORD AREA:

Oxford Baptist Institute
South Lamar St. Extension
Oxford, MS   38655

Presbyterian Day School
Sunflower Rd.
Cleveland, MS   38732

Mount Pleasant Christian
  Academy
Mount Pleasant, MS   38649

MERIDIAN AREA:

Calvary Christian School,
  Inc.
3905 Eighth St.
Meridian, MS   39301

Countryside Baptist Christian
  School
Highway 39 N.
Meridian, MS   39301

Saint Patrick Catholic
  School
2700 Davis St.
Meridian, MS   39301

HATTIESBURG AREA:

Central Baptist Schools
201 Freeman Rd.
Hattiesburg, MS   39401

Saint John's Episcopal
  School
North Fifth Ave.
Laurel, MS   39440

Immaculate Conception
  Catholic School
West 6th St.
Laurel, MS   39440

GREENWOOD AREA:

Greenwood Christian School
801 Sycamore Ave.
Greenwood, MS   38980

TUPELO AREA:

Lakeview Christian School
930 Shumacola Trail
Tupelo, MS   38801

LOUISVILLE AREA:

Grace Christian School
P.O. Box 183
Louisville, MS   39339

Green Valley Boy's Ranch
Route 7, Box 272V
Louisville, MS   39339

MEADVILLE AREA:

Franklin Christian Academy
P.O. Box 181
Roxie, MS   39661

SOUTHAVEN AREA:

Highway Baptist Christian
  Academy
P.O. Box 42
Southaven, MS   38671

Byhalia Christian School
Highway 309, S.
Byhalia, MS   38611

Mount Pleasant Christian
  Elementary Academy
Mount Pleasant, MS   38649

MACON AREA:

Magnolia Mennonite School
Route 1
Macon, MS   39341

GREENWOOD AREA:

Greenwood Christian School
801 Sycamore Ave.
Greenwood, MS   38930

CLEVELAND AREA:

Presbyterian Day School
West Sunflower Rd.
P.O. Box 367
Cleveland, MS   38732

MISSOURI

ST. LOUIS AREA:

Christian Academy of Greater
  St. Louis
11050 North Warson Rd.
St. Louis, MO   63114

Saint Louis Country Day
  School
425 Warson Rd.
St. Louis, MO   63124

Gateway Christian Schools
8221 Minnesota Ave.
St. Louis, MO   63111

Central Christian School
700 South Hanley Rd.
St. Louis, MO   63105

North County Christian
  Nazarene School
1309 North Elizabeth Ave.
Ferguson, MO   63135

Northwest Christian Academy
75 Williams Ave.
St. Louis, MO   63135

Lafayette Christian Academy
929 Big Bend Rd.
St. Louis, MO   63117

Covenant Christian School
  Evangelical Presbyterian
2143 North Ballas Rd.
St. Louis, MO   63131

Tower Grove Christian
  School
4257 Magnolia Ave.
St. Louis, MO   63110

Westminster Christian
  Academy
12006 Manchester Rd.
St. Louis, MO   63131

Berean Christian School
8625 State St.
P.O. Box 806
East St. Louis, MO 62203

Christian Fundamental School
3145 Lafayette
St. Louis, MO 63104

Bethel Evangelical Lutheran
  School
7001 Forsyth St.
University City, MO 63130

Zion Lutheran School
2005 Benton
St. Louis, MO 63106

Lutheran High School North
5401 Lucas & Hunt Rd.
St. Louis, MO 63121

Lutheran High School South
9515 Tesson Ferry Rd.
St. Louis, MO 63123

Christ Community Lutheran
  School
110 West Woodbine St.
Kirkwood, MO 63131

Saint Paul's Lutheran School
1300 North Ballas Rd.
Kirkwood, MO 63131

Christian Brothers Catholic
  High School
6501 Clayton Rd.
St. Louis, MO 63117

De Smet Jesuit Catholic High
  School
233 North New Ballas Rd.
St. Louis, MO 63141

Notre Dame Catholic High
  School
320 East Ripa St.
St. Louis, MO 63125

Mercy Catholic High School
1000 Pennsylvania St.
University City, MO 63130

Vianney Catholic High School
  for Boys
1311 South Kirkwood Rd.
Kirkwood, MO 63131

Principia Upper School
  Christian Science
13201 Clayton Rd.
St. Louis, MO 63131

SPRINGFIELD AREA:

Christian Schools of
  Springfield
2655 North Grant St.
Springfield, MO 65803

Christian Schools of
  Springfield
739 West Talmage St.
Springfield, MO 65803

Christian Heritage Schools
  of Missouri
2101 West Chestnut
  Expressway
Springfield, MO 65802

United Christian School
2501 West State St.
Springfield, MO 65802

Light & Life Christian
  School
Free Methodist
Oldfield, MO 65720

Christian Lighthouse Academy
2848 North Broadway
Springfield, MO 65803

Calvary Temple Christian
  School
444 West Grand St.
Springfield, MO 65804

Dawson Christian School
621 Baden
Mountain Grove, MO 65711

Immanuel Lutheran School
212 West Fourth
Lockwood, MO 65682

Seventh Day Adventist School
704 South Belview St.
Springfield, MO 65802

Springfield Catholic High
  School
601 South Jefferson St.
Springfield, MO 65806

KANSAS CITY AREA:

Tri-City Christian High
  School
1700 Blue Ridge Blvd.
Kansas City, MO 64126

Genesis High School
3911 Agnes Ave.
Kansas City, MO 64130

Baptist Christian Academy
16101 Salisbury Rd.
Salisbury, MO 65281

Kansas City East Christian
  School
11401 East 47th St.
Kansas City, MO 64133

Blue Ridge Christian School
8524 Blue Ridge Blvd.
Kansas City, MO 64138

Berean Baptist Christian
  Academy
4041 Denton Ave.
Kansas City, MO 64133

Carver Christian Day School
2547 Jackson Ave.
Kansas City, MO 64127

Englewood Christian School
10628 Winner Rd.
Kansas City, MO 64125

Fairmont Christian School
7th & Ash Ave.
Kansas City, MO 64133

Carver Bible Institute Day
  School
2360 East Linwood Blvd.
Kansas City, MO 64109

Immanuel Lutheran School
4200 Tracy Ave.
Kansas City, MO 64110

Calvary Lutheran School
7500 Oak St.
Kansas City, MO   64114

Holy Cross Lutheran School
2003 N. E. Englewood Rd.
Kansas City, MO   64118

Grandview School
 Assembly of God
12320 Grandview Blvd.
Kansas City, MO   64137

Cedarvale School
 Seventh Day Adventist
9933 East 56th St.
Kansas City, MO   64133

Saint Paul's Episcopal Day
 School
4043 Main St.
Kansas City, MO   64111

Loretto In Kansas City
 Upper & Middle Catholic
 Schools
12411 Wornall Rd.
Kansas City, MO   64145

Rockhurst Catholic High
 School
9301 State Line
Kansas City, MO   64114

Saint Pius X Catholic High
 School
1500 N. E. 42nd Terr.
Kansas City, MO   64116

Bishop Hogan Catholic High
 School
1221 East Meyer St.
Kansas City, MO   64131

Notre Dame De Sion
 Catholic High School
10631 Wornall Rd.
Kansas City, MO   64114

Bishop Miege Catholic High
 School
5041 Reinhardt Dr.
Kansas City, MO   64139

INDEPENDENCE AREA:

Independence Christian
 School
819 West Waldo St.
Independence, MO   64050

Harrisonville Christian
 School
1606 Chapel Dr.
Harrisonville, MO   64701

Messiah Lutheran School
 of Independence
Independence, MO   64050

Saint Mary's Catholic High
 School
622 North Main St.
Independence, MO   64050

FLORISSANT AREA:

Faith Christian School and
 Academy
2300 Parker Rd.
Florissant, MO   63033

Salem Lutheran School
5190 Parker St.
Hazlewood, MO   63042

Saint Thomas Aquinas
 Catholic High School
845 Dunn St.
Hazelwood, MO   63042

Rosary Catholic High School
1720 Redman St.
Hazelwood, MO   63042

JOPLIN AREA:

Joplin Christian School
9th & Moffet Sts.
Joplin, MO   64801

Central Christian Academy
423 Main St.
Joplin, MO   64801

Ozark Christian Elementary
614 North High
Neosho, MO   64850

College Heights Christian
 School
East Newman Rd.
Joplin, MO   64801

God's Training Academy
2225 North Saint Charles St.
Joplin, MO   64801

McCauley Regional Catholic
 High School
902 Pearl Ave.
Joplin, MO   64801

Mercy Catholic High School
369 South English St.
Marshall, MO   65340

ST. JOSEPH AREA:

Baptist Temple School
2606 Sycamore St.
St. Joseph, MO   64503

Christian Brothers Catholic
 High School
720 North Noges Blvd.
St. Joseph, MO   64506

Bishop LaBlond Catholic
 High School
36th & Frederick Sts.
St. Joseph, MO   64506

CAPE GIRARDEAU AREA:

Cape Christian School
1855 Perryville Rd.
Cape Girardeau, MO   63701

Faith Christian Academy
2530 Marsha Kay Dr.
Cape Girardeau, MO   63701

Liberty Baptist Christian
 School
207 Pindwood Ln.
Cape Girardeau, MO   63701

Trinity Lutheran School
55 North Pacific St.
Cape Girardeau, MO   63701

Notre Dame Catholic High
 School
1912 Ritter St.
Cape Girardeau, MO   63701

COLUMBIA AREA:

Faith Baptist Academy
3909 Brown Station Rd.
Columbia, MO 65201

Apostolic Christian Academy
211 Benton St.
Columbia, MO 65201

Seventh Day Adventist School
1100 College Park Dr.
Columbia, MO 65201

Columbia Catholic Middle
  School
105 Waugh St.
Columbia, MO 65201

ST. CHARLES AREA:

Bible Baptist Christian
  School
Highway 94 & Lakeview Dr.
St. Charles, MO 63301

St. Charles Christian School
1123 North Benton
P.O. Box 255
St. Charles, MO 63301

Heritage Academy
1524 Heritage Landing
St. Charles, MO 63301

St. Charles Mission School,
  Inc.
2054 Country Club Rd.
St. Charles, MO 63301

Catholic Academy of the
  Sacred Heart
619 North 2nd St.
St. Charles, MO 63301

SEDALIA AREA:

Calvary Temple Christian
  Academy
Driftwood & Heck Sts.
Sedalia, MO 65301

Cold Springs Christian School
Route 2
Warsaw, MO 65355

Saint Paul's Lutheran School
701 South Massachusetts St.
Sedalia, MO 65301

Sacred Heart Catholic High
  School
3rd & Vermont Sts.
Sedalia, MO 65301

HANNIBAL AREA:

First Assembly Christian
  School
1901 Missouri St.
Hannibal, MO 63401

Saint John's Lutheran School
1317 Lyon St.
Hannibal, MO 63401

Hannibal Catholic School
1113 Broadway
Hannibal, MO 63401

JEFFERSON CITY AREA:

Trinity Lutheran School
803 Swifts Hwy.
Jefferson City, MO 65101

Immanuel Lutheran School
Honey Creek, MO

Helias Catholic High School
1305 Swifts Hwy.
Jefferson City, MO 65101

CENTRALIA AREA:

Sunnydale Academy
  Seventh Day Adventist
Centralia, MO 65240

Plain View Amish School
Clark, MO 65243

RACINE AREA:

Racine Apostolic School
P.O. Box 855
Racine, MO 64858

KIRKSVILLE AREA:

Kirksville Bible School
1601 North Franklin
Kirksville, MO 63501

CHILLICOTHE AREA:

Meadowview Amish Elementary
  School
Jamesport, MO 64648

POPLAR BLUFF AREA:

South Missouri Christian
  School
921 Harper St.
P.O. Box 4768
Poplar Bluff, MO 63901

MONTANA

GREAT FALLS AREA:

Treasure State Academy
824 3rd Ave., N.
Great Falls, MT 59401

Seventh Day Adventist School
Southwest of City
Great Falls, MT

Teton Christian School
P.O. Box 719
Choteau, MT 59422

Saints Peter & Paul Catholic
  School
200 44th St., S.
Great Falls, MT 59405

Holy Family Catholic School
2820 Central Ave.
Great Falls, MT 59401

BILLINGS AREA:

Temple Baptist School
1620 13th St., W.
Billings, MT 59102

First Baptist School
Laurel, MT 59044

Trinity Lutheran School
2802 Belvedere Dr.
Billings, MT 59102

Billings Central Catholic
School
3 Broadwater Ave.
Billings, MT 59102

KALISPELL AREA:

New Covenant Christian
School
4099 Lower Valley Rd.
Somers, MT 59932

Trinity Lutheran School
5th Ave., N.W. & California
Kalispell, MT 59901

Kalispell Seventh Day
Adventist School
1275 Helena Flats Rd.
Kalispell, MT 59901

Saint Matthew's School
622 Main St.
Kalispell, MT 59901

BUTTE AREA:

Summit Valley Christian
School
1027 South Main St.
Butte, MT 59701

Christian Brothers Catholic
High School
105 South Idaho St.
Butte, MT 59701

CONRAD AREA:

Conrad Christian School
P.O. Box 1122
Conrad, MT 59425

BOZEMAN AREA:

Manhattan Christian Schools
P.O. Box 160, Route 1
Manhattan, MT 59741

Christian Center Schools
P.O. Box 244
Bozeman, MT 59715

Mount Ellis Academy
Seventh Day Adventist
3641 Bozeman Trail Rd.
Bozeman, MT 59715

Saint Mary's Catholic School
McLeod Island
Livingston, MT 59047

MILES CITY AREA:

Baptist Tabernacle School
20 North Stacy St.
Miles City, MT 59301

Seventh Day Adventist School
212 North Stacy St.
Miles City, MT 59301

Sacred Heart Catholic School
519 North Center St.
Miles City, MT 59301

LEWISTOWN AREA:

Christian & Missionary
Alliance School
301 Southwest Cottonwood
Lewistown, MT 59457

Big Sky Bible College
High School
Maiden Rd.
Lewistown, MT 59457

Saint Leo's Catholic High
School
301 Second Ave., N.
Lewistown, MT 59457

HELENA AREA:

Mount Helena Adventist
School
545 South California St.
Helena, MT 59601

Lewis and Clark Christian
Academy
1933 Colorado Gulch
Helena, MT 59601

MISSOULA AREA:

Valley Christian School
2526 Sunset Ln.
Missoula, MT 59801

Loyola Catholic High School
West Pine & Owens Sts.
Missoula, MT 59801

NEBRASKA

OMAHA AREA:

Temple Christian Academy
2702 North 61st St.
Omaha, NE 68104

Bellevue Christian Academy
Assembly of God
1400 Harvel Rd.
Bellevue, NE 68005

Marshall Drive Baptist Schools
Accelerated Christian
Education
4845 Marshall Dr.
Omaha, NE 68137

Good Shepherd Lutheran School
5071 Center St.
Omaha, NE 68106

Saint Paul Lutheran School
51st St. & Grand Ave.
Omaha, NE

Mount Calvary Lutheran School
5529 Leavenworth St.
Omaha, NE 68106

Gethsemane Lutheran School
4040 North 108th St.
Omaha, NE 68164

Cross Lutheran School
2902 South 20th St.
Omaha, NE 68108

Zion Lutheran School
4001 0 St. at 41st
Omaha, NE 68107

Brownell - Talbot Episcopal
School
400 North Happy Hollow Blvd.
Omaha, NE 68132

Dominican Catholic High
School
4725 North 28th St.
Omaha, NE 68111

Saint Michael Catholic High
  School
Elkhorn, NE 68022

Christ the King Catholic
  School
831 South 88th St.
Omaha, NE 68114

LINCOLN AREA:

Lincoln Christian School
5240 Normal Blvd.
Lincoln, NE 68506

Lincoln Lutheran Jr. High
  School
1100 North 56th St.
Lincoln, NE 68504

College View Academy
  Seventh Day Adventist
5420 Calvert St.
Lincoln, NE 68506

Concordia Lutheran High
  School
800 North Columbia St.
Seward, NE 68434

YORK AREA:

Emmanuel Lutheran School
Ninth and Beaver
York, NE 68467

GRAND ISLAND AREA:

Nebraska Christian Schools
P.O. Box 66
Central City, NE 68826

Christ Lutheran School
1300 North Grand Island Ave.
Grand Island, NE 68801

Trinity Lutheran School
13th & Locust Sts.
Grand Island, NE 68801

Seventh Day Adventist School
636 Shady Bend Rd.
Grand Island, NE 68801

Central Catholic High School
1200 North Ruby St.
Grand Island, NE 68801

NORFOLK AREA:

Park Avenue Christian School
401 East Park Ave.
Norfolk, NE 68701

Christ Lutheran School
511 South 5th St.
Norfolk, NE 68701

Saint Paul's Lutheran School
1010 Georgia Ave.
Norfolk, NE 68701

Norfolk Catholic High School
2300 Madison Ave.
Norfolk, NE 68701

NORTH PLATTE AREA:

Central Nebraska School of
  the Bible
513 West 11th St.
Cozad, NE 69130

Hope Baptist Academy
P.O. Box 415
Sutherland, NE 69165

Our Redeemer Lutheran
  School
1421 East D St.
North Platte, NE 69101

Seventh Day Adventist School
West Highway 30
North Platte, NE 69101

Saint Patrick Catholic Jr. -
  Sr. High School
South Park & Tabor Sts.
North Platte, NE 69101

SCOTTSBLUFF AREA:

Gering Christian Academy
  Church of Christ
1645 7th St.
Gering, NE 69341

Valley View School
  Seventh Day Adventist
Route 2
Scottsbluff, NE 69361

Saint Agnes Catholic School
205 East 23rd St.
Scottsbluff, NE 69361

BEATRICE AREA:

Christ Evangelical Lutheran
  School
Route 2
Beatrice, NE 68310

First Trinity Lutheran School
Route 2
Beatrice, NE 68310

Saint Paul's Lutheran School
930 Prairie Ln.
Beatrice, NE 68310

Saint Paul's Lutheran School
108 East Hwy. 4
Plymouth, NE 68424

Saint Peter's Lutheran School
Davenport, NE 68335

Saint Joseph's Catholic School
420 North 6th St.
Beatrice, NE 68310

Saint Michael's School
8th & East Fairbury Sts.
Beatrice, NE 68310

HASTINGS AREA:

Zion Lutheran School
601 South Marian Rd.
Hastings, NE 68901

Platte Valley Academy
  Seventh Day Adventist
Shelton, NE 68876

Saint Michael's Catholic
  School
Bellevue & C Sts.
Hastings, NE 68901

GRAND ISLAND AREA:

Zion Lutheran School
Saint Libory
Worms, NE   68872

COLUMBUS AREA:

Christ Lutheran School
Route 1
Columbus, NE   68601

Immanuel Lutheran School
1468 24th Ave.
Columbus, NE   68601

Trinity Lutheran School
705 West 6th St.
Madison, NE   68748

Saint John Lutheran School
Route 1
Madison, NE   68748

Zion Lutheran School
Leigh, NE   68643

Seventh Day Adventist School
9th & Prairie Sts.
Albion, NE   68620

Scotus Central Catholic High
  School
1554 18th Ave.
Columbus, NE   68601

Holy Family Catholic High
  School
Lindsey, NE   68644

FREMONT AREA:

Trinity Lutheran East School
16th & Luther Rd.
Fremont, NE   68025

Trinity Lutheran West School
250 North C St.
Fremont, NE   68025

Bergan Central Catholic High
  School
545 East 4th St.
Fremont, NE   68025

KEARNEY AREA:

Zion Lutheran School
2421 Ave. C
Kearney, NE   68847

Kearney Catholic High School
110 East 35th St.
Kearney, NE   68847

SUTTON AREA:

Sutton Christian School
P.O. Box 321
Sutton, NE   68979

NEVADA

LAS VEGAS AREA:

Clark County Christian Schools
3005 Cedar Ave.
Las Vegas, NV   89101

Grace Christian Day School
6208 Hargrove St.
Las Vegas, NV   89105

Christian School of North Las
  Vegas
2828 East Cheyenne Ave.
North Las Vegas, NV   89030

First Good Shepherd Lutheran
  School
301 South Maryland Pkwy.
Las Vegas, NV   89101

Las Vegas Jr. Academy
  Seventh Day Adventist
6059 West Oakey Blvd.
Las Vegas, NV   89102

Bishop Gorman Catholic High
  School
1801 South Maryland Pkwy.
Las Vegas, NV   89105

Saint Christopher's Catholic
  School
1840 North Bruce St.
North Las Vegas, NV   89101

Our Lady of Las Vegas
  Catholic School
3036 Alta Dr.
Las Vegas, NV   89107

RENO AREA:

Reno Christian Academy
148 Richards Way
Sparks, NV   89431

Christian Bible Centered
  Schools
East Plumb Ln. & Harvard
  Way
Reno, NV   89502

Sierra Christian School
627 Sunnyside Dr.
Reno, NV   89503

Sierra View School
3195 Everett Dr.
Reno, NV   89502

Reno Jr. Academy
  Seventh Day Adventist
1090 Bresson Ave.
Reno, NV   89502

Manogue Catholic High School
400 Bartlett St.
Reno, NV   89502

CARSON CITY AREA:

Seventh Day Adventist School
Carson City, NV   89701

Catholic School
Carson City, NV   89701

ELKO AREA:

Ruby Valley Christian School
Ruby Valley
Elko, NV   89801

FALLON AREA:

Seventh Day Adventist School
755 Esmeralda St.
Fallon, NV   89406

ELY AREA:

Sacred Heart Catholic School
1080 Ave. I
East Ely, NV   89315

WEST POINT AREA:

Saint John's Lutheran School
Beemer, NV   68716

NEW HAMPSHIRE

MANCHESTER AREA:

Granite Christian Academy
1569 Mammoth Rd.
Hooksett, NH   03106

Calvary Christian School
Hampstead Rd.
Derry, NH   03038

Kellogg Seventh Day Adventist
  School
Back River Rd.
Bedford, NH   03102

Trinity High School
581 Bridge St.
Manchester, NH   03104

Saint Joseph's Catholic Jr.
  High School
Pine St.
Manchester, NH   03103

CONCORD AREA:

First Baptist Church School
20 North State St.
Concord, NH   03301

New Hampton Baptist School
New Hampton, NH   03256

Tilton Methodist School
Tilton, NH   03276

Saint Paul's Episcopal School
Pleasant St.
Concord, NH   03301

Bishop Brady Catholic High
  School
Columbus Ave.
Concord, NH   03301

KEENE AREA:

Dublin Christian Academy
Box 98
Dublin, NH   03444

Community Christian School
West Swanzey, NH   03469

Saint Joseph's Catholic School
Keene, NH   03431

Thomas More Catholic School
Harrisville, NH   03450

LACONIA AREA:

Christian Fellowship School
254 Court St.
Laconia, NH   03246

Calvary Christian School
2 Yeaton Rd.
West Plymouth, NH   03264

Victory Christian School
Old State Rd., Box 89
Gilmanton Iron Works, NH
03837

Holderness Episcopal School
Holderness, NH   03245

Holy Trinity School
50 Church St.
Laconia, NH   03246

Saint Mary Catholic School
Elkins St.
Franklin, NH   03235

PORTSMOUTH AREA:

Bethel Christian Academy
Bedford Way
Portsmouth, NH   03801

Saint Patrick's Catholic School
125 Austin St.
Portsmouth, NH   03801

Boynton Episcopal School
Orford, NH   03777

BERLIN AREA:

Community Baptist School
108 Main St.
Gorham, NH   03581

West Catholic School
Blanchard St.
Berlin, NH   03570

Our Lady of the Mountains
  Catholic Academy
66 Main St.
Gorham, NH   03581

NASHUA AREA:

High Mowing Christian School
Abbot Hill
Wilton, NH   03086

Nashua Christian High School
3 Lund Rd.
Nashua, NH   03060

Greater Nashua Christian
  School
49 Fairview Ave.
Nashua, NH   03060

Tabernacle Christian Schools
Route 102, Derry Rd.
Hudson, NH   03051

Nashua Catholic Jr. High
  School
72 Vine St.
Nashua, NH   03060

ROCHESTER AREA:

Christian Day School
Rocky Hill Rd.
Somersworth, NH   03878

Rochester Catholic School
Rochester, NH   03867

CLAREMONT AREA:

Claremont Christian Academy
97 Maple Ave.
Claremont, NH   03743

Living Word School
Claremont, NH   03743

DOVER AREA:

Dover Catholic School
Central Ave.
Dover, NH 03820

NEW JERSEY

JERSEY CITY AREA:

T E T Christian Academy
695 Ocean Ave.
Jersey City, NJ 07305

Lutheran School of Hudson
 County
15 Brinkerhof St.
Jersey City, NJ 07304

Hudson Catholic High School
790 Bergen Ave.
Jersey City, NJ 07306

Saint Peter's Catholic
 Preparatory School
144 Grand St.
Jersey City, NJ 07302

Saint Michael's Catholic
 High School
175 Erie St.
Jersey City, NJ 07302

Saint Anthony's Catholic
 High School
175 8th St.
Jersey City, NJ 07302

Saints Peter & Paul
 Ukrainian School
16 Bentley Ave.
Jersey City, NJ 07304

Academy of Saint Aloysius
 High School
2495 Kennedy Blvd.
Jersey City, NJ 07601

Saint Ann's Polish School
205 Tonnele Ave.
Jersey City, NJ 07306

PASSAIC AREA:

Passaic Christian School
54-56 Pine St.
Passaic, NJ 07055

Covenant Christian School
Norwood & Manning Ave.
North Plainfield, NJ 07060

Parsippany Christian School
Littleton Rd.
P. O. Box 165
Parsippany, NJ 07054

Evangel Day School
656 North Broad St.
Elizabeth, NJ 07201

Saint Benedict's Catholic
 Preparatory School
520 High St.
Newark, NJ 07102

Archbishop Walsh Catholic
 High School
100 Linden Ave.
Irvington, NJ 07111

Essex Catholic High School
300 Broadway
Newark, NJ 07104

PATERSON AREA:

Eastern Christian Jr. High
 School
272 North 8th St.
Paterson, NJ 07508

Eastern Christian Sr. High
 School
50 Oakwood Ave.
North Haledon, NJ 07508

Midland Park Christian School
25 Baldwin Dr.
Midland Park, NJ 07432

Wyckoff Christian School
518 Sicomac Ave.
Wyckoff, NJ 07481

Sussex Christian School
51 Unionville Ave.
Sussex, NJ 07461

Calvary Christian School
491 Alps Rd.
Wayne, NJ 07470

Netherland Reformed Christian
 School
475 Lafayette Ave.
Wyckoff, NJ 07481

Ringwood Christian School
30 Carletondale Rd.
Ringwood, NJ 07456

Dawn Treader School
1 Market St.
Paterson, NJ 07501

Don Bosco Catholic Technical
 High School
202 Union Ave.
Paterson, NJ 07502

Don Bosco Catholic High
 School
Ramsey, NJ 07446

HOBOKEN AREA:

Mustard Seed Christian School
311 6th St.
Hoboken, NJ 07030

Brookdale Christian School
Broad & Mountain Ave.
Bloomfield, NJ 07003

Trinity Lutheran School
85 Summit Ave.
Garfield, NJ 07026

Hoboken Spanish Seventh Day
 Adventist School
901 Bloomfield St.
Hoboken, NJ 07030

Pope Paul VI Regional
 Catholic High School
775 Valley Rd.
Clifton, NJ 07015

Three Saints Russian
 Orthodox School
106 Cambridge Ave.
Garfield, NJ 07026

TRENTON AREA:

Trenton Christian Day
  School
32 Artic Pkwy.
P. O. Box 922
Trenton, NJ 08605

Mercer Christian Academy
2015 Pennington Rd.
Trenton, NJ 08618

Peddie Baptist School
Memorial Hall
Hightstown, NJ 08520

Pennington Methodist School
Pennington, NJ 08520

Faith Christian Academy
2111 Kuser Rd.
Trenton, NJ 08690

Bethany Lutheran School
1125 Parkside Ave.
Trenton, NJ 08618

Mount Sinai School
  Seventh Day Adventist
35 Arlington Ave.
Trenton, NJ 08620

Meadowview School
  Seventh Day Adventist
Chesterfield-Bordentown Rd.
Chesterfield, NJ 08620

Trinity Cathedral Day School
West State & Overbrook Ave.
Trenton, NJ 08618

Saint Anthony's Catholic High
  School
Leonard Ave.
Trenton, NJ 08610

Notre Dame Catholic High
  School
601 Lawrenceville Rd.
Trenton, NJ 08638

ATLANTIC CITY AREA:

Atlantic City Friends School
1216 Pacific Ave.
Atlantic City, NJ 08401

Atlantic Christian School
Box 2202
Ventor City, NJ 08406

Atlantic Christian School,
  Inc.
P. O. Box 271
Ocean City, NJ 08226

Greentree Christian Academy
811 North Main St.
Pleasantville, NJ 08232

CAMDEN AREA:

Gloucester County Christian
  School
Golf Club Rd.
P. O. Box 161
Pitman, NJ 08071

Ambassador Christian
  Academy
Richwood, NJ 08074

Faith Christian Schools
Haddon Ave. & Cuthbert
P. O. Box 326
Collingswood, NJ 08108

Woodbury Friends School
North Broad St.
Woodbury, NJ 08096

Moorestown Friends School
Page Ln.
Moorestown, NJ 08057

Camden Catholic High School
State Hwy. 38 & Cuthbert
Cherry Hill, NJ 08034

Center City Catholic Jr. High
  School
15 North 7th St.
Camden, NJ 08102

Saint Joseph's Catholic High
  School
1770 Mount Ephraim Ave.
Camden, NJ 08104

CHERRY HILL AREA:

Burlington County Christian
  School
Lewistown Rd.
P. O. Box 197
Juliustown, NJ 08042

Christian School of Camden
  County
800 King's Hwy.
Haddon Heights, NJ 08035

Baptist High School
3rd & Station Ave.
Haddon Heights, NJ 08035

Bethel Baptist Christian
  School
1704 Springdale Rd.
Cherry Hill, NJ 08003

Ambassador Christian
  Academy
408 Ganttown Rd.
Turnerville, NJ 08012

Calvary Baptist School
Walnut Ave. & Burnt Mill
  Rd.
Kirkwood, NJ 08043

Haddonfield Friends School
Haddon Ave.
Haddonfield, NJ 08033

Martin Luther Christian Day
  School
U. S. Hwy. 130 & Terrace
  Ave.
Pennsauken, NJ 08110

Delaware Valley Jr. Academy
  Seventh Day Adventist
Sickel Ln.
Almonesson, NJ 08096

Bishop Eustace Catholic
  Preparatory School, Inc.
Marlton Pike
Pennsauken, NJ 08110

Gloucester Catholic High
  School
Ridgeway & Sussex Sts.
Gloucester, NJ 08030

Christ the King Catholic
School
156 Hopkins Ave.
Haddonfield, NJ   08030

HACKENSACK AREA:

Gateway Christian High
School
300 Park St.
Hackensack, NJ   07601

Hackensack Christian Schools
15 Conklin Pl.
Hackensack, NJ   07601

Saddle Brook Christian
School
585 Saddle River Rd.
Saddle Brook, NJ   07662

Bergen Catholic High School
1040 Oradell Ave.
Oradell, NJ   07649

Dwight School
315 East Palisade Ave.
Englewood, NJ   07631

Saint Joseph Regional Catholic
High School
40 Chestnut Ridge Rd.
Montvale, NJ   07645

Holy Trinity Catholic School
43 Maple Ave.
Hackensack, NJ   07607

BRIDGETON AREA:

Bridgeton Christian School
27 Central Ave.
Bridgeton, NJ   08302

MADISON AREA:

American Christian School
126 South Hillside Ave.
Succasunna, NJ   07876

Lakeland Christian School
97 East Dewey Ave.
Wharton, NJ   07885

Blair Presbyterian Academy
Blairstown, NJ   07825

Saint John Baptist School
Mendham, NJ   07945

NEW BRUNSWICK AREA:

Timothy Christian School
2008 Ethel Rd.
Piscataway, NJ   08854

American Christian School
North Main St.
Stewartsville, NJ   08886

Green Brook Christian
Academy
170 Green Brook Rd.
Green Brook, NJ   08813

Our Savior Lutheran School
151 Milltown Rd.
East Brunswick, NJ   08816

Alma Preparatory School
Pillar of Fire
Zarephath, NJ   08890

Lake Nelson School
Seventh Day Adventist
555 South Randolph Rd.
Piscataway, NJ   08854

Saint Bartholomew's Catholic
School
470 Ryder's Ln.
East Brunswick, NJ   08816

VINELAND AREA:

Vineland Christian School
P. O. Box 32
Vineland, NJ   08360

Cumberland Christian School
1100 West Sherman Ave.
Vineland, NJ   08360

RIO GRANDE AREA:

Cape May County Christian
School
29 South Shore Rd.
Rio Grande, NJ   08242

ASBURY PARK AREA:

Trinity Christian School
P. O. Box 1198
Wall, NJ   07719

Ocean County Christian Day
School Association
204 Porter Ave.
Seaside Heights, NJ   08751

Providence Bible Academy
1102 Ocean Ave.
Sea Bright, NJ   07760

Central Jersey Christian
School
P. O. Box 470
Asbury Park, NJ   07712

Methodist Church School
580 Chestnut Ave.
Teaneck, NJ   07666

Christian Brothers Catholic
Academy for Boys
Newman Springs Rd.
Lincroft, NJ   07738

Red Bank Catholic High
School
10 Peters Pl.
Red Bank, NJ   07701

Mater Dei Catholic High
School
Church St.
New Monmouth, NJ   07748

Saint Anastasia Catholic
School
1095 Teaneck Rd.
Teaneck, NJ   07666

ELIZABETH AREA:

Covenant Christian School
135 Centennial Ave.
Cranford, NJ   07016

LONG BRANCH AREA:

Bayshore Christian School,
Inc.
P. O. Box 210
Atlantic Highlands, NJ   07716

BRIDGETON AREA:

Bridgeton Christian School
27 Central Ave.
Bridgeton, NJ   08302

PHILLIPSBURG AREA:

The Phillipsburg Christian
  Academy
Third & Cromwell Sts.
Phillipsburg, NJ   08865

GLASSBORO AREA:

Ambassador Christian
  Academy
Holly and Whitney
Glassboro, NJ   08028

Victory Christian School
New Brooklyn Rd.
Williamstown, NJ   08094

BURLINGTON AREA:

Life Center Academy
P.O. Box 457
Burlington, NJ   08016

NEWTON AREA:

Newton Christian School
P.O. Box 543
Newton, NJ   07860

Sussex County Christian High
  School
P.O. Box 282
Lafayette, NJ   07848

MANAHAWKIN AREA:

Lighthouse Christian Academy
129 North Main St.
Route 9
Manahawkin, NJ   08050

CAPE MAY AREA:

Heritage Christian Academy
123 Fishing Creek Rd.
Cape May, NJ   08204

EGG HARBOR CITY AREA:

The Pilgrim Academy
P.O. Box 322
Egg Harbor City, NJ   08125

Bethel Christian Day School
P.O. Box 196
Port Republic, NJ   08241

FLEMINGTON AREA:

Faith Christian School
R.D. 2, Box 278
Flemington, NJ   08822

NEW MEXICO

ALBUQUERQUE AREA:

Good News Christian School
9300 Pan American Freeway,
  N.E.
Albuquerque, NM   87109

Bella Vista Baptist Christian
  Academy
2800 Louisiana Blvd., N.E.
Albuquerque, NM   87110

Parkview Baptist School
1404 Lead Ave., S.E.
Albuquerque, NM   87106

Temple Baptist Academy
1620 San Pedro Dr., N.E.
Albuquerque, NM   87110

Menaul Presbyterian High
  School
301 Menaul Blvd., N.E.
Albuquerque, NM   87107

Harwood United Methodist
  School
114 Seventh St., N.W.
Albuquerque, NM   87101

Evangel Temple School
4501 Montgomery Blvd., N.E.
Albuquerque, NM   87110

Immanuel Lutheran School
300 Gold Ave., S.E.
Albuquerque, NM   87102

Crestview School
  Seventh Day Adventist
3400 Comanche Rd., N.E.
Albuquerque, NM   87107

Saint Pius X Catholic High
  School
2240 Louisiana Blvd., N.E.
Albuquerque, NM   87110

Lourdes Catholic High School
4500 2nd St., S.W.
Albuquerque, NM   87102

Holy Ghost Catholic School
6201 Ross Ave., S.E.
Albuquerque, NM   87108

San Felipe Catholic School
2000 Lomas Blvd., N.W.
Albuquerque, NM   87104

Nazarene Indian School
2315 Markham Rd., S.W.
Albuquerque, NM   87105

Paradise Christian School
4620 Paradise Blvd., N.W.
Albuquerque, NM   87114

Tijeras Christian School
  Baptist
Tijeras, NM   87059

SANTA FE AREA:

Temple Baptist Christian
  School
2103 Yucca St., Box 4006
Santa Fe, NM   87501

McCurdy United Methodist
  School
Santa Cruz, NM   87567

Saint Michael's Catholic High
  School
413 College St.
Santa Fe, NM   87501

Cristo Rey Catholic School
Calle Cristo Rey
Santa Fe, NM   87501

LAS CRUCES AREA:

College Heights Christian
School
1800 Locust St.
Las Cruces, NM 88001

Saint Luke's Episcopal
School
(La Union)
Canutillo, NM 88001

Holy Cross Catholic Jr. High
School
1330 North Miranda St.
Las Cruces, NM 88001

Immaculate Heart of Mary
Catholic School
865 East Idaho Ave.
Las Cruces, NM 88001

FARMINGTON AREA:

Christian Academy Jr. & Sr.
High School
2020 East 20th St.
Farmington, NM 87401

Grace Baptist School
2200 North Sullivan Ave.
Farmington, NM 87401

Navajo United Methodist
Mission School
1200 West Apache St.
Farmington, NM 87401

Berean Mission Navajo School
Huerfano, NM 87401

Sacred Heart Catholic School
404 North Allen Ave.
Farmington, NM 87401

CLOVIS AREA:

Clovis Nazarene School
1800 Norris St.
Clovis, NM 88101

Westbrook Christian Academy
1420 Thornton St.
Clovis, NM 88101

Sacred Heart Catholic
School
919 Meriwether St.
Clovis, NM 88101

CARLSBAD AREA:

Victory Christian Academy
2107 West Church St.
Carlsbad, NM 88220

Bethel Christian School
513 East Wood St.
Carlsbad, NM 88220

Saint Edward's Jr. High
School
805 Walter St.
Carlsbad, NM 88220

GRANTS AREA:

Grants Christian Academy
500 Jefferson St.
Grants, NM 87020

First Baptist School
224 Mountain Rd.
Grants, NM 87020

Saint Theresa's Catholic
School
400 East High St.
Grants, NM 87020

GALLUP AREA:

Rehoboth Christian School
P.O. Box 41
Rehoboth, NM 87322

Zuni Christian School
Box 445
Zuni, NM 87327

Crownpoint Christian School
Box 1298
Crownpoint, NM 87313

Cathedral Grade School
Los Lunas Rd.
Gallup, NM 87301

Saint Francis Catholic School
215 West Wilson Ave.
Gallup, NM 87301

ALAMOGORDO AREA:

Alamogordo Christian
Academy
Alamogordo, NM 88310

ROSWELL AREA:

Trinity Christian Academy
1200 West Alameda St.
Roswell, NM 88201

TUCUMCARI AREA:

Temple Baptist Academy
224 East Aber St.
Tucumcari, NM 88401

DEMING AREA:

Good Shepherd Christian
School
214 West Hemlock St.
Deming, NM 88030

RATON AREA:

Raton Catholic School
401 South 3rd St.
Raton, NM 87740

SILVER CITY AREA:

Saint Mary's Catholic
Interparochial School
1813 Alabama St.
Silver City, NM 88061

HOBBS AREA:

Saint Helena's Catholic
School
Bender Blvd.
Hobbs, NM 88240

LOS ALAMOS AREA:

Covenant Christian School
333 Bryce Ave.
Los Alamos, NM 76544

NEW YORK

NEW YORK CITY,
MANHATTAN AREA:

Alexander Robertson
  Presbyterian School
3 West 95th St.
New York, NY 10025

Friends Seminary
  College Prep School
222 East 16th St.
New York, NY 10003

Seventh Avenue Mennonite
  School
201 West 146th St.
New York, NY 10039

Collegiate School
  Reformed Church in America
241 West 77th St.
New York, NY 10024

Church of Christ Bible
  Institute
112 East 125th St.
New York, NY 10035

Saint Matthew Lutheran
  School
200 Sherman Way
New York, NY 10034

Y.M.C.A. Evening High
  School
15 West 63rd St.
New York, NY 10023

McBurney Y.M.C.A. School
15 West 63rd St.
New York, NY 10023

Y.W.C.A. School of New
  York
610 Lexington Ave.
New York, NY 10022

Episcopal School
234 East 22nd St.
New York, NY 10010

Saint Luke's Episcopal School
487 Hudson St.
New York, NY 10014

Trinity Episcopal School
139 West 91st St.
New York, NY 10024

Grace Episcopal Church
  School
86 Fourth Ave.
New York, NY 10003

Choir School of Saint Thomas
123 West 55th St.
New York, NY 10019

Cathedral of Saint John the
  Divine Episcopal School
1047 Amsterdam Ave.
New York, NY 10025

Richfield Springs Christian
  School
78 East James
New York, NY 13439

Rice High School
74 West 124th St.
New York, NY 10027

Saint Jean Baptist Catholic
  High School
173 East 75th St.
New York, NY 10021

Cathedral High School
350 East 56th St.
New York, NY 10022

Xavier Catholic High School
30 West 16th St.
New York, NY 10011

Saint Sergius Catholic High
  School
1190 Park Ave.
New York, NY 10028

Saint Michael's Catholic High
  School
425 West 33rd St.
New York, NY 10001

Regis Catholic High School
55 East 84th St.
New York, NY 10028

Immaculata Catholic High
  School
317 East 33rd St.
New York, NY 10016

Greek Cathedral School
319 East 74th St.
New York, NY 10021

YONKERS AREA:

Concordia Preparatory School
171 White Plains Rd.
Bronxville, NY 10708

Salesian Catholic High School
148 Main St.
New Rochelle, NY 10805

Iona Catholic Preparatory
  School
Wilmot Rd.
New Rochelle, NY 10804

MERRICK AREA:

South Shore Christian School
34 Smith St.
Merrick, NY 11566

Saint Andrews Episcopal
  School
50 Anchor Ave.
Oceanside, NY 11572

BROOKLYN AREA:

Saint John's Evangelical
  School
255 21st St.
Brooklyn, NY 11215

Saint John's Evangelical
  Lutheran School
88-24 Myrtle Ave.
Glendale, NY 11227

Brooklyn Friends School
375 Pearl St.
Brooklyn, NY 11201

Lutheran School of Bay Ridge
440 Ovington Ave.
Brooklyn, NY 11209

Saint Mark's Lutheran School
626 Bushwick Ave.
Brooklyn, NY 11206

Saint Stephen's Lutheran
  School
2806 Newkirk Ave.
Brooklyn, NY 11226

Redeemer Lutheran School
69-26 Cooper Ave.
Glendale, NY 11227

Brooklyn Seventh Day
  Adventist School
1260 Ocean Ave.
Brooklyn, NY 11230

Flatbush Seventh Day
  Adventist School
5810 Snyder Ave.
Brooklyn, NY 11203

Brooklyn Temple School
  Seventh Day Adventist
3 Lewis Ave.
Brooklyn, NY 11206

Hanson Place School
  Seventh Day Adventist
38 Lafayette Ave.
Brooklyn, NY 11217

Y. M. C. A. Technical Schools
119 Bedford Ave.
Brooklyn, NY 11211

Saint Ann's Episcopal
  School
129 Pierrepont St.
Brooklyn, NY 11201

Saint Ann's Episcopal School
131 Clinton St.
Brooklyn Heights, NY 11201

Brooklyn Catholic Preparatory
  School
1150 Carroll St.
Brooklyn, NY 11225

Saint Saviour Catholic High
  School
590 Sixth St.
Brooklyn, NY 11215

Saint John's Catholic
  Preparatory School
82 Lewis Ave.
Brooklyn, NY 11206

Saint Francis Catholic
  Preparatory School
186 North Sixth St.
Brooklyn, NY 11211

Cathedral Prep Seminary
555 Washington Ave.
Brooklyn, NY 11238

Saint Joseph's Catholic High
  School
97 Lawrence St.
Brooklyn, NY 11201

Xaverian Catholic High School
7100 Shore Rd.
Brooklyn, NY 11209

Bishop Ford Catholic High
  School
500 19th St.
Brooklyn, NY 11215

Bishop Kearney Catholic High
  School
Bay Pkwy. & 60th St.
Brooklyn, NY 11204

Bishop Loughlin Memorial
  Catholic High School
357 Clermont Ave.
Brooklyn, NY 11238

Saint Edward's Catholic High
  School
2470 Ocean Ave.
Brooklyn, NY 11229

Holy Ghost Ukrainian
  Catholic School
160 North 5th St.
Brooklyn, NY 11211

Resurrection Catholic School
2335 Geritson Ave.
Brooklyn, NY 11229

Holy Spirit Catholic School
525 Saint John's Pl.
Brooklyn, NY 11217

HUNTINGTON STATION AREA:

Huntington Christian
  Elementary School
319 West Hills Rd.
Huntington Station, NY 11746

QUEENS AREA:

Flushing Christian Schools
158-15 Oak Ave.
Flushing, NY 11358

Y. M. C. A School
138-46 Northern Blvd.
Flushing, NY 11358

Martin Luther High School
60-02 Maspeth Ave.
Maspeth, NY 11378

Queens Lutheran School
31-20 21st Ave.
Long Island City, NY 11105

Queens Lutheran School
33-57 58th St.
Woodside, NY 11377

Redeemer Lutheran School
  of Bayside
36-01 Bell Blvd.
Bayside, NY 11361

Our Savior Lutheran School
64-33 Woodhaven Blvd.
Rego Park, NY 11374

Immanuel Lutheran School
12-10 150th St.
(West Tiana Station)
Pine Neck, NY

Grace Lutheran School
100-05 Springfield Blvd.
Queens Village, NY 11429

Redeemer Lutheran School
220-16 Union Turnpike
Flushing, NY 11358

Greater New York
  Seventh Day Academy
41-32 58th St.
Woodside, NY 11377

Linden–Jamaica School
Seventh Day Adventist
173-04 Linden Blvd.
St. Albans, NY 11412

The Woodhull Episcopal
Preparatory School
196-10 Woodhull Ave.
Hollis, NY 11423

Saint Joseph's Episcopal
Day School
217-55 100th Ave.
Queens Village, NY 11429

Archbishop Molloy Catholic
High School
85-53 Manton St.
Jamaica, NY 11435

Mater Christi Catholic High
School
21-21 Cresent St.
Long Island City, NY 11105

Holy Cross Catholic High
School
26-20 Francis Lewis Blvd.
Flushing, NY 11358

MINEOLA AREA:

South Shore Christian School
2616 Martin Ave.
Bellmore, NY 11710

Long Island Bible Institute
84 Orchard St.
Oyster Bay, NY 11771

Friends Academy
Duck Pond Rd.
Locust Valley, NY 11560

Roslyn Presbyterian School
East Broadway
Roslyn, NY 11576

The Stony Brook School
Chapman Pkwy.
Stony Brook, NY 11790

Long Island Lutheran High
School
131 Brookville Rd.
(Brookville, Glen Head)
Long Island, NY 11545

Nassau Lutheran School
155 Washington Ave.
Mineola, NY 11501

Lutheran School for Deaf
First Mill Rd.
Mill Neck, NY 11765

Our Redeemer Lutheran
School
2025 Washington Ave.
Seaford, NY 11783

Grace Lutheran School
400 Hempstead Ave.
Malvern, NY 11565

Saint Paul's Episcopal School
295 Stewart Ave.
(Garden City)
Long Island, NY 11530

Advent-Tuller Episcopal
School
Walden St.
(Westbury)
Long Island, NY 11590

Saint Andrew's Episcopal
School
50 Anchor Ave.
Oceanside, NY 11572

Saint Dominic's Catholic
High School
110 Anstce
Oyster Bay, NY 11771

Holy Trinity High School
98 Cherry Ln.
Hicksville, NY 11801

Saint Agnes Cathedral High
School
North Village Ave.
Rockville Center, NY 11570

Maria Regina Diocesan
Catholic High School
1333 Admiral Ln.
Uniondale, NY 11553

Cathedral School of Saint
Mary
37 Cathedral Ave.
Garden City, NY 11530

Saint Thomas the Apostle
Catholic School
12 Westminster Rd.
West Hempstead, NY 11552

Transfiguration Parish Day
School
South Long Beach Ave. and
Pine
(Freeport)
Long Island, NY 11520

BRONX AREA:

Our Savior Lutheran High
School
1734 Williamsbridge Rd.
The Bronx, NY 10461

Grace Lutheran School
Valentine Ave. & East 199th
The Bronx, NY 10458

Saint Peter's Lutheran School
411 East 143rd St.
The Bronx, NY 10454

Bronx-Manhattan School
Seventh Day Adventist
1440 Plimpton Ave.
The Bronx, NY 10452

Saint Barnabas Catholic High
School
425 East 240th St.
The Bronx, NY 10470

Aquinas Catholic High School
Belmont Ave. & East 182nd
St.
The Bronx, NY 10457

All Hallows Catholic Institute
111 East 164th St.
The Bronx, NY 10452

Cardinal Hays Catholic High
School
650 Grand Concourse
The Bronx, NY 10451

Cardinal Spellman Catholic
High School
1991 Needham Ave.
The Bronx, NY 10466

Monsignor Scanlan Business
High School
955 Hutchinson River Pkwy.
The Bronx, NY   10465

MOUNT VERNON AREA:

Hope Town Christian
Residential School
Route 3
Carmel, NY   10512

Immanuel Evangelical
Lutheran School
17 East Grand St.
Mount Vernon, NY   10552

Malcolm Gordon Episcopal
School
Garrison, NY   10524

Saint Peter's Episcopal
School
East Main St.
Peekskill, NY   10566

STATEN ISLAND,
RICHMOND AREA:

Saint John's Lutheran School
663 Manor Rd.
Staten Island, NY   10314

Trinity Lutheran School
309 Saint Paul's Ave.
Staten Island, NY   10304

Eltingville Lutheran School
300 Genesee Ave.
Staten Island, NY   10312

Saint Peter's Boys High
School
200 Clinton Ave.
Staten Island, NY   10301

Moore Catholic High School
100 Merrill Ave.
Staten Island, NY   10314

Saint Joseph by-the-Sea
Catholic High School
5150 Hylan Blvd.
Staten Island, NY   10312

Saint Joseph's Hill Academy
High School
850 Hylan Blvd.
Staten Island, NY   10305

Notre Dame Catholic
Academy
78 Howard Ave.
Staten Island, NY   10301

BUFFALO AREA:

Christian Central Academy
895 North Forest Rd.
Buffalo, NY   14221

Central Christian Academy
4560 East Boncrest Dr.
Williamsville, NY   14221

New York Christian Institute
5375 Old Goodrich Rd.
Clarence, NY   14031

Center Road Baptist
Christian Academy
412 Center Rd.
West Seneca, NY   14224

Martin Luther School
1085 Egert Rd.
Egertsville, NY   14226

Trinity Lutheran School
146 Reserve Rd.
West Seneca, NY   14224

Cathedral School
1069 Delaware Ave.
Buffalo, NY   14209

Saint Francis Catholic High
School
Lake Shore
Athol Springs, NY   14010

Archbishop Carroll Catholic
High School
1409 East Delaware Ave.
Buffalo, NY   14209

Bishop Timon Catholic High
School
601 McKinley Pkwy.
Buffalo, NY   14219

Bishop Turner Catholic High
School
185 Lang Ave.
Buffalo, NY   14215

Saint John Newman Catholic
High School
Park Club Ln.
Williamsville, NY   14221

Canisius Catholic High School
1180 Delaware Ave.
Buffalo, NY   14209

Most Holy Redeemer Catholic
School
16 Alpine Pl.
Cheektowaga, NY   14225

Saints Peter & Paul Russian
Orthodox School
44 Benzinger St.
Buffalo, NY   14206

ROCHESTER AREA:

Rochester Christian Academy
3177 Lyell Rd.
Rochester, NY   14606

Rochester Christian School
260 Embury Rd.
Rochester, NY   14625

Rochester Christian High
School
163 Bunker Hill Rd.
Rochester, NY   14625

Covenant Christian School
P. O. Box 468
Penfield, NY   14526

Beaver Valley Christian
Academy
350 Adams St.
Rochester, NY   15074

Penfield Christian School
1796 Penfield Rd.
Penfield, NY   14526

Harley School
1981 Clover St.
Rochester, NY   14618

North Star Bible Baptist
  Christian Academy
1039 North Greece Rd.
Rochester, NY 14626

North Baptist Christian
  School
2052 Saint Paul St.
Rochester, NY 14621

Webster Christian School
675 Holt Rd.
Webster, NY 14580

Chapel Christian Academy
East Henrietta Rd.
Henrietta, NY 14467

Gates Baptist Temple School
4393 Lyell Rd.
Spencerport, NY 14559

Faith Temple School
1876 Elmwood Ave.
Rochester, NY 14620

Rochester Jr. Academy
  Seventh Day Adventist
Blair Rd.
Rochester, NY

Aquinas Catholic Institute
1127 Dewey Ave.
Rochester, NY 14613

Bishop Kearney Catholic High
  School
125 King's Hwy., S.
Rochester, NY 14617

Cardinal Mooney Catholic
  High School
800 Maiden Ln.
Rochester, NY 14615

McQuaid Jesuit Catholic High
  School
1800 Clinton Ave., S.
Rochester, NY 14618

Nazareth Catholic Academy
1001 Lake Ave.
Rochester, NY 14618

Saint Agnes Catholic High
  School
300 East River Rd.
Rochester, NY 14620

Our Lady of Mercy Catholic
  High School
1437 Blossom Rd.
Rochester, NY 14610

Saint John the Evangelist
  School
545 Humboldt St.
Rochester, NY 14610

Saint John Evangelist School
2376 Ridge Rd., W.
Rochester, NY 14626

Christ the King Catholic
  School
445 King's Hwy., S.
Rochester, NY 14617

Saint Josaphat's Ukrainian
  School
Stanton Ln.
Rochester, NY 14617

SYRACUSE AREA:

Faith Heritage Christian
  School
3740 Midland Ave.
Syracuse, NY 13205

Living Word Academy
Court Street Rd.
Syracuse, NY 13206

Parkview Academy
  Seventh Day Adventist
412 South Avery Ave.
Syracuse, NY 13219

Cathedral School
420 Montgomery St.
Syracuse, NY 13202

Christian Brothers Catholic
  Academy
Randell Rd.
Dewitt, NY 13214

Franciscan Catholic Academy
2500 Grant Blvd.
Syracuse, NY 13208

Saint John the Baptist
  Academy
1406 Park St.
Syracuse, NY 13208

Bishop Grimes Catholic
  High School
6653 Kirkville Rd.
East Syracuse, NY 13057

Bishop Ludden Catholic High
  School
815 Fay Rd.
Syracuse, NY 13212

Assumption Catholic High
  School
1115 North Townsend St.
Syracuse, NY 13208

Saint John the Baptist
  Ukrainian Catholic School
110 South Wilbur Ave.
Syracuse, NY 13204

ALBANY AREA:

Capital Christian Academy
5th Ave. & 101st St., N.
Troy, NY 12180

Pineview Christian Academy
Washington Ave. Extension
Albany, NY 12210

Alcove Christian Academy
P.O. Box 33
Alcove, NY 12007

Loudonville Christian School
374 Loudon Rd.
Loudonville, NY 12211

Covenant Christian School
Box 165
Duanesburg, NY 12056

Schenectady Christian School
36-38 Sacandaga Rd.
Scotia, NY 12302

Peoples Baptist School
12 Launfal St.
Albany, NY 12205

Tri-City Jr. Academy
  Seventh Day Adventist
Saint Agnes Hwy.
Cohoes, NY 12047

Christ the King Catholic
  High School
68-02 Metropolitan Ave.
Maryland Village, NY 12116

Christian Brothers Catholic
  Academy
1 De La Salle Rd.
Albany, NY 12208

Catholic Academy of the
  Holy Names Middle School
1065 New Scotland Rd.
Albany, NY 12208

Catholic Academy of the
  Holy Names Upper School
1075 New Scotland Rd.
Albany, NY 12208

Bishop Maginn Catholic High
  School
Slingerland St.
Albany, NY 12202

Mercy Catholic High School
310 South Manning Blvd.
Albany, NY 12208

Waterford Central Catholic
  School
12 Sixth St.
Waterford, NY 12188

Christ the King Catholic
  School
Sumpter & Seward Sts.
Guilderland, NY 12084

Saints Peter & Paul
  Catholic School
174 Ontario St.
Cohoes, NY 12047

Holy Spirit Catholic School
667 Columbia Street
  Turnpike
East Greenbush, NY 12061

NIAGARA FALLS AREA:

Niagara Christian Academy
601 28th St.
Niagara Falls, NY 14301

Faith Christian School
6301 Main St.
Williamsville, NY 14221

First Baptist Christian
  School
530 Meadow Dr.
North Tonawanda, NY 14120

Saint Mark's Evangelical
  Lutheran School
1135 Oliver St.
North Tonawanda, NY 14120

Niagara Lutheran Jr. High
  School
1110 Niagara St.
Niagara Falls, NY 14303

Stella Niagara Education
  Park
4421 Lower River Rd.
(Stella)
Niagara Falls, NY 14144

Trinity Lutheran School
1333 South Ave.
Niagara Falls, NY 14305

Saint Paul Lutheran School
453 Old Falls Blvd.
North Tonawanda, NY 14120

Saint Matthew's Lutheran
  School
875 Eggert Dr.
North Tonawanda, NY 14120

Saint Peter's Lutheran School
6168 Walmore Rd.
Sanborn, NY 14132

Deveaux Episcopal School
Lewiston Rd.
Niagara Falls, NY 14305

Niagara Catholic High School
520 66th St.
Niagara Falls, NY 14304

Saint Joseph's Catholic
  School
625 Tronolone Pl.
Niagara Falls, NY 14301

Saint Joseph's Catholic
  School
1469 Payne Ave.
North Tonawanda, NY 14120

Saint Francis of Assisi
  Catholic School
144 Broad St.
North Tonawanda, NY 14120

Prince of Peace Catholic
  School
1055 North Military Rd.
Niagara Falls, NY 14304

Ascension School
75 Keil St.
North Tonawanda, NY 14120

Monsignor McClancy
  Memorial Catholic High
  School
72-02 31st Ave.
John F. Kennedy Heights, NY
14085

WATERTOWN AREA:

Immaculate Heart Catholic
  Central High School
Ives Street Rd.
Watertown, NY 13601

JAMESTOWN AREA:

Kennedy Christian Academy
Jamestown-Randolph Rd.
Kennedy, NY 14747

First Baptist Church School
59 South Erie St.
Mayville, NY 14757

Houghton Academy
  Free Methodist
Houghton, NY 14744

Bethel Baptist School
200 Hunt Rd.
Jamestown, NY 14701

Saints Peter & Paul
  Catholic School
1135 North Main St.
Jamestown, NY 14701

ELMIRA AREA:

Elmira Christian Academy
235 East Miller St.
Elmira, NY 14904

Twin Tiers Baptist High
  School
Main St., P.O. Box 320
Breesport, NY 14816

Horseheads Christian School
306 Grand Central Ave.
Horseheads, NY 14845

Tioga Center Christian
  School
P.O. Box 116
Tioga Center, NY 13845

Twin Tiers Jr. Adventist
  Academy
811 Maple Ave.
Elmira, NY 14904

Saint Patrick Catholic Jr.
  High School
517 Park Pl.
Elmira, NY 14901

AUBURN AREA:

Auburn Christian School
89 Letchworth St.
Auburn, NY 13021

Adirondack Christian Day
  School
Route 86
Wilmington, NY 12997

Frontenac School
  Seventh Day Adventist
Spring St.
Union Springs, NY 13160

Blessed Trinity Catholic
  School
101 East Genesee St.
Auburn, NY 13021

Saints Peter & Paul Catholic
  School
130 Washington St.
Auburn, NY 13021

BINGHAMTON AREA:

Ross Corners Christian
  Academy
Box 404
Vestal, NY 13850

UTICA AREA:

Maranatha Christian
  Academy
Middle Settlement
New Hartford, NY 13413

NEWARK AREA:

East Palmyra Christian
  School
Box 31
East Palmyra, NY 14444

PATCHOQUE AREA:

West Sayville Christian
  School
37 Rollstone Ave.
West Sayville, NY 11796

GENEVA AREA:

Trinity Christian Academy
c/o Otto Krein
500 East Lake Rd.
Rushville, NY 14544

AMSTERDAM AREA:

Spa Christian School
P.O. Box 445
Ballston Spa, NY 12020

MIDDLETOWN AREA:

Goshen Christian School
R.D. 2, P.O. Box 469
Goshen, NY 10924

SCHROON LAKE AREA:

Mountainside Christian
  Academy
P.O Box 208
Schroon Lake, NY 12870

PLAINVIEW AREA:

Good Shepherd Lutheran
  School
99 Central Park Rd.
Plainview, NY 11803

CENTEREACH AREA:

North Shore Christian School
Box 227
Port Jefferson, NY 11776

NORTH CAROLINA

CHARLOTTE AREA:

Charlotte Christian School
7301 Sardis Rd.
Charlotte, NC 28211

Carolina Christian Day
  School
5832 Thrift Rd.
Charlotte, NC 28214

Covenant Christian Academy
1800 Fourth St., E.
Charlotte, NC 28204

Northside Christian Schools
333 Jeremiah Blvd.
Charlotte, NC 28213

Trinity Christian Academy
1019 Scaleybark Rd.
Charlotte, NC 28209

Bible Baptist School
2724 Margaret Wallace Rd.
Charlotte, NC 28212

Bible Presbyterian School
6237 Rumple Rd.
P.O. Box 26291
Charlotte, NC 28213

Paw Creek Christian Academy
1209 Little Rock Rd.
Charlotte, NC   28214

Ascension Lutheran School
1225 East Morehead St.
Charlotte, NC   28204

Berean Seventh Day
  Adventist School
1801 Double Oaks Rd.
Charlotte, NC   28206

Kilgore Seventh Day Adventist
  School
3900 Litchfield Rd.
Charlotte, NC   28211

Charlotte Catholic High
  School
3100 Park Rd.
Charlotte, NC   28209

Assumption Catholic School
2101 Shenandoah Ave.
Charlotte, NC   28205

STATESVILLE AREA:

Southview Christian School
Wallace Springs Rd.
Route 10, Box 38
Statesville, NC   28677

MORGANTON AREA:

Tabernacle Christian School
P.O. Box 429
Morganton, NC   28655

WINSTON-SALEM AREA:

Salem Baptist Christian Day
  School
429 South Broad St.
Winston-Salem, NC   27101

Salem Moravian Academy
Winston-Salem, NC   27102

Kerwin Christian School
4520 Old Hollow Rd.
Kernersville, NC   27284

Wesleyan Academy
P.O. Box 646
Kernersville, NC   27284

Edgewood Christian School,
  Inc.
4067 Reidsville Rd.
Winston-Salem, NC   27101

Woodland Baptist Christian
  School
3665 Patterson Ave.
Winston-Salem, NC   27105

Immanuel Christian School
Lewisville-Clemmons Rd.
Winston-Salem, NC   27107

South Park Baptist Schools
2925 South Main St.
Winston-Salem, NC   27107

Calvary Baptist Day School
5000 Country Club Rd.
Winston-Salem, NC   27104

Gospel Light Christian School
P.O. Box 7
Walkerton, NC   27051

Saint John's Lutheran Day
  School
2415 Silas Creek Pkwy.
Winston-Salem, NC   27103

Ephesus Jr. Academy
  Seventh Day Adventist
240 North Dunleith Ave.
Winston-Salem, NC   27101

Bishop McGuinnes Memorial
  Catholic High School
1730 Link Rd.
Winston-Salem, NC   27103

Saint Leo's Catholic School
335 Springdale Ave.
Winston-Salem, NC   27104

LENOIR AREA:

Lenoir Community Church
  School
1002 N.E. Lower Creek Dr.
Lenoir, NC   28645

Patterson Episcopal School
Ledgerwood Station
Lenoir, NC   28645

GREENSBORO AREA:

Vandalia Christian Schools
3919 Pleasant Garden Rd.
Greensboro, NC   27406

Christian Heritage Schools
4607 Tower Dr.
Greensboro, NC   27410

John Wesley High School
1906 Boulevard St.
Greensboro, NC   27406

Brightwood Christian Academy
Highway 29 N.
Route 5
Greensboro, NC   27406

Community Baptist Elementary
  School
509 Wall Rd.
Reidsville, NC   27320

New Garden Friends School
840 Neal St.
Greensboro, NC   27403

Grace Lutheran School
1315 East Washington St.
Greensboro, NC   27401

Tri-City Jr. Academy
  Seventh Day Adventist
Clinard Farm Rd.
Greensboro, NC

East Market Street School
  Seventh Day Adventist
1802 East Market St.
Greensboro, NC   27401

Notre Dame Catholic High
  School
901 Summit Ave.
Greensboro, NC   27405

WILMINGTON AREA:

Wilmington Christian Academy
608 South College Rd.
Wilmington, NC   28403

Hanover Baptist Christian
  Academy
4702 South College Rd.
Wilmington, NC   28403

Harrell's Christian Academy
P.O. Box 88
Harrells, NC 28444

Ephesus School
  Seventh Day Adventist
1002 Castle St.
Wilmington, NC 28401

Saint Mary's Catholic School
217 South 4th St.
Wilmington, NC 28401

RALEIGH AREA:

Raleigh Christian Academy
2110 Trawick Rd.
Raleigh, NC 27604

Wake Christian Academy
5550 Fayetteville Rd.
Raleigh, NC 27603

Mid-Way Christian Middle &
  Upper Schools
6910 Fayetteville Rd.
Raleigh, NC 27603

Friendship Christian Schools
5510 Falls of Neuse Rd.
Raleigh, NC 27609

Southern Christian Academy
Rolesville Rd.
Knightdale, NC 27545

Cathedral School
204 Hillsboro St.
Raleigh, NC 27603

Cardinal Gibbons Catholic
  High School
2401 Western Blvd.
Raleigh, NC 27606

Saint Timothy's School
4523 Six Forks Rd.
Raleigh, NC 27609

GASTONIA AREA:

Gaston Christian School
2000 Dixon Rd.
Gastonia, NC 28052

First Wesleyan Church School
208 South Church St.
Gastonia, NC 28052

Temple Christian School
405 South Sherman St.
Gastonia, NC 28052

Gospel Baptist Christian
  School
107 North Washington St.
Gastonia, NC 28052

Cramerton Christian Academy
Lowell, NC 28052

Saint Michael's Catholic
  School
Saint Michael's Ln.
Gastonia, NC 28052

ASHEBORO AREA:

Fayetteville Street Christian
  School
901 North Fayetteville St.
Asheboro, NC 27203

Faith Christian Schools
Box 49, Route 1
Ramseur, NC 27316

DURHAM AREA:

Cresset Christian Middle &
  Upper Schools
3707 Garrett Rd.
Durham, NC 27707

Central Baptist Academy
Cole Mill Rd.
Durham, NC 27705

Council Christian Academy
  Foundation
Redwood Rd.
Durham, NC 27704

Fellowship Christian School
P.O. Box 11648
Durham, NC 27703

Liberty Baptist Christian
  Schools
1606 Liberty St.
P.O. Box 11186
Durham, NC 27703

Carolina Friends School
Creech Rd.
Durham, NC 27704

Saint Mary's Country Day
  School
Pleasant Green Rd.
Durham, NC 27705

Immaculata Catholic School
721 Burch Ave.
Durham, NC 27701

SALISBURY AREA:

Salisbury Christian School
Route 5
Salisbury, NC 28144

North Hills Christian School
2740 West Innes St.
Salisbury, NC 28144

Gospel Light Baptist School
Airport Rd.
Salisbury, NC 28144

Monroe Christian School
Goldmine Rd., Route 6
Monroe, NC 28110

Lincoln Congregational
  Academy
King's Mountain, NC 28086

Seventh Day Adventist School
325 Malcolm Rd.
Salisbury, NC 28144

Sacred Heart Catholic School
123 North Ellis St.
Salisbury, NC 28144

ASHEVILLE AREA:

Asheville Christian Academy
P.O. Box 9038, Bell Rd.
Asheville, NC 28805

Faith Christian Day School
P.O. Box 1149
Hendersonville, NC 28739

Asheville Baptist Tabernacle
  Christian School
3 Camp Ground Rd.
Asheville, NC 28805

Ben Lippen School
  Fundamentalist
10 Ben Lippen School Rd.
Asheville, NC 28806

Allen Methodist High School
Asheville, NC 28801

Mount Pisgah Academy
Monte Vista Rd.
Candler, NC 28715

Gibbons Hall School for
  Boys
12 Oakland Rd.
Asheville, NC 28801

Asheville Catholic High
  School
285 Victoria Rd.
Asheville, NC 28801

Saint Eugene's Catholic
  School
12 Culvern St.
Asheville, NC 28804

HICKORY AREA:

Tabernacle Christian School
29th Ave., N.W.
Route 6
Hickory, NC 28601

Concordia Christian Day
  School
115 5th Ave., S.E.
Conover, NC 28613

Glade Valley School
  Presbyterian
P.O. Box 506
Glade Valley, NC 28627

Saint Stephen's Lutheran
  School
2304 Springs Rd.
Hickory, NC 28601

Johnston School
  Seventh Day Adventist
172 23rd St., N.W.
Hickory, NC 28601

ROCKY MOUNT AREA:

Falls Road Baptist School,
  Inc.
113 Trevathan St.
Rocky Mount, NC 27801

Grace Christian School
509 Kingston Ave.
Rocky Mount, NC 27801

New Christian Academy, Inc.
Sharpsburg, NC 27878

Catholic School of Our Lady
  of Perpetual Help
315 Hammond St.
Rocky Mount, NC 27801

NEW BERN AREA:

Calvary Baptist Christian
  School
1821 Rhem Ave.
Box 698
New Bern, NC 28560

Ruth's Chapel Christian
  School
2709 Oaks Rd.
New Bern, NC 28560

Beaufort Christian Academy
Broad St., Box 409
Beaufort, NC 28516

Grace Christian School
Route 2, Box 391
Morehead City, NC 28557

Maranatha Baptist School
Alliance, NC 28509

New Bern Adventist Academy
511 West St.
New Bern, NC 28560

Saint Paul's Catholic School
306 Bern St.
New Bern, NC 28560

HIGH POINT AREA:

Mount Calvary Christian
  School
903 East Kearns Ave.
High Point, NC 27260

Alamance Christian School
Box 128
Graham, NC 27253

Christ the King Catholic
  School
1601 Kivett Dr.
High Point, NC 27260

FAYETTEVILLE AREA:

Cumberland Christian
  School
Hope Mills Rd.
Fayetteville, NC 28304

Berean Baptist Christian
  School
520 Glensford Dr.
Fayetteville, NC 28304

Eutaw Baptist School
Scotty Hill & Cain Rd.
Fayetteville, NC 28303

GREENVILLE AREA:

Greenville Christian
  Academy
264 By-Pass West
Greenville, NC 27834

Calvary Christian School
1412 Holbert St.
Greenville, NC 27834

Mount Calvary Christian
  Academy
P.O. Box 157
Hookerton, NC 28538

Terra Ceia Christian School
Route 2
P.O. Box 159
Pantego, NC 27860

Saint Peter's Catholic School
2700 East 4th St.
Greenville, NC 27834

KINSTON AREA:

Bethel Christian Academy
Route 2, P.O. Box 385
Highway 258 N.
Kinston, NC 28501

Grace Christian School
1800 Old Snow Hill Rd.
Kinston, NC 28501

Christ the King Catholic
  School
705 Perry St.
Kinston, NC 28501

SHELBY AREA:

Shelby Christian School
Shelby, NC 28150

Manna Christian School
P.O. Box 1937
Shelby, NC 28150

Broad River Academy
900 Mark Dr.
Shelby, NC 28150

Joy Christian School
P.O. Box 252
Conetoe, NC 27819

JACKSONVILLE AREA:

Pine Valley Christian
  School
304 Western Blvd.
Jacksonville, NC 28540

Tabernacle School
Route 1
Maysville, NC 28555

The Gramercy School
Route 3, P.O. Box 239
Newport, NC 28570

Grace Baptist Christian
  School
Route 2, P.O. Box 391
Country Club Rd.
Morehead City, NC 28557

Holy Spirit Catholic School
7 East Dr.
Jacksonville, NC 28540

ELIZABETH CITY AREA:

Emmanuel Christian School
109 Chadbury Ave.
Elizabeth City, NC 27909

Immanuel Christian School
West Queen Extension
Edenton, NC 27932

Saint Catherine's Catholic
  School
605 South Martin St.
Elizabeth City, NC 27909

THOMASVILLE AREA:

Carolina Christian Academy
Academy Dr.
Thomasville, NC 27360

Free Pilgrim Academy
Route 2, P.O. Box 99-E
Thomasville, NC 27360

Palmer Memorial Institute
Sedalia, NC 27342

BURLINGTON AREA:

Burlington Day School
1615 Greenwood Terr.
Burlington, NC 27215

Sonlight Christian School
Route 1, P.O. Box 135A
Walnut Cove, NC 27052

Alamance Christian School
P.O. Box 128
Graham, NC 27253

Church of the Blessed
  Sacrament Catholic School
400 West Davis St.
Burlington, NC 27215

WILSON AREA:

Wilson Christian School, Inc.
Route 2, P.O. Box 3816
Wilson, NC 27893

Temple Christian Academy
Forrest Hills Rd.
Wilson, NC 27893

GOLDSBORO AREA:

Goldsboro Christian School
1700 East Beech St.
P.O. Box 1957
Goldsboro, NC 27530

Faith Christian Academy
Raleigh Hwy., W.
P.O. Box 1159
Goldsboro, NC 27530

Duplin Christian Academy
Route 3, Box 176
Warsaw, NC 28398

CHAPEL HILL AREA:

Carrboro Christian Academy
1110-B West Main St.
Carrboro, NC 27510

Saint Thomas More Catholic
  School
15-501 B-Pass
Chapel Hill, NC 27514

LEXINGTON AREA:

Grace Christian School
Haywood Rd.
Route 3, Box 300
Lexington, NC 27292

Sheets Memorial Christian
  School
207 Holt St.
Lexington, NC 27292

Union Grove Christian School
Route 8, Box 100
Lexington, NC 27292

CONCORD AREA:

Bethany Christian School
Old Airport Rd.
Concord, NC 28025

First Assembly School
Rockaldin Circle
Concord, NC 28025

MONROE AREA:

Monroe Christian School
Route 6, Goldmine Rd.
Monroe, NC 28110

Broad River Christian
  School
Mooresboro, NC 28114

NORTH DAKOTA

FARGO AREA:

Central Christian School
1002 South 10th St.
Fargo, ND 58103

Oak Grove Lutheran High
School
124 North Terr.
Fargo, ND 58102

Grace Lutheran School
1025 South 14th Ave.
Fargo, ND 58103

Richards School
Seventh Day Adventist
1301 North 7th St.
Wahpeton, ND 58075

Shanley Catholic High School
705 North 13th Ave.
Fargo, ND 58102

Saint Mary's Cathedral
School
619 North 7th St.
Fargo, ND 58102

Holy Spirit Catholic School
1441 North 8th St.
Fargo, ND 58102

Saint Anthony of Padua
Catholic School
719 South 9th St.
Fargo, ND 58103

Saint John's Catholic School
122 North 2nd St.
Wahpeton, ND 58075

Saint Catherine's Catholic
School
540 3rd Ave., N.E.
Valley City, ND 58072

BISMARCK AREA:

Dakota Adventist Academy
North of City
Bismarck, ND 58501

Shiloh Christian School
325 Telstar Dr.
Bismarck, ND 58501

Saint Mary's Catholic High
School
1025 North 2nd St.
Bismarck, ND 58501

Cathedral of Holy Spirit
School
508 Raymond St.
Bismarck, ND 58501

JAMESTOWN AREA:

Our Savior's Lutheran School
325 5th Ave., S.E.
Jamestown, ND 58401

Seventh Day Adventist School
116 15th Ave., N.E.
Jamestown, ND 58401

Saint John's Catholic Academy
215 Fifth St., S.E.
Jamestown, ND 58401

GRAFTON AREA:

Pleasant Valley School
Park River, ND 58270

Saint Joseph's Catholic School
9th & 10th Ave.
Devil's Lake, ND 58301

GRAND FORKS AREA:

Saint James Academy
1600 Fourth Ave., N.
Grand Forks, ND 58201

Holy Family Catholic School
1004 18th Ave., S.
Grand Forks, ND 58201

(See also East Grand Forks,
Minn.)

DICKINSON AREA

Trinity High School
Northwest of City
Dickinson, ND 58601

Saint Joseph's Catholic
School
237 S.E. 1st St.
Dickinson, ND 58601

Saint Patrick's Catholic
School
145 3rd Ave., W.
Dickinson, ND 58601

MANDAN AREA:

Christ the King Catholic
School
1100 N.W. 3rd St.
Mandan, ND 58554

Saint Joseph Catholic School
106 N.E. 3rd St.
Mandan, ND 58554

MINOT AREA:

Bishop Ryan Catholic High
School
316 11th Ave., N.W.
Minot, ND 58701

OHIO

CLEVELAND AREA:

Cleveland Christian School
10902 Avon Ave.
Cleveland, OH 44105

Christian Schools of Ohio
15401 Detroit Ave.
Cleveland, OH 44107

Baptist Christian High School
27200 Emery Rd.
Cleveland, OH 44128

Baptist Christian School
12601 Cedar St.
Cleveland, OH 44106

Westside Baptist Christian
School
9407 Madison Ave.
Cleveland, OH 44102

The West Cleveland
  Christian School
15135 Triskett St.
Cleveland, OH 44111

Heritage Christian School
4431 Tiedeman Rd.
Cleveland, OH 44144

Willo-Hill Christian School
4200 State Route 306
Willoughby, OH 44094

Friends School in Cleveland
10819 Magnolia Dr.
Cleveland, OH 44106

Lutheran High School West
3850 Linden Rd.
Rocky River, OH 44116

Messiah Lutheran School
21485 Lorain Ave.
Cleveland, OH 44126

Saint Thomas Lutheran
  School
21211 Detroit Ave.
Cleveland, OH 44116

Cleveland Jr. Academy
  Seventh Day Adventist
17822 Euclid Ave.
Cleveland, OH 44112

Lakewood School
  Seventh Day Adventist
1382 Arthur St.
Lakewood, OH 44107

Trinity High School
12425 Granger Rd.
Cleveland, OH 44125

Cleveland Central Catholic
  High School
6550 Baxter Ave.
Cleveland, OH 44105

Benedictine Catholic High
  School
2900 East Blvd.
Cleveland, OH 44104

Erieview Catholic High School
1736 Superior Ave.
Cleveland, OH 44114

Holy Name Catholic High
  School
8328 Broadway
Cleveland, OH 44105

Lake Catholic High School
6733 Reynolds St.
Mentor, OH 44060

Saint Joseph Catholic High
  School
18491 Lake Shore Blvd.
Cleveland, OH 44119

Incarnate Word Academy
6618 Pearl St.
Cleveland, OH 44130

Saint Ignatius Catholic High
  School
1911 West 30th St.
Cleveland, OH 44113

Saint Edward High School
13500 Detroit Ave.
Cleveland, OH 44107

Byzantine Catholic High
  School
1900 Carlton Rd.
Cleveland, OH 44107

Saint Stephen's Catholic
  Byzantine Rite School
432 Lloyd Rd.
Cleveland, OH 44132

Saint Gregory's Greek Rite
  Catholic School
West 129th & Madison Sts.
Cleveland, OH 44111

Regina Catholic High School
1857 South Green St.
Cleveland, OH 44121

Christ the King Catholic
  School
16005 Terrace Rd.
Cleveland, OH 44112

Holy Redeemer Catholic
  School
15720 Kipling Ave.
Cleveland, OH 44110

COLUMBUS AREA:

Columbus Christian School
5521 Groveport Rd.
Columbus, OH 43207

Columbus Christian School
1850 Bostwick Rd.
Columbus, OH 43227

Central Christian Academy
192 South Central St.
Columbus, OH 43223

Maranatha Christian School
4663 Trabue Rd.
Columbus, OH 43228

Northside Christian School
3865 North High St.
Columbus, OH 43214

Northside Christian School
1955 Schrock Rd.
Columbus, OH 43229

Worthington Christian Schools
6670 Worthington-Galena Rd.
Columbus, OH 43085

High Street Christian Academy
7399 North High St.
Columbus, OH 43085

Linden Christian School
1911 Oakland Park
Columbus, OH 43224

Heritage Temple Baptist
  School
470 East Welch Ave.
Columbus, OH 43207

Winchester Christian
  Academy
470 Groveport Rd.
Columbus, OH 43207

Plainview Christian School
8270 Amish Pike
Plain City, OH 43064

Saint Paul's Evangelical
Lutheran School
322 East Stewart St.
Columbus, OH   43206

Worthington School
Seventh Day Adventist
860 Griswald St.
Columbus, OH   43085

Eastwood Jr. Academy
Seventh Day Adventist
270 Napoleon Ave.
Columbus, OH   43213

Trinity Middle School
1543 Roxbury Rd.
Columbus, OH   43212

John XXIII Catholic Jr. High
School
508 Berkeley Rd.
Columbus, OH   43205

Saint Joseph Catholic
Academy
331 East Rich St.
Columbus, OH   43215

Christ the King Catholic
School
2855 East Livingston Ave.
Columbus, OH   43209

CINCINNATI AREA:

Greater Cincinnati Christian
High School
7350 Dixie Hwy.
Fairfield, OH   45014

Landmark Christian High
School
500 Oak Rd.
(Evendale)
Cincinnati, OH   45013

Christian School of Greater
Cincinnati
P.O Box 4176
Cincinnati, OH   45204

Lord's Covenant Christian
School
839 North Bend Rd.
Cincinnati, OH   45224

Norwood Baptist Christian
School
2041 Courtland Ave.
Cincinnati, OH   45212

Immanuel Christian School
2929 Springdale Rd.
Cincinnati, OH   45239

Deer Park Baptist School
4220 East Galbreath Rd.
Cincinnati, OH   45236

Beautiful Savior Lutheran
School
11981 Pippin Rd.
Cincinnati, OH   45231

Lutheran School of Our
Redeemer
6969 Montgomery Rd.
Cincinnati, OH   45236

Immanuel Lutheran Christian
Day School
1285 Main St.
Cincinnati, OH   45210

Saint Paul Lutheran School
5433 Madison Rd.
Cincinnati, OH   45227

Grace Lutheran School
Verdin & Boudinot Aves.
Cincinnati, OH   45211

Bethany School
495 Albion St.
Cincinnati, OH   45246

Sharonville Church of God
School
10830 Sharondale Rd.
Cincinnati, OH   45241

God's Bible School
1810 Young St.
Cincinnati, OH   45210

McNicholas Catholic High
School
6532 Beechmont Ave.
Cincinnati, OH   45230

La Salle Catholic High School
3091 West North Bend Rd.
Cincinnati, OH   45239

Cardinal Pacelli Catholic
School
927 Ellison St.
Cincinnati, OH   45226

Saint Xavier Catholic High
School
600 West North Bend Rd.
Cincinnati, OH   45224

Marian Catholic High School
2121 Madison Rd.
Cincinnati, OH   45208

Mount Notre Dame Catholic
High School
711 East Columbia Ave.
Cincinnati, OH   45215

Mother of Mercy Catholic
High School
3036 Werk Rd.
Cincinnati, OH   45211

Our Lady of the Angels
Catholic High School
4320 Bertus St.
Cincinnati, OH   45217

DAYTON AREA:

Dayton Christian High School
325 Homewood Ave.
Dayton, OH   45405

Dayton Christian School
2528 Wilmington Pike
Dayton, OH   45419

Xenia Christian Day School
1120 South Detroit St.
Xenia, OH   45385

Temple Christian School
1707 Ohmer St.
Dayton, OH   45410

Sugar Grove Christian School
7875 South Kessler-Frederick
Rd.
Milton, OH   43541

Xenia Christian School
100 Jasper Rd.
Xenia, OH 45385

Spring Valley Academy
  Seventh Day Adventist
1461 East Spring Valley
  Pike
Dayton, OH 45459

Archbishop Alter Catholic
  High School
940 East David
Dayton, OH 45429

TOLEDO AREA:

Toledo Christian School
South 22nd & Monroe Sts.
Toledo, OH 43602

Emmanuel Baptist High
  School
4607 Laskey St.
Toledo, OH 43623

Boulevard Christian School
1501 South Coy Rd.
Toledo, OH 43616

Calvary Christian School
3251 Glendale Ave.
Toledo, OH 43610

Borderline Christian School
6023 Bonsels Pkwy.
Toledo, OH 43615

State Line Christian School
6320 Lewis Ave.
Toledo, OH 43612

Sylvania Christian Academy
5242 McGregor Ln.
Toledo, OH 43623

Trinity Lutheran School
4560 Glendale Ave.
Toledo, OH 43614

Saint Philip Lutheran School
428 North Erie St.
Toledo, OH 43624

Zion Lutheran School
630 Cuthbert Rd.
Toledo, OH 43607

Seventh Day Adventist School
540 Independence Rd.
Toledo, OH 43607

Central Catholic High School
2550 Cherry St.
Toledo, OH 43608

Saint John's High School
5901 Airport Hwy.
Toledo, OH 43615

Cardinal Stritch Catholic
  High School
3225 Pickle St.
Toledo, OH 43616

Saint Francis de Sales
  Catholic High School
2323 West Bancroft St.
Toledo, OH 43607

Rosary Cathedral Catholic
  School
2535 Collingwood St.
Toledo, OH 43610

Christ the King Catholic
  School
4100 Harvest Ln.
Toledo, OH 43623

AKRON AREA:

Akron Christian School
508 Newton St.
Tallmadge, OH 44278

Akron Wesleyan Methodist
  Christian School
1504 Hardin Dr.
Barberton, OH 44203

Cuyahoga Valley Christian
  Academy
4687 Wyoga Lake Rd.
Cuyahoga Falls, OH 44222

Reimer Road Baptist
  Christian School
3163 Akron-Wadsworth Rd.
Barberton, OH 44203

Chapel Hill Christian School
1090 Howe Rd.
Cuyahoga Falls, OH 44221

Shadyside Christian School
220 South Balch St.
Akron, OH 44302

Zion Lutheran School
139 South High St.
Akron, OH 44308

Archbishop Hoban Catholic
  High School
400 Elbon St.
Akron, OH 44306

Saint Vincent - Saint Mary's
  Catholic High School
21 North Walnut St.
Akron, OH 44303

Christ the King Catholic
  School
1558 Creighton St.
Akron, OH 44310

Saint Paul's Catholic School
1580 Brown St.
Akron, OH 44301

Saint John the Baptist Catholic
  School
1025 Clay St.
Akron, OH 44301

Saint Matthew's Catholic
  School
Woolf and Benton Sts.
Akron, OH 44312

Saint Peter's Catholic School
812 Bircuta St.
Akron, OH 44307

YOUNGSTOWN AREA:

Youngstown Christian Academy
554 South Meridian Ave.
Youngstown, OH 44509

Lighthouse Christian School
350 State Route 7
Columbiana, OH 44408

Calvary Christian Academy
1812 Oak Hill Ave.
Youngstown, OH 44507

Salem Bible Academy
Woodsdale Rd., Route 2
Salem, OH 44460

Youngstown Christian School
125 Wychwood Ln.
Youngstown, OH 44512

Lakeside School
  Seventh Day Adventist
1228 Niles St.
Vienna S.E., OH 44473

Ursuline Catholic High School
750 Wick Ave.
Youngstown, OH 44505

Saints Peter & Paul
  Catholic School
421 Covington St.
Youngstown, OH 44510

Saint John the Baptist
  Slovak School
151 Reel Ave.
Youngstown, OH 44511

Saint Anne Byzantine Rite
  School
4310 Kirk Rd.
Youngstown, OH 44511

HAMILTON AREA:

Hamilton Christian School
40 Wrenwood Dr.
Hamilton, OH 45013

Landmark Christian High
  School
500 Oak Rd.
Evendale, OH 45013

Tri-County Christian School
7350 Dixie Hwy.
Fairfield, OH 45015

Ross Bible Chapel School
2846 Hamilton-Cleves Hwy.
Hamilton, OH 45013

Badin Catholic High School
571 Hamilton-New London
  Pike
Hamilton, OH 45013

Notre Dame Catholic
  Education Center
926 South 2nd St.
Hamilton, OH 45011

CANTON AREA:

Stark County Christian
  Academy
2651 Market Ave., N.
Canton, OH 44714

Heritage Christian School
2107 6th St., S.W.
Canton, OH 44706

Trinity Christian School
1379 Garfield Ave., S.W.
Canton, OH 44706

Hartville Christian School
1379 Garfield Ave., S.W.
Canton, OH 44706

Brunnerdale High School
  Seminary
4001 Brunnerdale Ave., N.W.
Canton, OH 44718

Central Catholic High School
4824 Tuscarawas West
Canton, OH 44708

Saint Thomas Aquinas Catholic
  High School
2121 Reno Dr.
Canton, OH 44708

Saint Joseph's Catholic School
126 Columbus Ave., N.W.
Canton, OH 44708

LORAIN AREA:

Liberty Christian Schools
1313 Tower Blvd.
Lorain, OH 44053

Elyria Christian Academy
145 Academy Ct.
Elyria, OH 44035

Open Door Christian School
43275 Telegraph Rd.
Elyria, OH 44035

Lorain Catholic High School
Tower Blvd. & Falbo Ave.
Lorain, OH 44052

Catholic High School
Poplar St.
Elyria, OH 44053

Saint Nicholas Byzantine
  Rite Catholic School
3150 Clifton Ave.
Lorain, OH 44055

MANSFIELD AREA:

Mansfield Christian School
500 Logan Rd.
Mansfield, OH 44907

Temple Christian School
1185 Ashland Rd.
P.O. Box 2001
Mansfield, OH 44905

Saint Peter's Catholic High
  School
104 West First St.
Mansfield, OH 44903

MIDDLETOWN AREA:

Middletown Christian School
3023 North Union St.
P.O. Box 777
Middletown, OH 45042

Heritage Baptist Christian
  Schools
4700 Central St.
Middletown, OH 45042

Ridgeville Christian Schools
946 East Lower Springboro
  Rd.
Springboro, OH 45066

NEWARK AREA:

Licking County Christian
  Academy
81 Licking View Dr.
Newark, OH 43055

Mount Vernon Academy
  Seventh Day Adventist
Mount Vernon, OH 43050

Newark Catholic High School
855 West Church St.
Newark, OH 43055

STEUBENVILLE AREA:

Jefferson County Christian
  School
416 South 5th St.
Steubenville, OH 43952

Wintersville Christian
  Academy
Fernwood Rd.
Wintersville, OH 43952

Immaculate Heart Catholic
  Academy
Wintersville, OH 43952

ATHENS AREA:

Apostolic Lighthouse
  Christian School
P.O. Box 116
Albany, OH 45710

LIMA AREA:

Lima Christian Academy
3360 West Elm St.
Lima, OH 45805

Temple Christian Day School
982 Brower Rd.
Lima, OH 45801

Maranatha Christian Academy
P.O. Box 83
Minster, OH 45865

Mennonite Christian Day
  School
Grubb Rd.
Lima, OH 45807

Seventh Day Adventist
  School
1976 Spencerville Rd.
Lima, OH 45805

Lima Central Catholic High
  School
720 South Cable Rd.
Lima, OH 45805

ZANESVILLE AREA:

Zanesville Christian School
2400 Chandlersville Rd.
Zanesville, OH 43701

Y-City Christian School
2960 Maysville Pike
Zanesville, OH 43701

Wesley Christian Academy
2375 East Pike St.
Zanesville, OH 43701

Malta Christian Day School
P.O. Box 162
Malta, OH 43758

Friends Boarding School
Route 1
Barnesville, OH 43713

Rosecrans High School
1040 Main St.
Zanesville, OH 43701

Saint Thomas School
139 North Fifth St.
Zanesville, OH 43701

Saint Nicholas School
1030 Main St.
Zanesville, OH 43701

ASHLAND AREA:

Ashland Christian School
1144 West Main St.
Ashland, OH 44805

SANDUSKY AREA:

Erie County Christian
  Academy
1320 East Strub Rd.
Sandusky, OH 44870

Heritage Christian Schools
3706 Milan Rd.
Sandusky, OH 44870

Temple Baptist Schools
3333 Columbus St.
Sandusky, OH 44870

Celeryville Christian School
Route 2
Willard, OH 44890

Saint Mary's Catholic High
  School
410 West Jefferson St.
Sandusky, OH 44870

Saints Peter & Paul Catholic
  School
514 Jackson St.
Sandusky, OH 44870

MASSILLON AREA:

Massillon Christian School
965 Overlook Ave., S.W.
Massillon, OH 44646

Calvary Christian Academy
8151 Stuhldreher St.
Massillon, OH 44646

Central Christian High
  School
P.O. Box 9
Kidron, OH 44636

Indian Hills Christian Schools
P.O. Box 505
New Philadelphia, OH 44663

Shiloh Christian Day School
Star Route
Millersburg, OH 44654

Zion Christian School
P.O. Box 41
Benton Rural Station
Millersburg, OH 44654

Saint Joseph's Catholic
  School
330 Fourth St., S.E.
Massillon, OH 44646

Saint Mary's Catholic School
726 First St., N.E.
Massillon, OH 44646

SPRINGFIELD AREA:

Springfield Christian Schools
924 East Home Rd.
Springfield, OH 45503

Central Catholic High School
1200 East High St.
Springfield, OH 45505

CIRCLEVILLE AREA:

Trueway Christian School
138 Plum St.
Ashville, OH 43103

WARREN AREA:

Howland Christian Schools
8957 East Market St.
Warren, OH 44484

Bethany Christian Academy
1244 Tod Ave., N.W.
Warren, OH 44485

Warren Christian School
2640 Parkman Rd., N.W.
Warren, OH 44485

John F. Kennedy Catholic
  High School
2550 Central Parkway Ave.,
  S.E.
Warren, OH 44483

MARION AREA:

Marion Christian School
131 Marion-Cardington Rd.,
  E.
Marion, OH 43302

MENTOR AREA:

Mentor Christian School
8600 Lake Shore Blvd.
P.O. Box 486
Mentor, OH 44060

FINDLAY AREA:

Fellowship Christian School
West Fellowship Dr.
Arlington, OH 45814

Heritage Christian School
2000 Broad Ave.
Findlay, OH 45840

LANCASTER AREA:

Greencastle Christian School
2940 Amanda-Northern
Carroll, OH 43112

ALLIANCE AREA:

Hartville Christian High
  School
10515 Market Ave., N.W.
Hartville, OH 44632

FREMONT AREA:

Faith Christian School
P.O. Box 243
Clyde, OH 43410

MARIETTA AREA:

Devola Christian School
101 Masonic Park Rd.
Marietta, OH 45750

GREENVILLE AREA:

Faith Christian School
P.O. Box 475
Greenville, OH 45331

NEVADA AREA:

Wyandot Christian School
Route 1
Nevada, OH 44849

OKLAHOMA

OKLAHOMA CITY AREA:

Oklahoma Christian Schools,
  Inc.
2820 South Blvd.
Oklahoma, OK 73119

Oklahoma Christian Schools,
  Inc.
4500 East 2nd St.
Edmond, OK 73034

Westminster Day School
  Middle Division
4400 North Shartel St.
Oklahoma City, OK 73118

Westminster Day School
540 N.W. 44th St.
Oklahoma City, OK 73118

Christian Heritage Academy
1139 S.W. 48th St.
Oklahoma City, OK 73109

Galilean Christian School
3030 Overholser Dr.
Oklahoma City, OK 73127

Christian Center School
9625 North May Ave.
Oklahoma City, OK 73120

Edmond Baptist Schools
1921 East 15th St.
Edmond, OK 73034

Bethany Baptist Schools
2800 North Division St.
Bethany, OK 73008

Independence Christian
  School
3215 N.W. 48th St.
Oklahoma City, OK 73112

Wesleyan Christian School
3745 S.W. 25th St.
Oklahoma City, OK 73115

Life Christian School
11301 S.E. 104th St.
Midwest City, OK 73110

Jefferson Heights Baptist
  Academy
1100 S.W. 66th St.
Oklahoma City, OK 73139

Cherokee Hills Christian
  School
6601 North McArthur St.
Oklahoma City, OK 73132

Windsor Hills Baptist School
5517 N.W. 23rd St.
Oklahoma City, OK 73127

Amazing Grace Chapel
School
5500 N.W. 23rd St.
Oklahoma City, OK 73127

Immanuel Lutheran School
1800 N.W. 36th St.
Oklahoma City, OK 73118

Gethsemane Lutheran School
6301 N.W. Expressway
Oklahoma City, OK 73132

Zion Lutheran Schools
201 N.W. 8th St.
Oklahoma City, OK 73102

Parkview Adventist School
4201 North Eastern Ave.
Oklahoma City, OK 73111

Saint John's Episcopal
School
5201 North Brookline Ave.
Oklahoma City, OK 73112

Trinity Episcopal School
6400 North Pennsylvania
Ave.
Oklahoma City, OK 73116

Casady Episcopal School
9500 Pennsylvania Ave.
Oklahoma City, OK 73132

Apostolic Faith Tabernacle
School
208 S.E. 62nd St.
Oklahoma City, OK 73149

Living Word Academy
901 N.W. 10th St.
Oklahoma City, OK 73106

Bishop McGuinness Catholic
High School
801 N.W. 50th St.
Oklahoma City, OK 73118

Mount Saint Mary's Catholic
High School
2801 South Shartel St.
Oklahoma City, OK 73109

Christ the King Catholic
School
1900 Guilford Ln.
Oklahoma City, OK 73120

NORMAN AREA:

Norman Christian School--
Living Word Academy
726 McGee Dr.
Norman, OK 73069

Robinson Street Christian
School
801 East Robinson St.
Norman, OK 73071

TULSA AREA:

Tulsa Christian Academy
2805 West 48th St.
Tulsa, OK 74107

Heritage Academy of Tulsa
1719 South Owasso St.
Tulsa, OK 74120

Moody Christian Academy
7301 East 15th St.
Tulsa, OK 74112

Mingo Valley Christian
School
11416 East 20th St.
Tulsa, OK 74128

Sheridan Christian School
205 South Sheridan Rd.
Tulsa, OK 74112

Southpark Christian School
10811 East 41st St.
Tulsa, OK 74145

Green Country Christian
Academy
11391 East Admiral Pl.
Tulsa, OK 74116

Green Country Christian
Academy
3434 South Garnett Rd.
Tulsa, OK 74145

Eastwood Baptist School
System
8740 East 11th St.
Tulsa, OK 74112

Heritage Baptist Schools
415 West 11th St.
Sand Springs, OK 74063

Winnetka Heights Christian
School
1020 West 49th St.
Tulsa, OK 74107

Temple Christian School
6308 East Apache St.
Tulsa, OK 74115

Faith Christian Academy
2121 East Third St.
Tulsa, OK 74104

Mount Olive Evangelical
Lutheran School
12425 East 31st St.
Tulsa, OK 74145

Rhema Bible Training Center
1025 West Kenosha Ave.
Tulsa, OK 74106

Seventh Day Adventist
Academy
900 South New Haven Ave.
Tulsa, OK 74112

Trinity Episcopal Day School
501 South Cincinnati Ave.
Tulsa, OK 74103

Holland Hall Episcopal
Middle School
2640 South Birmingham Pl.
Tulsa, OK 74114

Holland Hall School
56666 East 81st St.
Tulsa, OK 74136

Bishop Kelley Catholic High
School
3905 South Hudson Ave.
Tulsa, OK 74107

Saint Francis Religious
  Education Center
2510 East Admiral Blvd.
Tulsa, OK 74110

Monte Cassino Catholic High
  School
2206 South Lewis Ave.
Tulsa, OK 74114

Saints Peter & Paul Catholic
  School
1428 North 67th East Ave.
Tulsa, OK 74115

LAWTON AREA:

Lawton Christian School
112th & Old Cache Rd.
Lawton, OK 73505

Lawton Christian Academy
6201 N.W. Elm St.
Lawton, OK 73505

Carriage Hills Christian
  School
3211 East Gore Ave.
Lawton, OK 73501

Seventh Day Adventist
  School
1610 N.W. 19th St.
Lawton, OK 73501

Saint Mary's Catholic School
611 A St.
Lawton, OK 73502

ENID AREA:

Enid Christian School
3601 Owen K. Garriott St.
Enid, OK 73701

Emmanuel Christian School
2505 West Garroth Rd.
Enid, OK 73701

Oklahoma Mennonite Bible
  Academy
Meno, OK 73760

Jabbok Brethren in Christ
  Bible School
Thomas, OK 73669

MUSKOGEE AREA:

Boulevard Christian School
810 East Okmulgee Blvd.
Muskogee, OK 74401

Markoma Bible Academy
Route 1, Box 278
Tahlequah, OK 74464

Muskogee Catholic Christian
  Learning Center
323 North Virginia St.
Muskogee, OK 74401

Saint Joseph Catholic
  Academy
226 South 7th St.
Chickasha, OK 73018

BROKEN ARROW AREA:

Faith Christian Academy
1108 North 6th St.
Broken Arrow, OK 74012

Bible Baptist School
510 West College St.
Broken Arrow, OK 74012

Saint John's School
Keeler & 8th Sts.
Bartlesville, OK 74003

Saint James School
Madison Blvd. & Douglas Ln.
Bartlesville, OK 74003

Saint Anne's Catholic School
301 South 9th St.
Broken Arrow, OK 74012

DUNCAN AREA:

Duncan Christian School
1702 Jones St.
Duncan, OK 73533

Apostolic Christian School
512 Maple
Duncan, OK 73533

Assumption Catholic School
710 Hickory St.
Duncan, OK 73533

SHAWNEE AREA:

Tecumseh Christian Academy
P.O. Box C
Tecumseh, OK 74873

Saint Gregory's Catholic
  High School
Shawnee, OK 74801

PONCA CITY AREA:

Lutheran School
North 5th & Liberty Sts.
Ponca City, OK 74601

Saint Mary's Catholic School
415 South 7th St.
Ponca City, OK 74601

DURANT AREA:

Bryan County Christian
  Academy
602 East Mason St.
Durant, OK 74701

OREGON

PORTLAND AREA:

Portland Christian High
  School
11251 S.E. Market St.
Portland, OR 97216

Portland Christian School
11845 S.E. Market St.
Portland, OR 97216

Columbia Christian High
  School
200 N.E. 91st Ave.
Portland, OR 97220

West Hills Christian School
7945 S.W. Capital Hill Rd.
Portland, OR 97219

Wesley Christian Academy
14020 N.E. Thompson St.
Portland, OR 97230

Abundant Life Christian
School
9643 North Ivanhoe St.
Portland, OR 97203

Neighborhood Christian
Schools
4525 S. E. 63rd St.
Portland, OR 97206

Crossroads Christian School
2505 N. E. 102nd Ave.
Portland, OR 97220

The Open Community School
4635 N. E. 9th Ave.
Portland, OR 97211

Catlin Gabel School
8825 S. W. Barnes Rd.
Portland, OR 97225

Liberty Christian Academy
8490 S. E. King Rd.
Portland, OR 97222

Montessori Pacific Christian
School
18370 S. W. Shaw St.
Aloha, OR 97005

North Clackamas Christian
School
19651 South Molalla St.
Oregon City, OR 97045

Progress Christian Academy
12930 S. W. Scholls Ferry Rd.
Tigard, OR 97223

Temple Christian School
7600 N. E. Glisan St.
Portland, OR 97213

Neighborhood Christian
Schools
11509 S. E. 27th St.
Milwaukie, OR 97222

Concordia Lutheran High
School
2811 N. E. Hollman St.
Portland, OR 97211

Lutheran High School
16301 S. E. Division St.
Portland, OR 97236

Trinity Lutheran School
5520 N. E. Killingsworth St.
Portland, OR 97218

Grace Lutheran School
7610 N. E. Fremont St.
Portland, OR 97213

Portland Adventist Academy
1500 S. E. 96th Ave.
Portland, OR 97216

Oregon Episcopal School
6300 S. W. Nicol Rd.
Portland, OR 97223

Central Catholic High School
2401 S. E. Stark St.
Portland, OR 97214

Jesuit Catholic School
9000 S. W. Beaverton-Hillsdale
Hwy.
Portland, OR 97225

Saint Mary's Catholic
Cathedral School
110 N. W. 17th Ave.
Portland, OR 97209

MEDFORD AREA:

Medford Christian School
2715 Table Rock Rd.
Medford, OR 97501

Grace Baptist Christian School
649 Crater Lake Ave.
Medford, OR 97501

New Dimension Christian
School
1008 West Main St.
Medford, OR 97501

Rogue River Jr. Academy
Seventh Day Adventist
3675 State Rd., S.
Medford, OR 97501

Rogue Valley Ranch School
1828 Pine Gate Way
Central Point, OR 97502

Saint Mary's Catholic High
School
816 Black Oak Dr.
Medford, OR 97501

Sacred Heart Catholic School
431 South Ivy St.
Medford, OR 97501

EUGENE AREA:

Eugene Christian School
4500 West Amazon Dr.
Eugene, OR 97405

Norvale Park Christian
Academy
2600 Belmont St.
Eugene, OR 97402

Fairfield Nazarene Christian
School
1052 Fairfield St.
Eugene, OR 97402

Santa Clara Christian School
815 Irving Rd.
Eugene, OR 97402

Delight Valley Christian
School
33087 Saginaw Rd., E.
Cottage Grove, OR 97424

Fern Ridge Christian Academy
24918 Warthen Rd.
Veneta, OR 97487

South Lane Christian School
77820 Mosby Creek Rd.
Cottage Grove, OR 97424

Christ's Center School
530 West 7th St.
Junction City, OR 97448

Canyonville Bible Academy
The Christian High School
Canyonville, OR 97417

Montessori School
2255 Oakmont Way
Eugene, OR 97401

Homestead Ranch School
46300 Big Fall Creek Rd.
Fall Creek, OR 97438

Grace Lutheran School
710 East 17th Ave.
Eugene, OR 97401

West Lane School
  Assembly of God
22540 Fir St.
Noti, OR   97461

Emerald Jr. Academy
  Seventh Day Adventist
35582 Zephyr Way
Pleasant Hill, OR   97401

John F. Kennedy Catholic
  High School
Mount Angel, OR   97362

Marist Catholic High School
1900 Kingsley Rd.
Eugene, OR   97401

O'Hara Catholic School
715 West 18th Ave.
Eugene, OR   97401

SALEM AREA:

Salem Academy
250 College Dr., N.W.
Salem, OR   97304

Salem Private Schools
930 Chemawa Rd., N. E.
Salem, OR   97303

Montessori's Children's
  House
1945 37th Ave., N. W.
Salem, OR   97304

Berean Baptist School
1755 Lockhaven Dr., N. E.
Salem, OR   97303

Church of the Nazarene
  School
1550 Market St., N. E.
Salem, OR   97301

Western Mennonite School
9045 Wallace Rd., N.W.
Salem, OR   97304

Livingston School
  Seventh Day Adventist
5771 Fruitland Rd., N. E.
Salem, OR   97301

Serra Catholic High School
942 Lancaster Dr., N. E.
Salem, OR   97308

Sacred Heart Catholic Mid
  High School
3750 Lancaster Dr., N. E.
Salem, OR   97303

ROSEBURG AREA:

Roseburg Christian School
751 S. E. Main St.
Roseburg, OR   97470

Nazarene School of Roseburg
3013 Stewart Pkwy.
Roseburg, OR   97470

First Christian Church School
432 S. E. Kane St.
Roseburg, OR   97470

Roseburg Jr. Academy
  Seventh Day Adventist
1653 N.W. Troost St.
Roseburg, OR   97470

Saint Joseph's Catholic
  School
630 West Stanton St.
Roseburg, OR   97470

HILLSBORO AREA:

Grace Lutheran School
4435 S. E. Tualatin Valley
  Hwy.
Hillsboro, OR   97123

Laurelwood Academy
  Seventh Day Adventist
Route 2
Gaston, OR   97119

Seventh Day Adventist School
McMinnville, OR   97128

Seventh Day Adventist School
367 N. E. Grant St.
Hillsboro, OR   97123

Saint Matthew's Catholic
  School
447 S. E. 3rd St.
Hillsboro, OR   97123

Roman Catholic School
McMinnville, OR   97128

CORVALLIS AREA:

Corvallis Baptist Academy
605 N. W. 25th St.
Corvallis, OR   97330

Sunrise Christian School
440 S.W. 9th St.
Corvallis, OR   97330

Lutheran School of Zion
2800 N.W. Tyler St.
Corvallis, OR   97330

ALBANY AREA:

Santiam Christian High School
800 34th St., S. E.
Albany, OR   97321

Central Valley Jr. Academy
  Seventh Day Adventist
Route 1
Tangent, OR   97389

Saint Mary's Catholic School
815 Broadalbin St., S.W.
Albany, OR   97321

SPRINGFIELD AREA:

Nazarene Christian School of
  Springfield
1761 North E St.
Springfield, OR   97477

Saint Alice Catholic School
1510 F St.
Springfield, OR   97477

BEND AREA:

Central Oregon Christian
  Academy
802 D St., Box 587
Madras, OR   97741

Central Oregon Christian
  School
1 S.W. Broadway
Bend, OR   97701

Northwest Baptist Institute
21129 S. E. Reed Market Rd.
Bend, OR 97701

Prineville Christian School
450 South Fairview St.
Prineville, OR 97754

Christ Our Redeemer
  Lutheran School
20145 Powers Rd.
Bend, OR 97701

Newport Avenue School
  Church of Christ
554 N.W. Newport Ave.
Bend, OR 97701

Three Sisters Jr. Academy
  Seventh Day Adventist
21155 Deschutes Hwy.
Bend, OR 97701

Saint Francis Catholic
  School
720 N.W. Bond St.
Bend, OR 97701

THE DALLES AREA:

Chenoweth Baptist School
1122 Oak St., W.
The Dalles, OR 97058

Christian Academy
  Evangelical Church of North
  America
1001 East 12th St.
The Dalles, OR 97058

Hood River Alliance Academy
2650 Montello
Hood River, OR 97031

Seventh Day Adventist School
3339 East 13th St.
The Dalles, OR 97058

Saint Mary's Catholic
  Academy
1112 Cherry Heights Rd.
The Dalles, OR 97058

Mount Hood Christian School
3445 S. E. Hillyard Rd.
Gresham, OR 97030

PENDLETON AREA:

Pendleton Christian School
4450 S.W. Quinney St.
Pendleton, OR 97801

Milton-Stateline School
  Seventh Day Adventist
Crockett Rd., Route 3
Milton-Freewater, OR 97862

Hermiston Jr. Academy
  Seventh Day Adventist
Route 2, Box 2301
Hermiston, OR 97838

ASHLAND AREA:

Rogue Valley Christian
  School
840 Faith Ave.
Ashland, OR 97520

Central Assembly Christian
  School
310 North 10th St.
Central Point, OR 97502

KLAMATH FALLS AREA:

Seventh Day Adventist School
Main & Williams Sts.
Klamath Falls, OR 97601

Sacred Heart Catholic High
  School
429 North 8th St.
Klamath Falls, OR 97601

COOS BAY AREA:

Seventh Day Adventist
  School
1251 Clark St.
North Bend, OR 97459

MEDFORD AREA:

Grace Christian School
c/o Mr. Norman Holden
649 Crater Lake Ave.
Medford, OR 97501

WILLAMINA AREA:

Neskowin Valley School
P.O. Box 868
Neskowin, OR 97149

PENNSYLVANIA

PHILADELPHIA AREA:

Philadelphia-Montgomery
  Christian Academy
35 Hillcrest Ave.
Erdenheim, PA 19118

Philadelphia-Montgomery
  Christian Academy
1701 Jarrettown Rd.
Dresher, PA 19025

Northwest Christian School
6220 Wissahickon Ave.
Philadelphia, PA 19144

Northeast Christian School
Rising Sun Ave. & Comly St.
Philadelphia, PA 19120

Delaware County Christian
  School
Malin Rd.
Newtown Square, PA 19073

Upper Christian School
13th & Potter Sts.
Chester, PA 19013

The Christian Academy
704 South Old Middletown Rd.
Media, PA 19063

Cedar Grove Christian School
Rising Sun Ave. & Tabor
  Ave.
Philadelphia, PA 19120

Roxborough Community
  Christian School
8232 Ridge Ave.
Philadelphia, PA 19128

Valley Christian School
2364 Huntington Pike
Huntington Valley, PA 19006

Covenant Christian School
283 West Valley Forge Rd.
King of Prussia, PA   19406

Spruce Hill Christian School
4115 Baltimore Ave.
Philadelphia, PA   19118

Faith Christian School
1200 Easton Rd.
Roslyn, PA   19001

Calvary Christian School
P. O. Box 1086
Brookhaven, PA   19015

Lower Bucks Christian
   Academy
501 Trenton Rd.
Penn Del, PA   19047

Philadelphia Christian
   Academy
6007 Larchwood
Philadelphia, PA   19143

Darby Christian School
Ridge Ave. & Main St.
Darby, PA   19023

Grace Christian Academy
7372 Henry Ave.
Philadelphia, PA   19128

Timothy Academy
2719 North Reese Rd.
Philadelphia, PA   19133

Lower Bucks Christian
   Academy
321 Main St.
Hulmeville, PA   19047

The Christian Academy
3515 Edgemont Ave.
Brookhaven, PA   19015

Manna Bible Institute
700 East Church Ln.
Philadelphia, PA   19144

Friends Central School
68th St. & City Line
(Overbrook)
Philadelphia, PA   19151

Friends Select School
17th St. & Parkway
Philadelphia, PA   19103

William Penn Charter School
3000 West School House Ln.
Philadelphia, PA   19144

Germantown Friends School
31 West Coulter St.
Philadelphia, PA   19144

Friends School
851 Buck Ln.
Haverford, PA   19041

Abington Friends School
Jenkintown, PA   19046

Academy of the New Church
   Swedenborgian
Bryn Athyn, PA   19009

Redeemer Lutheran School
Ryan Ave. & Sackett St.
Philadelphia, PA   19152

Saint Peter's Episcopal
   School
319 Lombard St.
Philadelphia, PA   19147

Episcopal Academy
376 North Latches Ln.
Merion, PA   19066

Christ Memorial Episcopal
   School
Chestnut at 43rd Sts.
Philadelphia, PA   19104

All Saints Episcopal School
State Rd.
Andalusia, PA   19020

Northeast Catholic High
   School for Boys
Torresdale & Kensington
   Aves.
Philadelphia, PA   19124

Roman Catholic High School
Broad & Vine Sts.
Philadelphia, PA   19107

West Catholic High School
   for Boys
49th & Chestnut Sts.
Philadelphia, PA   19139

Norwood Catholic Academy
8891 Germantown Ave.
Philadelphia, PA   19118

Saint Joseph's Catholic
   Preparatory School
18th & Thompson Sts.
Philadelphia, PA   19121

Saint Aloysius Catholic
   Academy
Bryn Mawr, PA   19010

Saint Nicholas Ukrainian
   Catholic School
860 North 24th St.
Philadelphia, PA   19130

Archbishop Ryan High School
   for Boys
11101 Academy Rd.
Philadelphia, PA   19154

Bishop Neumann Catholic
   High School
26th & Moore Sts.
Philadelphia, PA   19145

The Lankenau School
   Lutheran
3201 West School House Ln.
Philadelphia, PA   19144

Cardinal Dougherty Catholic
   High School
64th & 2nd Sts.
Philadelphia, PA   19126

Saint Maria Goretti Catholic
   High School
10th & Moore Sts.
Philadelphia, PA   19148

Cathedral School
18th & Wood Sts.
Philadelphia, PA   19103

Christ the King Catholic
   School
Chesterfield Rd. & Morrell
Philadelphia, PA   19114

PITTSBURGH AREA:

Pittsburgh Allegheny
  Wesleyan School
807 Ross Ave.
Pittsburgh, PA 15221

North Hills Christian School
P.O. Box 11161
Pittsburgh, PA 15237

Wilkinsburg Christian School
1608 Graham Blvd.
Pittsburg, PA 15235

The Wesley Institute
44 Highland Rd.
Bethel Park, PA 15102

Trinity Christian School
P.O. Box 17070
9100 Frankstown Rd.
Pittsburgh, PA 15235

South Hills Christian School
Route 88
Finleyville, PA 15332

Robinson Township Christian
  School
c/o Roger Schild
77 Phillips Ln.
McKees Rocks, PA 15136

Beaver County Christian
  School
611 Penn Ave.
New Brighton, PA 15066

First Evangelical Lutheran
  School
600 Clay St.
Pittsburgh, PA 15215

Saint Matthew's Lutheran
  School
600 East North Ave.
Pittsburgh, PA 15212

Pittsburgh New Church School
299 Le Roi Rd.
Pittsburg, PA 15208

Pathfinder School
Donati Rd.
Bethel Park, PA 15102

Saint Edmund's Episcopal
  School
5705 Darlington Rd.
Pittsburgh, PA 15217

Saint Paul's Cathedral High
  School
144 North Craig St.
Pittsburg, PA 15213

Central Catholic High School
4720 Fifth Ave.
Pittsburgh, PA 15213

Monongahela Valley Catholic
  High School
Coyle Curtain Rd.
Monongahela, PA 15063

Hilltop Catholic High School
205 Orchard Pl.
Pittsburgh, PA 15207

North Catholic High School
1400 Troy Hill Rd.
Pittsburgh, PA 15212

Saint John the Baptist
  Cathedral School
427 10th Ave.
Munhall, PA 15120

Holy Cross School
$7825\frac{1}{2}$ Hamilton Ave.
Pittsburgh, PA 15208

Saint Thomas High School
1025 Braddock Ave.
Pittsburgh, PA 15218

South Hills Catholic High
  School
1000 McNeilly Rd.
Pittsburgh, PA 15226

Divine Providence Catholic
  Academy
158 Larimer Ave.
Pittsburgh, PA 15206

Lawrenceville Catholic High
  School
37th & Butler Sts.
Pittsburgh, PA 15201

Mount Alvernia Catholic High
  School
Evergreen Ave.
(Millvale)
Pittsburgh, PA 15209

Saint Elizabeth Catholic High
  School
Grove Pl.
Pittsburgh, PA 15219

Vicentian Catholic High School
Peebles & McKnight Rds.
(North Hills)
Pittsburgh, PA 15237

Byzantine Catholic School
3605 Perrysville Ave.
Pittsburgh, PA 15214

ALIQUIPPA AREA:

Rhema Christian School
Jack St., Extended
Aliquippa, PA 15001

Beaver County Christian
  School
601 Penn Ave.
New Brighton, PA 15066

ERIE AREA:

Temple Christian Schools
6015 West Ridge Rd.
Erie, PA 16506

Harborcreek Christian School
4719 Buffalo Rd.
Erie, PA 16510

Bethel Christian School
757 East 26th St.
Erie, PA 16504

Bethel Baptist School
1781 West 38th St.
Erie, PA 16508

Seventh Day Adventist School
6679 Wattsburg Rd.
Erie, PA 16509

Cathedral Prep School
225 West 9th St.
Erie, PA 16501

Holy Trinity Catholic School
641 East 22nd St.
Erie, PA   16503

Spirit of Christ School
1022 East 10th St.
Erie, PA   16503

Saint Peter's Cathedral
  School
160 West 11th St.
Erie, PA   16501

ALLENTOWN AREA:

Allentown Christian School
3436 Winchester Rd.
Allentown, PA   18104

Leigh Christian Academy
  Evangelical Free Church
Wescosville, PA   18090

Leigh Christian Academy
689 South Hillview Rd.
Allentown, PA   18104

Pocono Boy Singers Choir
  School
East Stroudsburg, PA   18301

Allentown Central Catholic
  High School
4th & Chew Sts.
Allentown, PA   18102

Holy Spirit Catholic Middle
  School
510 Ridge Ave.
Allentown, PA   18102

Perkiomen Schwenkfelder
  School
Seminary Ave.
Pennsburg, PA   18073

NORRISTOWN AREA:

Penn Square Christian Day
  School
2633 Hillcrest Ave.
Norristown, PA   19401

Open Door Christian Academy
Fort Washington Ave. and
  Susquehanna
Fort Washington, PA   19034

Conestoga Christian School
Route 2
Elverson, PA   19520

Valley Forge Christian
  Academy
Valley Park & Whitehorse
  Rds.
Phoenixville, PA   19460

The Chapel Christian
  Academy
378 Ridge Pike, W.
Limerick, PA   19468

Calvary Baptist Schools
Valley Forge Rd.
Lansdale, PA   19446

Pine Forge School
  Seventh Day Adventist
Pine Forge, PA   19548

Saint Pius X Catholic High
  School
Keim Rd. & Briar Ln.
Pottstown, PA   19464

Saint Peter's Catholic School
1126 South St.
Pottstown, PA   19464

LANCASTER AREA:

Christian School Association
  of Lancaster
651 Lampeter Rd.
Lancaster, PA   17602

Calvary Baptist Christian
  School
530 Milton Rd.
Lancaster, PA   17603

Mount Calvary Christian
  School
Holly St. & Hillside Ave.
Elizabethtown, PA   17022

West Fallowfield Christian
  School
Route 1
Atglen, PA   19310

Hess Christian Day School
506 Owl Hill Rd.
Lititz, PA   17543

Manheim Christian Day School
R.D. 6
Manheim, PA   17545

Breezy View Christian School
Breezy View Rd.
R.D. 1
Columbia, PA   17512

Linden Hall Moravian School
Lititz, PA   17543

Lancaster Mennonite High
  School
2176 Lincoln Hwy., E.
Lancaster, PA   17602

New Danville Mennonite School
Long Ln.
Lancaster, PA   17603

Locust Grove Mennonite School
2257 Old Philadelphia Pike
Lancaster, PA   17602

Reamstown Mennonite School
Reamstown, PA   17567

Weavertown Mennonite School
R.D. 1
Bird In Hand, PA   17505

Linville Hill Mennonite School
P.O. Box 447A
R.D. 1
Paradise, PA   17562

Kraybille Mennonite
  Elementary School
Route 1
Mount Joy, PA   17552

Lititz Area Mennonite School
Lititz, PA   17543

Sporting Hill Mennonite School
393 West Lexington Rd.
Lititz, PA   17543

Crossroad Mennonite School
R.D. 1
New Holland, PA   17557

Blue Rock Mennonite School
79 Blue Rock Rd.
Millersville, PA   17551

Valley View Mennonite School
Route 1
Narvon, PA   17555

Parkesburg Mennonite School
Route 2, Box 274
Parkesburg, PA   19365

Little Britain Mennonite
  School
R. D. 2
Quarryville, PA   17566

Brick Amish School
R. D. 1
Christiana, PA   17509

Lancaster Seventh Day
  Adventist School
1721 Conard Rd.
Lancaster, PA   17602

Catholic High School
650 Juliet Ave.
Lancaster, PA   17601

Saint Anthony's Catholic
  Parochial School
521 East Orange St.
Lancaster, PA   17602

NEW CASTLE AREA:

New Castle Parkstown
  Christian Academy
R. D. 2, P. O. Box 646
New Castle, PA   16101

Lawrence County Christian
  School
P. O. Box 202
Volant, PA   16156

STATE COLLEGE AREA:

Centre City Christian Academy
P. O. Box 124
Pleasant Gap, PA   16823

INDIANA AREA:

Calvary Baptist Academy
R. D. 1, P. O. Box 170
Clymer, PA   15729

Independent Wesleyan School
P. O. Box 156
Dixonville, PA   15734

POTTSTOWN AREA:

Conestoga Christian School
R. D. 1, P. O. Box 124
Morgantown, PA   19543

High Point Baptist Academy
Geigertown, PA   19523

OIL CITY AREA:

Pleasant View Christian
  School
R. D. 1
Sandy Lake, PA   16145

COATESVILLE AREA:

Calvary Christian School
1400 Olive St.
Coatesville, PA   19320

SCRANTON AREA:

Northeastern Christian School
820 Monroe Ave.
Scranton, PA   18510

Calvary Christian School
Maplewood, PA   18519

Calvary Christian School
Hollister Ave.
Scranton, PA   18508

Calvary Christian School
R. D. 2
Lake Ariel, PA   18436

Scranton Catholic Preparatory
  School
1000 Wyoming Ave.
Scranton, PA   18509

Bishop Klonowski Catholic
  High School
901 Prospect Ave.
Scranton, PA   18505

Sacred Heart Catholic High
  School
Church St. & Seventh Ave.
Carbondale, PA   18407

BETHLEHEM AREA:

Moravian Academy
Green Pond Campus
Bethlehem, PA   18017

Moravian Academy Middle
  School
Church Street Campus
Bethlehem, PA   18015

Central Assembly Christian
  Academy
Bethlehem, PA

Northampton Christian School
Cherryville Rd.
Northampton, PA   18067

Bethlehem Catholic High
  School
Madison & Dewb. Aves.
Bethlehem, PA   18017

Notre Dame Catholic High
  School
3417 Church Rd.
Easton, PA   18042

LEWISBURG AREA:

Northumberland Christian
  School
2nd & Queen Sts.
Northumberland, PA   17857

Penn View Bible Institute
P. O. Box 97
Penn's Creek, PA   17862

Lewisburg Christian School
Buffalo and Airport Rds.
Lewisburg, PA   17837

Maranatha Christian Day
  School
Route 2
Watsontown, PA   17777

HARRISBURG AREA:

Christian School of
  Harrisburg
2000 Blue Mountain Pkwy.
Harrisburg, PA   17112

Bible Baptist Christian
  Academy
600 North 48th St.
Harrisburg, PA   17111

Bible Baptist School
201 West Main St.
Shiremanstown, PA   17011

Grace Baptist Christian
  School
777 West North St.
Carlisle, PA   17013

Middletown Christian Day
  School
Spruce & East Emaus Sts.
Middletown, PA   17057

Bethany Christian Academy
Route 15 & Slate Hill Rd.
Camp Hill, PA   17011

Trinity High School
Route 15 & Simpson Ferry Rd.
Shiremanstown, PA   17011

Bishop McDevitt Catholic
  High School
2200 Market St.
Harrisburg, PA   17103

WILLIAMSPORT AREA:

Williamsport Christian School
1730 Four Mile Dr.
Williamsport, PA   17701

Lycoming Christian School
1421 Sherman St.
Williamsport, PA   17701

Mountain Christian Academy
Route 2, P.O. Box 283
Montgomery, PA   17752

Pleasant View Wesleyan
  Christian Academy
Route 3
Muncy, PA   17756

Faith Tabernacle Christian
  Academy
36 East Fourth St.
P.O. Box 596
Williamsport, PA   17701

Walnut Street Baptist
  Christian School
1313 Walnut St.
Jersey Shore, PA   17740

Mountain View School
  Seventh Day Adventist
East Southern Ave.
South Williamsport, PA
17701

Bishop Neumann Catholic
  High School
901 Penn St.
Williamsport, PA   17701

ALTOONA AREA:

Altoona Christian Academy
1532 4th St.
Altoona, PA   16601

Emmanuel Christian Academy
R.D. 1
Claysburg, PA   16625

Altoona Bible Institute
1111 14th Ave.
Altoona, PA   16601

Bishop Guilfoyle Catholic High
  School
6th Ave. & 11th St.
Altoona, PA   16601

McNelis Catholic School
  Cathedral Extension
13th Ave. & 13th St.
Altoona, PA   16601

LEBANON AREA:

Grace Brethren Christian
  School
430 East Lincoln Ave.
Lebanon, PA   17042

Christian School of Grace
  Baptist Church
777 West North St.
Carlisle, PA   17013

Gingrich's Mennonite School
Route 4
Lebanon, PA   17042

Millbach Mennonite School
Route 1, Box 122
Newmanstown, PA   17073

Lebanon District Mennonite
  School
c/o R.S. Musselman
Route 1
P.O. Box 303
Bethel, PA   19507

Saint Paul the Apostle
  Catholic School
116 West Main St.
Annville, PA   17003

Saint Mary's Catholic School
12 North 8th St.
Lebanon, PA   17042

Valley View Parochial School
R.D. 1, Box 393
Belleville, PA   17004

QUAKERTOWN AREA:

Quakertown Christian School
143 Rocky Ridge Rd.
Quakertown, PA   18951

Penn View Christian School
420 Cowpath Rd.
Souderton, PA   18964

Upper Bucks Christian School
754 East Rockhill Rd.
Sellersville, PA   18960

Faith Christian Academy
P.O. Box 83
North Main St.
Sellersville, PA   18960

Buckingham Friends School
York Rd.
Lahaska, PA   18931

Plumstead Mennonite Christian
  School
P.O. Box 216
Old Easton Rd.
Plumsteadville, PA   18949

Christ's Home School
800 York Rd.
Warminster, PA 18974

KINGSTON AREA:

Westmoor Christian Academy
57 South Goodwin Ave.
Kingston, PA 18704

Wyoming Methodist Seminary
  Preparatory School
1560 Wyoming Ave.
Kingston, PA 18704

Bishop Hoban Catholic High
  School
159 South Pennsylvania Blvd.
Wilkes-Barre, PA 18701

Holy Saviour Catholic School
35 Worrall St.
Wilkes-Barre, PA 18702

Holy Trinity Catholic School
414 East South St.
Wilkes-Barre, PA 18702

WEST CHESTER AREA:

West Chester Christian
  School
1237 Paoli Pike
West Chester, PA 19380

Westtown Friends School
Westtown, PA 19395

Episcopal Church Farm School
Box S
Paoli, PA 19301

Malvern Catholic Preparatory
  School
Warren Ave.
Malvern, PA 19355

READING AREA:

Reading Jr. Academy
  Seventh Day Adventist
309 Kenhorst Blvd.
Reading, PA 19607

Blue Mountain School
  Seventh Day Adventist
Route 3, P.O. Box 560
Hamburg, PA 19526

Central Catholic High School
Hill Rd. & Clymer St.
Reading, PA 19602

Holy Name Catholic High
  School
955 East Wyomissing Blvd.
Reading, PA 19602

YORK AREA:

Christian School of York
907 Greenbriar Rd.
Route 1
York, PA 17407

Red Lion Christian School
Route 3
Red Lion, PA 17356

Hometown Christian School
R.D. 1, Box 472A
Glen Rock, PA 17327

New Freedom Christian
  Schools
222 North Constitution Ave.
New Freedom, PA 17349

Saint Francis Catholic
  Preparatory School
Spring Grove, PA 17352

MONROEVILLE AREA:

Monroeville Christian Academy
4271 Northern Pike
Monroeville, PA 15146

Beaver County Christian
  School
3300 6th Ave.
Beaver Falls, PA 15010

North American Martyrs
  School
2526 Haymaker Rd.
Monroeville, PA 15146

Greater Work Academy
c/o Ronald Malamisuro
301 College Park Dr.
Monroeville, PA 15146

MEADVILLE AREA:

Calvary Baptist Christian
  Academy
543 Randolph St.
Meadville, PA 16335

Calvary Baptist Christian
  School
South & Sixth Aves.
Union City, PA 16438

Saint Joseph's Catholic
  Academy High School
512 West Main St.
Titusville, PA 16354

JOHNSTOWN AREA:

Johnstown Mennonite School
Holsopple, PA 15935

CHAMBERSBURG AREA:

Mercersburg Academy
  United Church of Christ
Mercersburg, PA 17236

Rowe Strasburg Christian
  Day School
Star Route 2
Shippensburg, PA 17257

Shalom Christian Academy
126 Social Island Rd.
Chambersburg, PA 17201

MCKEESPORT AREA:

Wilson Christian Academy
2910 Liberty Way
McKeesport, PA 15133

BUTLER AREA:

Homeacre Christian Academy
P.O. Box 908
Butler, PA 16001

HANOVER AREA:

Hanover Mennonite School
c/o Walter Danner, Treasurer
R. D. 1
Hanover, PA 17331

MONESSEN AREA:

Chapel Christian School
318 Ridge Rd.
Belle Vernon, PA 15012

SUNBURY AREA:

Millmont Christian Day School
Box 71H, R. D. 1
Millmont, PA 17845

Sunbury Christian Academy
200 Island Blvd.
Sunbury, PA 17801

Elysburg Christian Meadowview Academy
c/o Robert E. Lee
P. O. Box 94
Elysburg, PA 17824

Locust Grove Christian Day
School
c/o Homer L. Weaver
R. D. 2
Mount Pleasant Mills, PA
17853

LATROBE AREA:

William Tyndale Christian
School
P. O. Box 688
Latrobe, PA 15650

BLOOMSBURG AREA:

Bloomsburg Christian School
518 Park St.
Bloomsburg, PA 17815

Turbotville Christian School
Route 1, Box 76-A
Turbotville, PA 17772

CANONSBURG AREA:

West Middletown Christian
School
P. O. Box 42
West Middletown, PA 15379

LEWISTOWN AREA:

Delaware Mennonite School
R. D. 1
Thompsontown, PA 17094

DU BOIS AREA:

Du Bois Christian Academy
Maple Ave. Extension
Du Bois, PA 15801

GROVE CITY AREA:

Christian Public School of
Western Pennsylvania
P. O. Box 423
Harrisville, PA 16038

EAST STROUDSBURG AREA:

Pocono Christian School
P. O. Box 642
East Stroudsburg, PA 18301

CLARION AREA:

New Bethlehem Christian
School
R. D. 1
New Bethlehem, PA 16242

WELLSBORO AREA:

Cannon Christian School
R. D. 2, P. O. Box 410 C
Wellsboro, PA 16901

HAZELTON AREA:

Immanuel Christian School
P. O. Box 182
Hazelton, PA 18201

LEVITTOWN AREA:

Lower Bucks Christian
Academy
501 Trenton Rd.
Levittown, PA 19057

PORTERSVILLE AREA:

Portersville Christian School
R. D. 1
Portersville, PA 16051

ROGERSVILLE AREA:

West Greene High School
Principal Paul Polink
Rogersville, PA 15359

ROME AREA:

Union Valley Christian School
Route 1
Rome, PA 18837

STONEBORO AREA:

Stoneboro Wesleyan School
R. D. 1
Stoneboro, PA 16153

RHODE ISLAND

PROVIDENCE AREA:

Saint Paul's Christian Day
School
12 Carter St.
Providence, RI 02907

Zion Gospel Temple School
846 Broadway
East Providence, RI 02914

Moses Brown Friends School
250 Lloyd Ave.
Providence, RI 02906

Lincoln Friends School
301 Butler Ave.
Providence, RI 02906

Providence Country Day
School
2117 Pawtucket Ave.
East Providence, RI 02914

Abbie Loveland Tuller
Episcopal School
72 Prospect St.
Providence, RI 02906

Saint Dunstan's Episcopal Day
  School
19 Benefit St.
Providence, RI   02904

Notre Dame Catholic Regional
  School
107 Summit Ave.
West Warwick, RI   02893

Saint Patrick's Catholic High
  School
622 Woonasquatckt Ave.
North Providence, RI   02908

Bishop McVinney Catholic
  Regional Middle School
155 Harrison St.
Providence, RI   02907

Saint Patrick Word of God
  School
244 Smith St.
Providence, RI   02908

WOONSOCKET AREA:

South County Christian Day
  School
3 Branch St.
Peace Dale, RI   02883

Saint Andrew's Episcopal
  School
Federal Rd.
West Barrington, RI   02890

Curtis Corner Christian
  Academy
Tower Hill Rd.
Wakefield, RI   02879

Prout Memorial High School
Tower Hill Rd.
Wakefield, RI   02879

Mount Saint Charles Catholic
  Academy
Bernon Heights
Woonsocket, RI   02871

Catholic School of Saint
  Gregory the Great
Cory's Ln.
Portsmouth, RI   02871

BARRINGTON AREA:

Barrington Christian Academy
Old County Rd.
Barrington, RI   02806

Saint Luke's School
Waldron Ave.
Barrington, RI   02806

NEWPORT AREA:

Jesus Saviour School
437 Broadway
Newport, RI   02840

Saint George's Episcopal
  School
Academic Office
Newport, RI   02840

Saint Michael's Episcopal
  School
180 Rhode Island Ave.
Newport, RI   02840

Newport County Catholic
  Regional School
80 Memorial Blvd., W.
Newport, RI   02840

PAWTUCKET AREA:

Woodlawn Catholic Regional
  School
61 Hope St.
Pawtucket, RI   02860

Saint Rafael Catholic Academy
123 Walcott St.
Pawtucket, RI   02860

Saint Leo's Catholic School
723 Central Ave.
Pawtucket, RI   02861

Saint Mary's Catholic School
167 George St.
Pawtucket, RI   02860

CRANSTON AREA:

Cranston Johnston Catholic
  Regional School
43 Poplar Dr.
Cranston, RI   02905

Saint Paul's Catholic School
1789 Broad St.
Cranston, RI   02905

Saint Matthew's Catholic
  School
1301 Elmwood Ave.
Cranston, RI   02905

Saint Mary's Catholic School
85 Chester Ave.
Cranston, RI   02905

CENTRAL FALLS AREA:

Holy Trinity Catholic School
325 Cowden St.
Central Falls, RI   02863

Saint Matthew's Catholic
  School
901 Lonsol Ave.
Central Falls, RI   02863

Mercymount Country Day
  School
Wrentham Rd.
Cumberland, RI   02864

Saint Patrick's Catholic
  School
269 Broad St.
Cumberland, RI   02864

PEACE DALE AREA:

South County Christian Day
  School
3 Branch St.
Peace Dale, RI   02883

SOUTH CAROLINA

COLUMBIA AREA:

Columbia Christian Schools
2739 Covenant Rd.
Columbia, SC   29204

Harbor Christian Schools
Highway 378 Frontage Rd.
West Columbia, SC   29169

Berean Baptist Christian
  Schools
626 Brooks Ave.
West Columbia, SC   29169

Grace Baptist Christian
  School
416 Denham Ave.
West Columbia, SC   29169

Palmetto Baptist Academy
1510 South Beltline
Columbia, SC   29205

Columbia Jr. Academy
  Seventh Day Adventist
241 River Chase Way
Columbia, SC

Ursuline Catholic High School
1505 Assembly St.
Columbia, SC   29201

Saint Andrew's Jr. High
  School
Bluefield Dr.
Columbia, SC   29210

Saint Joseph's Catholic School
3700 Devine St.
Columbia, SC   29205

Saint Peter's Catholic School
1513 Assembly St.
Columbia, SC   28201

CHARLESTON AREA:

Palmetto Christian School
6337 Rivers Ave.
Charleston Heights, SC   29405

Citadel Square Christian
  School
328 Meeting St.
Charleston, SC   29403

Northside Christian School
7800 Northside Dr.
Charleston Heights, SC   29405

Trident Baptist Academy
South Moncks Corner
Hwy. 17A
Charleston, SC   29461

First Baptist Church School
61 Church St.
Charleston, SC   29401

Charlestown Heights Baptist
  Academy
2002 Grayson St.
Charleston Heights, SC   29405

Westview Baptist Christian
  School
609 Wappo Rd.
Charleston, SC   29407

Ferndale Baptist Christian
  School
400 Piedmont Ave., N.
Charleston, SC   29403

Rantowles Baptist School
Route 1, P.O. Box 224
Meggett, SC   29460

Dear Park Baptist School
2301 University Blvd.
Charleston, SC   29405

First Baptist Church School
681 McCants Dr.
Mount Pleasant, SC   29464

Northwood Christian School
  Assembly of God
8717 Rivers Ave.
Charleston Heights, SC   29405

Christian School of Church
  Creek
2234 Plainview Rd.
Charleston, SC   29407

Charleston Jr. Academy
  Seventh Day Adventist
2518 Savannah Hwy.
Charleston, SC   29407

Porter-Gaud Episcopal
  Upper School
Albemarle Rd.
Charleston, SC   29407

Bishop England High School
203 Calhoun St.
Charleston, SC   29403

Cathedral of Saint John the
  Baptist School
120 Broad St.
Charleston, SC   29401

Divine Redeemer Catholic
  School
1104 Fort Dr.
Charleston, SC   29406

Holy Spirit Catholic School
1055 Yeamans Hall Rd.
Charleston, SC   29407

SPARTANBURG AREA:

Tabernacle Baptist School
Route 8
Spartanburg, SC

Community Bible Day School
Route 6
Spartanburg, SC

Eddlemon Memorial School
1217 Reidville Rd.
Spartanburg, SC   29301

Saint Paul's Catholic Jr.
  High School
152 Alabama St.
Spartanburg, SC   29302

FLORENCE AREA:

Emmanuel Baptist School
Route 1, P.O. Box 170
Hartsville, SC   29550

GREENVILLE AREA:

Greenville Christian School
State Park Rd.
Greenville, SC   29609

Washington Avenue Christian
  School
200 North Washington Ave.
Greenville, SC   29611

Shannon Forest Christian
  School
Garlington Rd., Route 2
Greenville, SC   29607

Boulevard Christian School
2701 Wade Hampton Blvd.
Greenville, SC 29607

Northside Baptist Christian
  Day School
515 Tindal Rd.
Greenville, SC 29605

Southside Christian School
2315 Augusta Rd.
Greenville, SC 29605

Tabernacle Christian Schools
3931 White Horse Rd.
Greenville, SC 29611

Hampton Park Christian
  Jr. High School
State Park Rd., Route 9
Greenville, SC 29609

Mitchell Road Christian
  Academy
207 Mitchell Rd.
Greenville, SC 29607

Bob Jones Academy
Greenville, SC 29601

Westside Christian School
306 Haigler St.
Abbeville, SC 29620

Saint Michael Lutheran School
2619 Augusta Rd.
Greenville, SC 29605

Trinity Lutheran Day School
421 North Main St.
Greenville, SC 29601

Seventh Day Adventist School
1700 East North St.
Greenville, SC 29607

Christ Church Episcopal
  School
100 Cavalier Dr.
Greenville, SC 29601

Our Lady of the Rosary
  Catholic School
2 James Dr.
Greenville, SC 29605

ANDERSON AREA:

Oakwood Christian School
301 Rogers St.
Anderson, SC 29621

Temple Christian School
404 Warner Rd.
Anderson, SC 29621

Beverly Hills Christian School
Fretwell Dr.
Anderson, SC 29621

Saint Joseph Catholic School
1200 Cornelia Rd.
Anderson, SC 29621

FLORENCE AREA:

Florence Christian School
Highway 301 N.
P.O. Box 3296
Florence, SC 29501

Florence Baptist Temple
  School
2308 South Irby St.
Florence, SC 29501

Calvary Christian School
P.O. Box 766
Walterboro, SC 29488

All Saints Episcopal School
1425 Cherokee Rd.
Florence, SC 29501

Saint Anthony's Catholic
  School
2536 West Hoffmeyer Rd.
Florence, SC 29501

SUMTER AREA:

Sumter Christian Schools
420 South Pike W.
Sumter, SC 29150

Trinity Christian School
P.O. Box 1855
Sumter, SC 29150

Temple Baptist Christian
  Schools
Pinewood Rd.
Sumter, SC 29150

Saint Jude's Catholic High
  School
Sumter, SC 29150

NEWBERRY AREA:

Prosperity Christian School
P.O. Box 362
Prosperity, SC 29127

EASLEY AREA:

Easley Christian School
Saco Lowell Rd., Box 546
Easley, SC 29640

Landmark Baptist Christian
  Academy
Route 8, P.O. Box 97B
Rice's Creek Rd.
Easley, SC 29640

Grace Emmanuel Christian
  School
West Kirksey Dr.
Greenwood, SC 29646

AIKEN AREA:

South Aiken Baptist Christian
  School
908 Dougherty Rd.
Aiken, SC 29801

Mead Hall Episcopal Day
  School
129 Pendleton St.
Aiken, SC 29801

Saint Angela Catholic Academy
308 Berrie Rd.
Aiken, SC 29801

ROCK HILL AREA:

Trinity Christian School
505 University Dr.
Rock Hill, SC 29730

Heritage Academy
Fort Mill, SC 29715

GAFFNEY AREA:

Gaffney Christian Academy
Medallion Park Rd., Box 46
Gaffney, SC 29340

Heritage Christian School
U.S. 29 Hwy., N.
Gaffney, SC 29340

ORANGEBURG AREA:

Orangeburg Baptist
 Tabernacle School
North Rd.
Orangeburg, SC 29115

Garden City Christian
 School
630 Broughton St., S.W.
Orangeburg, SC 29115

Orangeburg Christian Schools
Ron Jezowski, Principal
P.O. Box 1325
Orangeburg, SC 29115

GEORGETOWN AREA:

First Baptist Church School
Cleland St.
Georgetown, SC 29440

Andrews Christian School
106 East Oakland St.
Andrews, SC 29510

LAURENS AREA:

Faith Christian School
1607 Greenwood Rd.
Laurens, SC 29360

Union Church and Bible
 School
P.O. Drawer A
Union, SC 29379

PICKENS AREA:

Oolenoy Valley Christian
 School
Route 3
Pickens, SC 29671

SOUTH DAKOTA

SIOUX FALLS AREA:

Sioux Falls Christian High
 School
1000 South Sycamore Dr.
Sioux Falls, SD 57103

Calvin Christian School
700 South Sneve Ave.
Sioux Falls, SD 57103

Faith Christian Academy
622 South Sycamore Dr.
Sioux Falls, SD 57103

Sioux Falls Netherland
 Reformed Christian School
c/o Harold Schilling
4905 West Fortieth St.
Sioux Falls, SD 57106

Good Shepherd Lutheran
 School
4800 Southeastern Dr.
Sioux Falls, SD 57103

Augustana Lutheran School
Canton, SD 57013

Lutheran School Association
22nd & Spring Sts.
Sioux Falls, SD 57105

Seventh Day Adventist School
3807 West 57th St.
Sioux Falls, SD 57106

All Saints School
101 West 17th St.
Sioux Falls, SD 57104

Christ the King Catholic
 School
1801 South Lake Ave.
Sioux Falls, SD 57105

Saint Joseph Cathedral School
601 West 4th St.
Sioux Falls, SD 57104

Saint Lambert's School
1000 South Bahnson St.
Sioux Falls, SD 57103

Saint Mary's Catholic School
2000 South 4th St.
Sioux Falls, SD 57105

PIERRE AREA:

Seventh Day Adventist School
1206 East Robinson St.
Pierre, SD 57501

Saint Joseph Catholic School
210 East Broadway
Pierre, SD 57501

RAPID CITY AREA:

Rapid City Christian Liberty
 Academy, Inc.
Hermosa, SD 57744

Memorial Christian School
Keystone Route, Box 200
Rapid City, SD 57701

Bethel Baptist Christian
 Schools
2212 Lance St.
Rapid City, SD 57701

Zion Lutheran School
501 Quincy St.
Rapid City, SD 57701

Seventh Day Adventist School
305 North 39th St.
Rapid City, SD 57701

Saint Martin's Academy High
 School
West of City
Rapid City, SD 57701

Perpetual Help Catholic
 School
431 Oakland St.
Rapid City, SD 57701

HURON AREA:

James Valley Christian High
 School
Route 2
Huron, SD 57350

Sunshine Bible Academy
Route 5
Miller, SD   57362

Platte Christian School
Box 368
Platte, SD   57369

Wessington Springs Academy
  Free Methodist
Wessington Springs, SD
57382

Saint Martin's Catholic School
522 Oregon St., S. E.
Huron, SD   57350

ABERDEEN AREA:

Trinity Lutheran School
923 South Dakota St.
Aberdeen, SD   57401

Plainview Academy
  Seventh Day Adventist
Redfield, SD   57469

Roncalli Catholic High School
1400 North Dakota St.
Aberdeen, SD   57401

Roncalli Catholic Jr. High
  School
505 S. E. 3rd Ave.
Aberdeen, SD   57401

HOT SPRINGS AREA:

Calvary Christian Academy
1938 Canton Ave.
Hot Springs, SD   57747

Bethesda Lutheran School
15th & Baltimore Sts.
Hot Springs, SD   57747

Seventh Day Adventist School
245 South Chicago St.
Hot Springs, SD   57747

Saint Ambrose Catholic School
750 Main St.
Deadwood, SD   57732

MOBRIDGE AREA:

Good Shepherd Bible School
516 East 6th Ave.
Mobridge, SD   57601

Northwestern Lutheran
  Academy
West 10th Ave.
Mobridge, SD   57601

Zion Lutheran School
West 5th Ave. & 9th St.
Mobridge, SD   57601

Seventh Day Adventist School
203 East 10th Ave.
Mobridge, SD   57601

MITCHELL AREA:

Dakota Christian High School
Box 31
New Holland, SD   57364

New Holland Christian Grade
  School
Box 19
New Holland, SD   57364

Faith Bible School
1015 East 6th St.
Mitchell, SD   57301

BROOKINGS AREA:

Christian School
223 East 6th St.
Volga, SD   57071

Mount Marty Catholic High
  School
Yankton, SD   57078

Saint Agnes Catholic School
909 East Lewis St.
Vermillion, SD   57069

Sacred Heart Catholic School
511 Capital St.
Yankton, SD   57078

WATERTOWN AREA:

Saint Martin's Lutheran
  School
1200 N. E. 2nd St.
Watertown, SD   57201

Harmony Hill Educational
  Center
South Hwy. 81
Watertown, SD   57201

Immaculate Conception
  Catholic School
103 S. E. 3rd St.
Watertown, SD   57201

TENNESSEE

MEMPHIS AREA:

Evangelical Christian School
  of Memphis, Inc.
7600 Macon Rd.
Cordova, TN   38018

Trinity Baptist Christian
  School
837 Craft Rd.
Memphis, TN   38116

Hammond Hills Baptist High
  School
3869 Thomas St.
Memphis, TN   38127

Sky-View Baptist High School
3000 University Ave.
Memphis, TN   38127

Briarcrest Baptist High
  School
842 Sweetbrier Rd.
Memphis, TN   38117

Central Baptist School
5470 Raleigh-La Grange Rd.
Memphis, TN   38134

Thrifthaven Baptist Schools
3925 Chelsea Ave.
Memphis, TN   38108

Woodlawn Terrace Baptist
  Academy
6083 Old Millington Rd.
P. O. Box 27141
Memphis, TN 38127

First Assembly Christian
  Academy
4070 Macon Rd.
Memphis, TN 38122

Frayser Baptist Schools, Inc.
3833 Mountain Terr.
Memphis, TN 38127

Southmoor Baptist Schools
3528 Sharpe Ave.
Memphis, TN 38111

C. H. Spurgeon Academy
4700 Macon Rd.
Memphis, TN 38122

Bethel Baptist Schools
4655 Apple Cove St.
Memphis, TN 38109

Oakhaven Baptist Academy
3885 Tchulahoma Rd.
Memphis, TN 38118

Randall Christian Academy
2898 South Perkins Rd.
Memphis, TN 38118

Elliston Baptist Academy
4179 Elliston Rd.
Memphis, TN 38111

Glenmore Academy, Inc.
3101 Knight Rd.
Memphis, TN 38118

Rose Hill Christian Academy
3774 Raleigh-Millington Rd.
Memphis, TN 38128

First Assembly Christian
  School
255 North Highland
P. O. Box 11487
Macon, TN 38048

Macon Road Baptist School
1082 Berclair St.
Memphis, TN 38122

Frayser Assembly of God
  Christian School
3284 Millington Rd.
Memphis, TN 38127

Audubon Park Baptist School
4060 Park Ave.
Memphis, TN 38111

Bartlett Baptist School
5868 State Rd.
Memphis, TN 38128

Marie's Kensington Day School
3124 Winchester St.
Memphis, TN 38117

Presbyterian Day School
4055 Poplar Ave.
Memphis, TN 38111

Whitehaven Presbyterian
  School
1005 Shelby Dr., E.
Memphis, TN 38116

Woodland Presbyterian School
5217 Park Ave.
Memphis, TN 38117

Christ Methodist Day School
4488 Poplar Ave.
Memphis, TN 38117

Whitehaven Methodist Day
  School
4523 Elvis Presley Blvd.
Memphis, TN 38116

Harding Academy of Memphis
  Church of Christ
1000 Cherry Rd.
Memphis, TN 38117

Lutheran High School
8760 Bayliss Rd.
Memphis, TN 38108

Immanuel Lutheran School
6319 Raleigh-Lagrange Rd.
Memphis, TN 38128

Messiah Lutheran School
3743 Austin Peay Hwy.
Memphis, TN 38128

Eastdale Lutheran Academy
8760 Bayliss Rd.
Memphis, TN 38108

Memphis Jr. Academy
  Seventh Day Adventist
50 North Mendenhall Rd.
Memphis, TN 38117

Grace - Saint Luke's
  Episcopal School
246 South Belvedere Blvd.
Memphis, TN 38104

Saint Mary's Episcopal School
4645 Walnut Grove Rd.
Memphis, TN 38117

Memphis Catholic High School
61 McLean Blvd., N.
Memphis, TN 38104

Bishop Byrne High School
1475 Shelby Dr., E.
Memphis, TN 38116

Christian Brothers Catholic
  High School
650 East Pkwy., S.
Memphis, TN 38104

Saint Dominic Catholic School
  for Boys
30 Avon Rd.
Memphis, TN 38117

NASHVILLE AREA:

Nashville Christian School
5807 Charlotte Ave.
Nashville, TN 37209

Goodpasture Christian High
  School
619 Due West Ave.
Nashville, TN 37206

David Lipscomb High School
  Church of. Christ
Granny White Pike
Nashville, TN 37204

Whispering Hills Christian
  Academy
477 McMurray Dr.
Nashville, TN 37211

Donelson Christian School
Stafford Dr.
Nashville, TN 37214

Saint Paul Christian Academy
5035 Hillsboro Rd.
Nashville, TN 37215

Woodbine Christian Academy
2204 Foster Ave.
Nashville, TN 37211

Ezell-Harding Christian
  School
574 Bell Rd.
Nashville, TN 37217

Pioneer Christian Academy
Jackson St.
Whites Creek, TN 37189

Greater Nashville Jr.
  Academy
3307 Brick Church Pike
Nashville, TN 37207

Father Ryan Catholic High
  School
2300 Elliston Pl.
Nashville, TN 37203

Saint Bernard Catholic High
  School
2020 24th Ave., S.
Nashville, TN 37212

Christ the King Catholic
  School
3105 Belmont Blvd.
Nashville, TN 37212

SPRINGFIELD AREA:

Springfield Christian Academy
Highway 41 S.
Springfield, TN 37172

Victory Christian Academy
Murfreesboro Hwy.
Shelbyville, TN 37160

MURFREESBORO AREA:

Middle Tennessee Christian
  School
Lebanon Hwy.
Murfreesboro, TN 37130

Franklin Road Christian
  School
Franklin Rd., Route 7
Murfreesboro, TN 37130

CLARKSVILLE AREA:

Bible Baptist Christian
  Academy
1485 Golf Club Ln.
Clarksville, TN 37040

Clarksville Academy
710 North Second St.
Clarksville, TN 37040

OAK RIDGE AREA:

Saint Mary's Catholic School
327 Vermont Ave.
Oak Ridge, TN 37830

CHATTANOOGA AREA:

Chattanooga Christian Schools
  Evangelical Presbyterian
P.O. Box 144
Lookout Mountain, TN 37350

Tennessee Temple Baptist
  High School
Union Ave.
Chattanooga, TN 37404

Tiftonia Christian School
518 Browns Ferry Rd.
Chattanooga, TN 37419

Wesleyan Christian School
3504 Walthall Ave.
Chattanooga, TN 37407

Trinity Christian Schools
7706 Colemere Dr.
Chattanooga, TN 37416

Brainerd Baptist School
300 Brookfield Ave.
Chattanooga, TN 37411

Hamill Road Christian School
1928 Hamill Rd.
Hixson, TN 37343

McCallie Presbyterian School
Missionary Ridge
Chattanooga, TN 37404

Lutheran School
800 Belvoir Ave.
Chattanooga, TN 37412

Collegedale Academy
  Seventh Day Adventist
Collegedale, TN 37315

Standifer Gap School
  Seventh Day Adventist
Standifer Gap Rd.
Chattanooga, TN 37416

Seventh Day Adventist School
1514 McBrien Rd.
Chattanooga, TN 37412

Sewanee Episcopal Military
  Academy
Sewanee, TN 37375

Saint Andrew's Episcopal
  School
Saint Andrews, TN 37372

Notre Dame Catholic High
  School
2701 Vermont Ave.
Chattanooga, TN 37404

All Saints Catholic Academy
310 East 8th St.
Chattanooga, TN 37403

KNOXVILLE AREA:

Knoxville Baptist Christian
  School
2434 Fifth Ave., N.E.
Knoxville, TN 37917

Harrison-Chilhowee Baptist
  Academy
Seymour, TN 37865

New Beverly Baptist School
3225 New Beverly Church Rd.
Knoxville, TN 37918

Temple Christian School
Beaver Creek Dr.
P.O. Box 159
Powell, TN 37849

First Lutheran School
1207 Broadway, N.E.
Knoxville, TN 39717

Knoxville Jr. Academy
  Seventh Day Adventist
3611 Kingston Pike
Knoxville, TN 37919

Knoxville Catholic High School
1610 Magnolia Ave., N.E.
Knoxville, TN 37917

BRISTOL AREA:

Gateway Baptist Christian
  School
1864 Holston Dr.
(Virginia-Tennessee)
Bristol, TN 37620

Gateway Baptist Christian
  School
Highway 11E
Bluff City, TN 37618

Johnson City Christian School
Route 7
Johnson City, TN 37601

The Cities Christian Schools,
  Inc.
P.O. Box 1113 TCAS
Blountville, TN 37617

Saint Ann Episcopal School
Euclid Ave.
(Virginia-Tennessee)
Bristol, TN 37620

KINGSPORT AREA:

Kingsport Christian Academy
P.O. Box 3706
Kingsport, TN 37664

Tri-Cities Christian Schools
1200 East Center St.
Kingsport, TN 37660

Washington College Academy
  Presbyterian
Limestone, TN 37681

Rock Christian Academy
Greenwood Dr.
Jonesboro, TN 37659

JACKSON AREA:

Jackson Christian School
1490 Campbell St.
Jackson, TN 38301

Malesius Baptist Academy
480 Old Malesius Rd.
Jackson, TN 38301

Faith Christian School
1643 East Chester St.
Jackson, TN 38301

Hines Memorial School
  Seventh Day Adventist
1902 Campbell St.
Jackson, TN 38301

CLEVELAND AREA:

Cross Christian Academy
South Lee Hwy.
Cleveland, TN 37311

Calvary Christian School
695 Ocoee St., S.E.
Cleveland, TN 37311

Bowman Hills Adventist School
300 Westview Dr.
Cleveland, TN 37311

GALLATIN AREA:

Gallatin Christian Academy
1012 Nashville Pike
Gallatin, TN 37066

Hendersonville Christian
  Academy
355 Old Shackle Island Rd.
Hendersonville, TN 37075

Franklin Christian School
Route 1, Arno Rd.
Franklin, TN 37064

Highland Academy
  Seventh Day Adventist
Highway 109 S.
Portland, TN 37148

Bush's Chapel School
South Tunnel
Gallatin, TN 37066

PARIS AREA:

Amish Community Mennonite
  School
Cottage Grove, TN 38224

Seventh Day Adventist School
1126 East Wood St.
Paris, TN 38242

LEBANON AREA:

Friendship Christian School
Coles Ferry Pike
P.O. Box 727
Lebanon, TN 37087

Mount Juliet Christian Academy
Mount Juliet Rd.
P.O. Box 226
Mount Juliet, TN 37122

F. C. Boyd, Sr., Christian
  School
McMinnville, TN 37110

Seventh Day Adventist School
McMinnville, TN 37110

GREENEVILLE AREA:

Greeneville Christian Academy
Newport Hwy., P.O. Box 427
Greeneville, TN 37743

Christ Academy
Friendsville, TN 37737

Seventh Day Adventist School
Takoma Ave.
Greeneville, TN 37743

COLUMBIA AREA:

Columbia Christian Academy
1101 West 7th St.
Columbia, TN 38401

Saint Paul's Catholic School
Tullahoma, TN 37388

MILAN AREA:

Apostolic Christian School
P.O. Box 25
Bradford, TN 38316

JACK'S CREEK AREA:

Jack's Creek Christian School
P. O. Box 35
Jack's Creek, TN 38347

TEXAS

HOUSTON AREA:

Houston Christian Schools
125 West Little York Rd.
Houston, TX 77022

Northwest Christian Schools
 of Greater Houston
6720 West Tidwell Rd.
Houston, TX 77092

Central Christian School
2217 Bingle Rd.
Houston, TX 77055

Broadway Baptist High School
1020 Coral St.
Houston, TX 77012

Bellaire Christian School
6643 Chetwood St.
Houston, TX 77036

Marian Christian High School
11101 South Gessner St.
Houston, TX 77036

Cypress Community Christian
 School
11711 Cypress St.
North Houston, TX 77012

Greenwood Village Christian
 School
11250 Bentley St.
Houston, TX 77016

Northland Christian School
2700 West F M 1960
Houston, TX 77068

Lindale Christian School
6502 Enid St.
Houston, TX 77022

Timbergrove Christian
 Academy
2025 West 11th St.
Houston, TX 77008

Second Baptist School
6410 Woodway Dr.
Houston, TX 77027

Heritage Baptist Academy
149 Winkler Dr.
Houston, TX 77087

Baptist Temple School
200 West 20th St.
Houston, TX 77017

Long Point Baptist School
8009 Long Point Rd.
Houston, TX 77055

Berean Baptist School
10250 North Freeway
Houston, TX 77037

Braeburn Baptist School
5539 Pine St.
Houston, TX 77036

Faith Christian Academy
3519 Burke St.
Houston, TX 77070

North Shore Baptist Academy
6511 Uvalde St.
Houston, TX 77015

Telephone Road Christian
 Academy
5025 Telephone Rd.
Houston, TX 77017

Melrose Baptist Day School
8902 Irvington Blvd.
Houston, TX 77022

Pine Grove Baptist School
3518 Aldine-Bender
Houston, TX 77039

River Oaks Baptist School
2300 Willowick St.
Houston, TX 77027

Sharpstown Christian School
8405 Bonhomme St.
Houston, TX 77036

Westbury Christian School
10424 Hillcroft St.
Houston, TX 77035

South Shaver Baptist School
5300 South Shaver St.
Houston, TX 77034

Asbury Methodist Day School
1010 Strawbridge Ln.
Houston, TX 77040

Gospel Assembly Christian
 School
8712 Airline Dr.
Houston, TX 77037

Lutheran High School
6901 Woodridge St.
Houston, TX 77017

Trinity-Messiah Lutheran
 School
800 Houston Ave.
Houston, TX 77007

Lutheran North School
215 Rittenhouse Rd.
Houston, TX 77022

Christ the Lord Lutheran
 School
4410 Kirkwood St.
Houston, TX 77022

Immanuel Lutheran School
306 East 15th St.
Houston, TX 77008

Messiah Lutheran School
5103 Rose St.
Houston, TX 77007

Our Savior Lutheran School
4425 North Shepherd Dr.
Houston, TX 77018

Trinity Lutheran School
18926 Klein Church Rd.
Houston, TX

Saint John's Lutheran School
404 66th St.
Houston, TX 77011

Saint Mark Lutheran School
1515 Hillendahl St.
Houston, TX 77055

Saint Matthew Lutheran School
5315 Main St.
Houston, TX 77004

Bethany Lutheran School
522 Lindale St.
Houston, TX 77022

Mount Olive Lutheran School
2524 Garland St.
Houston, TX 77017

Pilgrim Lutheran School
8601 Chimney Rock Rd.
Houston, TX 77035

Tomball Lutheran School
911 Hicks St.
Houston, TX 77007

Houston Jr. Academy
 Seventh Day Adventist
4303 Yupon St.
Houston, TX 77006

North Houston School
 Seventh Day Adventist
626 East Canino Rd.
Houston, TX 77022

Gulfhaven Jr. Academy
 Seventh Day Adventist
10716 Sabo Rd.
Houston, TX 77034

Bellfort Jr. Academy
 Seventh Day Adventist
5878 Bellfort Freeway
Houston, TX 77033

Freeway Forest School
 Assembly of God
12330 Viceroy St.
Houston, TX 77034

Church of the Holy Spirit
12535 Perthshire St.
Houston, TX 77024

Calvary Episcopal School
1201 Austin St.
Richmond, TX 77469

Saint Stephen's Episcopal
 School
1805 West Alabama St.
Houston, TX 77006

Saint Mark's Episcopal
 School
3816 Bellaire Blvd.
Houston, TX 77025

Saint Thomas Episcopal
 School
4900 Jackwood St.
Houston, TX 77035

Saint Francis Episcopal Day
 School
345 Piney Point Rd.
Houston, TX 77024

Annunciation Orthodox School
3511 Yoakum Ave.
Houston, TX 77006

Saint Thomas Catholic High
 School
4500 Memorial Dr.
Houston, TX 77007

Incarnate Word Catholic
 Academy
609 Crawford St.
Houston, TX 77002

Mount Carmel Catholic High
 School
6700 Mount Carmel Dr.
Houston, TX 77017

Strake Jesuit Catholic
 Preparatory School
8900 Bellaire Blvd.
Houston, TX 77036

Marian Catholic High School
4621 Fournace Pl.
Houston, TX

Marion Catholic High School
4600 Richmond St.
Bellaire, TX 77401

Saint Pius X Catholic
 School
811 Donovan St.
Houston, TX 77018

Duchesne Academy of the
 Sacred Heart
10202 Memorial Dr.
Houston, TX 77024

PASADENA AREA:

Pasadena Christian School
402 Shaver St.
Pasadena, TX 77502

Southeast Christian Schools
9020 Gulf Freeway
Pasadena, TX 77502

Easthaven Baptist School
9321 Edgebrook St.
(Houston)
Pasadena, TX 77075

Zion Lutheran School
1117 South Main St.
Pasadena, TX 77502

Apostolic Temple School
2630 Allen-Genoa Rd.
Pasadena, TX 77502

Saint Barnabas Episcopal
 Day School
705 Williams St.
Pasadena, TX 77502

Saint Augustine Catholic
 School
5500 Laurel Creek Rd.
(Houston)
Pasadena, TX 77017

Saint Pius V Catholic School
812 South Main St.
Pasadena, TX 77502

BAYTOWN AREA:

Baytown Christian Academy
302 West Cedar Bayou,
 Lynchburg Rd.
Baytown, TX 77521

DALLAS AREA:

Dallas Christian Jr. & Sr.
  High School
4900 Barnes Bridge Rd.
Mesquite, TX 75149

Dallas Christian Academy
2380 Dunloe Dr.
Dallas, TX 75228

Metropolitan Christian School
8501 Bruton St.
Dallas, TX 75217

East Dallas Christian School
2360 Laughlin Dr.
Dallas, TX 75228

North Dallas Christian School
10550 Marsh Ln.
Dallas, TX 75229

Heritage Christian Academy
12200 Ford at L B J Freeway
Dallas, TX 75234

Scofield Christian Day School
4105 Junius St.
Dallas, TX 75246

Christian Academy of Oak
  Cliff, Inc.
4100 West Jefferson Blvd.
Dallas, TX 75211

Christway Academy
419 North Cedar Ridge Dr.
Dallas, TX 75211

Trinity Christian Academy
P.O. Box 636
Addison, TX 75001

Tyler Street Christian School
927 West 10th
Dallas, TX 75208

Evangelical Methodist
  Christian School
P.O. Box 516
Duncanville, TX 75116

First Baptist Academy
1704 Patterson St.
Dallas, TX 75201

Golden Triangle Christian
  Academy
2806 Mitchell St.
Greenville, TX 75401

Oak Cliff Christian School
2127 South Corinth Street Rd.
Dallas, TX 75203

Conaway Private Schools
2508 Highland Rd.
Dallas, TX 75228

Scofield Christian Day School
7730 Abrams St.
Dallas, TX 75231

American Christian Academy
3201 West Davis St.
Dallas, TX 75211

Evangel Temple Christian
  School
S.W. Third and Hwy. 303
Grand Prairie, TX 75050

Beverly Hills Baptist Christian
  School
810 North Westmoreland St.
Dallas, TX 75211

Brook Hollow Christian School
135 West Wintergreen Rd.
(Brook Hollow)
Dallas, TX 75247

Buckner Boulevard Baptist
  School
2525 North Buckner Blvd.
Dallas, TX 75228

Canyon Creek Baptist Day
  School
2800 Custer Pkwy.
Dallas, TX 75216

Chapel Hill Baptist Schools
11611 Webb's Chapel Rd.
Dallas, TX 75229

Hutchins Baptist School
100 North Hills Dr.
Dallas, TX 75203

Lancaster Christian Academy
1575 Dewberry Blvd.
(Lancaster)
Dallas, TX

Royal Haven Baptist School
10919 Royal Haven
Dallas, TX 75229

Trinity Christian Academy
16700 Addison Rd.
Dallas, TX 75203

Temple Christian School
8421 Bohannon St.
Dallas, TX 75217

Tyler Street Christian
  Academy
927 West 10th St.
Dallas, TX 75208

Our Redeemer Lutheran
  School
7611 Park Ln.
Dallas, TX 75225

Calvary Lutheran School
9807 Church Rd.
Dallas, TX 75238

Grace Lutheran School
1523 South Beckley St.
Dallas, TX 75224

Bethel Lutheran School
11211 East Northwest Hwy.
Dallas, TX 75238

Holy Cross Lutheran School
11425 Marsh Ln.
Dallas, TX 75229

Zion Lutheran School
6121 East Lovers Ln.
Dallas, TX 75214

Dallas Jr. Academy
  Seventh Day Adventist
4025 North Central Expressway
Dallas, TX 75204

City Temple Jr. Academy
1600 Bonnie View
Dallas, TX 75203

Oak Cliff Jr. Academy
  Seventh Day Adventist
825 West Pentagon Pkwy.
Dallas, TX 75224

Burton Jr. Academy
  Seventh Day Adventist
4611 Kelly Elliott Rd.
Dallas, TX 75215

Episcopal School of Dallas
5002 West Lovers Ln.
Dallas, TX 75209

Saint Mark's School of Texas
  Boys Prep School
10600 Preston Rd.
Dallas, TX 75230

Good Shepherd Episcopal Day
  School
11122 Midway Rd.
Dallas, TX 75229

Day School of the Episcopal
  Church of the Transfiguration
14115 Hillcrest Rd.
Dallas, TX 75240

Saint John's Episcopal School
848 Harter St.
Dallas, TX 75218

Saint James Episcopal School
727 Hill St.
Dallas, TX 75223

Jesuit Preparatory School
12345 Inwood Rd.
Dallas, TX 75247

Bishop Dunne Catholic High
  School
3900 Rugged Dr.
Dallas, TX 75224

Bishop Lynch Catholic High
  School
9750 Ferguson
Dallas, TX 75228

Saint Paul the Apostle
  Catholic School
720 South Floyd Rd.
Dallas, TX 75204

MESQUITE AREA:

Christian Life Temple School
2930 Peachtree Rd.
Mesquite, TX 75149

IRVING AREA:

Irving Christian Academy
115 South MacArthur Blvd.
Irving, TX 75060

Garland Christian Academy
1522 Lavon Dr.
Garland, TX 75040

Love of God Christian Day
  Schools, Inc.
804 West Pioneer Dr.
P.O. Box 486
Irving, TX 75061

Alpha Academy Christian School
701 State St.
Garland, TX 75040

Beltline Road Baptist Christian
  School
3333 North Beltline Rd.
Irving, TX 75062

Miller Road Christian School
2004 16th St.
Garland, TX 75041

Berean Christian Academy
1012 East 6th St.
Irving, TX 75060

Shady Grove Christian Academy
1829 West Shady Grove Rd.
Irving, TX 75060

Plymouth Park Baptist School
1714 North Story Rd.
Irving, TX 75061

Cistercian Catholic Preparatory
  School
1 Cistercian Rd.
Irving, TX 75062

FORT WORTH AREA:

Fort Worth Christian School
7517 Bogart Dr.
Fort Worth, TX 76118

Texas State Academy
2000 Carson St.
Fort Worth, TX 76117

Apostolic Christian School
516 Hudgins Ave.
Fort Worth, TX 76111

Castleberry Baptist Christian
  School
1200 Roberts Cut-Off Rd.
Fort Worth, TX 76114

Rolling Hills Christian Schools
4800 South Riverside Dr.
Fort Worth, TX 76119

Seminary South Assembly Day
  School
501 West Seminary Dr.
Fort Worth, TX 76115

South Campus Christian
  Academy
6851 Wichita St.
Fort Worth, TX 76119

Southside Christian School
2101 Hemphill St.
Fort Worth, TX 76110

Southwest Christian School,
  Inc.
4600 Altamesa Blvd.
Fort Worth, TX 76133

Westridge Christian School
9001 Weatherford Hwy.
Fort Worth, TX 76116

Gospel Assembly Academy
2806 N.W. 27th St.
Fort Worth, TX 76106

Liberty Christian Academy
2809 Layton Ave.
P.O. Box 14143
Fort Worth, TX 76117

Bethel Baptist Christian Schools
506 East Randol Mill Rd.
Fort Worth, TX 76112

Foresthill Avenue Academy
6300 Nell Ave.
Fort Worth, TX 76140

Fort Worth Bible Church Day
  School
6917 Brentwood Stair Rd.
Fort Worth, TX 76112

Christian Character Academy
Route 2, P.O. Box 45D
Aledo, TX 76008

Boulevard Baptist School
315 North Burleson Blvd.
Fort Worth, TX 76119

Christian Temple School
4500 Booth Calloway Rd.
Fort Worth, TX 76118

First Methodist Day School
530 Elm St.
Hurst, TX 76053

Glenview Baptist Schools
5612 Glenview Dr.
Fort Worth, TX 76118

Meadowbrook Christian School
6801 Meadowbrook Dr.
Fort Worth, TX 76112

Redeemer Lutheran School
4513 Williams Rd.
Fort Worth, TX 76116

Saint Paul Lutheran Day School
1800 West Freeway
Fort Worth, TX 76102

Zion Lutheran School
1112 Eagle Dr.
Fort Worth, TX 76111

Saint Luke's Episcopal Day
  School
4301 Meadowbrook Dr.
Fort Worth, TX 76103

Saint Vincent Episcopal School
3201 West Pipe Line Rd.
Fort Worth, TX 76118

All Saints' Episcopal School
8200 Tumblewood Trail
Fort Worth, TX 76108

Saint Andrew's Catholic School
3304 Dryden Rd.
Fort Worth, TX 76109

Saint Peter the Apostle
  Catholic School
1201 South Cherry Ln.
Fort Worth, TX 76108

ARLINGTON AREA:

Metroplex Christian Schools
1013 Gibbins Rd.
Arlington, TX 76011

Bethel Christian School
2300 East Park Row Dr.
Arlington, TX 76010

Covenant Christian Academy
715 Cheek Sparger Rd.
P.O. Box 632
Colleyville, TX 76034

Pantego Christian Academy
2203 West Park Row Dr.
Arlington, TX 76013

Saint Alban's Episcopal School
Arlington, TX

Saint Maria Goretti Catholic
  School
1200 South Davis Dr.
Arlington, TX 76013

SAN ANTONIO AREA:

San Antonio Christian School
5703 Blanco Rd.
San Antonio, TX 78216

Christian Heritage Schools,
  Inc.
937 West Magnolia Ave.
San Antonio, TX 78201

Gateway Christian Schools
6623 Five Palms Dr.
San Antonio, TX 78242

Mexican Baptist Bible Institute
8019 South Panam Expressway
San Antonio, TX 78224

Bethel Mexican Baptist School
2101 Ruiz St.
San Antonio, TX 78207

Southwest Christian Academy
3737 Roosevelt Ave.
San Antonio, TX 78214

Sunnybrook Christian Academy
1620 Pinn Rd.
San Antonio, TX 78227

Oakhill Christian School
8308 Fredericksburg Rd.
San Antonio, TX 78229

Temple Baptist School
1905 N.W. Loop 410
San Antonio, TX 78213

Bethesda Temple School
2210 Basse Rd.
San Antonio, TX 78213

Lakeview Baptist School
4001 West Martin St.
San Antonio, TX 78207

Trinity United Methodist
  Weekday School
6800 Wurzbach Rd.
San Antonio, TX 78240

Pilgrim Congregational School
500 Pilgrim Dr.
San Antonio, TX 78213

Redeemer Lutheran School
2507 Fredericksburg Ave.
San Antonio, TX 78212

Concordia Lutheran School
1826 Basse Rd.
San Antonio, TX 78213

Seventh Day Adventist Jr.
  Academy
1250 Holbrook Dr.
San Antonio, TX 78218

Texas Episcopal Military
  Institute
800 College Blvd.
San Antonio, TX 78209

Saint Luke's Episcopal School
11 Saint Luke's St.
San Antonio, TX 78209

Antonian Catholic High School
6425 West Ave.
San Antonio, TX 78213

Central Catholic High School
1403 North Saint Mary's St.
San Antonio, TX 78215

Saint Gerard's Catholic
 Regional High School
South New Braunfels Ave.
San Antonio, TX 78210

Holy Cross Catholic High
 School
426 North San Felipe Ave.
San Antonio, TX 78228

Christ the King Catholic School
2626 Perez St.
San Antonio, TX 78207

AUSTIN AREA:

Austin Christian Academy
 Northside
8647 Rockwood Ln.
Austin, TX 78758

Christian Heritage Academy
7500 Woodrow Ave.
Austin, TX 78757

Strickland School
 First Evangelical Free Church
4425 Red River St.
Austin, TX 78757

Wesleyan Christian School
735 Turkey Creek Rd.
Austin, TX 78732

Allandale Christian School
2615 Allandale Rd.
Austin, TX 78756

Brentwood Christian School
6701 Arroyo Seca
Austin, TX 78757

Harvest Time Christian
 Academy
7612 Cooper Ln.
Austin, TX 78745

Hyde Park Baptist School
3901 Speedway
Austin, TX 78751

First Cumberland School
6800 Woodrow Ave.
Austin, TX 78757

Redeemer Lutheran School
1500 Anderson Ln.
Austin, TX 78757

Holy Word Lutheran School
10601 Bluff Bend Rd.
Austin, TX 78753

Saint Paul Lutheran School
3501 Red River Rd.
Austin, TX 78705

Trinity Lutheran School
1207 West 45th St.
Austin, TX 78756

Martin's Lutheran Day School
606 West 15th St.
Austin, TX 78701

Hope Lutheran School
6414 North Hampton
Austin, TX 78705

San Marcos Baptist Academy
San Marcos, TX 78666

Episcopal Church of the
 Resurrection School
2008 Justin Ln.
Austin, TX 78757

Saint Andrew's Episcopal
 School
1112 West 31st St.
Austin, TX 78757

Saint Austin's Catholic School
1911 San Antonio St.
Austin, TX 78705

Saint Louis Catholic School
2114 Saint Joseph Ave.
Austin, TX 78757

GREENVILLE AREA:

Greenville Christian School,
 Inc.
P.O. Box 1030
Greenville, TX 75401

EL PASO AREA:

El Paso Christian Academy
7959 Esther Rd.
El Paso, TX 79907

Christian Heritage School
645 Steadham St.
El Paso, TX 79927

Latin American Bible Institute
301 South Schutz St.
El Paso, TX 79907

Northeast Christian Academy
9901 McCombs St.
El Paso, TX 79924

Valley View Christian School
1500 Mescalero Dr.
El Paso, TX 79925

Horizon Christian School
14802 Duanesburg St.
El Paso, TX 79927

Lydia Patterson Institute
 United Methodist
517 South Florence St.
El Paso, TX 79901

El Paso Jr. Academy
 Seventh Day Adventist
8080 Meraz St.
El Paso, TX 79907

Cathedral High School
1309 North Stanton St.
El Paso, TX 79902

Father Yermo Catholic High
 School
250 Washington St.
El Paso, TX 79905

Saint Clement Pro-Cathedral
 School
600 Montana Ave.
El Paso, TX 79902

Loretto Catholic Middle School
1300 Hardaway St.
El Paso, TX 79903

MERCEDES AREA:

Immanuel Lutheran School
701 West Third
Mercedes, TX 78570

LAREDO AREA:

Laredo Christian Academy
1719 Malinche St.
Laredo, TX 78040

Christian Union Institute
1613 Madison St.
Laredo, TX 78040

Holding Institute
 United Methodist
101 Holding Blvd.
Laredo, TX 78040

Schreiner Presbyterian
 Institute
Kerrville, TX 78028

Faith Academy
1220 McClelland St.
Laredo, TX 78040

Saint Augustine Catholic High
 School
1300 Galveston St.
Laredo, TX 78040

Saint Augustin Downtown
 School
215 San Augustin St.
Laredo, TX 78040

BROWNSVILLE AREA:

First Baptist Day School
555 East Elizabeth St.
Brownsville, TX 78520

Saint Paul's Episcopal School
1626 East Taft St.
Brownsville, TX 78521

Episcopal Day School
34 North Coria St.
Brownsville, TX 78520

Incarnate Word Catholic
 Academy
224 Resaca Blvd.
Brownsville, TX 78520

Saint Joseph's Catholic
 Academy
101 Saint Joseph Dr.
Brownsville, TX 78520

Villa Maria Catholic High
 School
244 Resaca Blvd.
Brownsville, TX 78520

Villa Maria Catholic Jr.
 High School
700 West Jefferson St.
Brownsville, TX 78520

MCALLEN AREA:

Saint Paul Lutheran School
300 Pecan Ave.
McAllen, TX 78501

CORPUS CHRISTI AREA:

Corpus Christi Christian
 School, Inc.
3101 McArdie St.
Corpus Christi, TX 78415

Park Avenue Christian School,
 Inc.
915 Park Ave.
Corpus Christi, TX 78401

First Baptist Church School
3115 Ocean Dr.
Corpus Christi, TX 78404

Rebekah Christian School
Old Brownsville Rd.
Corpus Christi, TX 78405

Parkdale Baptist School
3875 South Staples St.
Corpus Christi, TX 78411

Travis Baptist School
4001 Schanen St.
Corpus Christi, TX 78413

Weber Road Baptist Christian
 School
4234 Weber Rd.
Corpus Christi, TX 78411

Faith Temple School
4425 South Staples St.
Corpus Christi, TX 78411

Grace School
3530 Gollihar Rd.
Corpus Christi, TX 78415

Saint Luke's United Methodist
 Day School
3151 Reid St.
Corpus Christi, TX 78404

Trinity Lutheran School
808 Louisiana St.
Corpus Christi, TX 78404

Saint James Episcopal School
701 Upper South Broadway
Corpus Christi, TX 78401

Incarnate Word Catholic High
 School
2910 South Alameda St.
Corpus Christi, TX 78404

Saint Joseph's Catholic Jr.
 High School
2121 Mary St.
Corpus Christi, TX 78405

Christ the King Catholic School
1625 Arlington St.
Corpus Christi, TX 78415

GALVESTON AREA:

Galveston Christian Academy
5801 S St.
Galveston, TX 77550

Saint John's Lutheran School
39th and L Sts.
Galveston, TX 77550

Trinity Episcopal School
720 Tremont St.
Galveston, TX 77550

O'Connell High School Sr.
1320 Tremont St.
Galveston, TX 77550

O'Connell High School Jr.
2601 Ursuline St.
Galveston, TX 77550

Dominican Middle School
901 13th St.
Galveston, TX 77550

Saint Patrick's Catholic School
3401 Broadway
Galveston, TX   77550

Our Lady of Guadelupe
  Catholic School
4416 M St.
Galveston, TX   77550

BEAUMONT AREA:

Christian Schools of Beaumont
2455 Commerce St.
Beaumont, TX   77703

Beaumont Christian Academy
730 Langham Rd.
Beaumont, TX   77701

New Life Tabernacle School
6655 Highway 105
Beaumont, TX   77708

Touch Christian Academy
8325 Walker Rd.
Beaumont, TX   77708

Trinity United Methodist Day
  School
3430 Harrison St.
Beaumont, TX   77706

All Saints' Episcopal School
4108 Delaware St.
Beaumont, TX   77706

Cathedral School
2350 Eastex Freeway
Beaumont, TX   77703

AMARILLO AREA:

Amarillo Christian Schools
4100 Republic St.
Amarillo, TX   79109

West Texas Christian School
1805 Magnolia St.
Amarillo, TX   79107

Rhema Christian School System
900 Alta Vista St.
Amarillo, TX   79106

San Jacinto School
  Church of Christ
823 South Mississippi St.
Amarillo, TX   79106

Trinity Lutheran School
5005 West Interstate Expressway
Amarillo, TX   79106

Amarillo Adventist Academy
5804 Erik St.
Amarillo, TX   79106

Saint Andrew's Episcopal Day
  School
1601 South Georgia St.
Amarillo, TX   79102

Alamo Catholic High School
1800 North Spring St.
Amarillo, TX   79107

Saint Lawrence Catholic School
2300 North Spring St.
Amarillo, TX   79107

LUBBOCK AREA:

New Life Christian Academy
2102 5th St.
Lubbock, TX   79401

Western Hills Baptist Academy
5505 Wayne Ave.
Lubbock, TX   79414

Trinity Bible Institute
7002 Canton Ave.
Lubbock, TX   79413

All Saints' Episcopal School
2801 42nd St.
Lubbock, TX   79413

Christ the King Catholic High
  School
4011 54th St.
Lubbock, TX   79413

Saint John Neumann's Catholic
  School
5838 22nd St.
Lubbock, TX   79407

WICHITA FALLS AREA:

Northwest Christian Academy
Sheppard Expressway at
  Airport
Wichita Falls, TX   76309

Heritage Christian Academy
1507 23rd St.
Wichita Falls, TX   76301

Bible Baptist Christian School
908 Austin St.
Wichita Falls, TX   76301

Saint Paul Lutheran School
2222 Brook St.
Wichita Falls, TX   76301

Episcopal School
3801 West Campus
Wichita Falls, TX   76308

Notre Dame Catholic Jr. -
  Sr. High School
2821 Lansing St.
Wichita Falls, TX   76309

WACO AREA:

Trinity Christian School
2517 Mt. Carmel St.
Waco, TX   76710

Trinity Lutheran School
6125 Bosque Blvd.
Waco, TX   76710

Saint Mark Lutheran School
2000 Clay St.
Waco, TX   76706

Saint Paul's Episcopal School
515 Columbus St.
Waco, TX   76702

Saint Alban's Episcopal School
321 North 30th St.
Waco, TX   76710

Reicher Catholic High School
212 North 23rd St.
Waco, TX   76708

Saint Mary's Catholic School
1301 Washington St.
Waco, TX 76702

STEPHENVILLE AREA:

Stephenville Christian School
P.O. Box 112A, Star Route
Stephenville, TX 76401

ABILENE AREA:

Abilene Christian High School
1600 Campus Ct.
Abilene, TX 79601

Evangel Christian Academy
2943 South 6th
Abilene, TX 79605

Temple Christian School
1164 Minter St.
Abilene, TX 79603

Faith Christian Schools
2300 South 20th St.
Abilene, TX 79605

Seventh Day Adventist School
Route 1
Abilene, TX 79604

Christ House School
701 Mesquite St.
Abilene, TX 79601

Saint John's School
1385 South Bowie St.
Abilene, TX 79605

ODESSA AREA:

Odessa Christian School
2000 Doran St.
Odessa, TX 79761

Midland Christian Day School
Midland, TX 79701

Grace Christian School
2409 Walnut St.
Odessa, TX 79761

Sherwood Baptist School
505 East 42nd St.
Odessa, TX 79761

The Hillander School
Midland, TX 79701

Trinity School
Midland, TX 79701

Saint Ann's Catholic School
Midland, TX 79701

SAN ANGELO AREA:

Riverside Christian Academy
20 East Bowie St.
San Angelo, TX 76903

Trinity Lutheran School
1326 Kenwood Dr.
San Angelo, TX 76903

Catholic School of San Angelo
2315 A & M Aves.
San Angelo, TX 76903

TYLER AREA:

Tyler Christian Academy
3100 West Erwin St.
Tyler, TX 75702

East Texas Christian Academy
1801 Shiloh Rd.
Tyler, TX 75703

Longview Christian Academy
2200 Loop 281 W.
Longview, TX 75601

Mission Temple Christian
  Academy
New Kilgore Hwy.
Tyler, TX 75701

Trinity Baptist Day School
604 West 4th St.
Tyler, TX 75701

Trinity Lutheran School
2001 Hunter St.
Tyler, TX 75701

Agape Force Prep School
Lindale St.
Tyler, TX 75701

All Saints' Episcopal School
118 South Bois d'Arc St.
Tyler, TX 75702

Trinity Day School
906 Padon St.
Longview, TX 75601

Saint Mary's Catholic School
405 Hollybrook Dr.
Longview, TX 75601

DENTON AREA:

Denton Christian School
Interstate Hwy. 35E
Denton, TX 76201

Maranatha Christian Academy
1301 Audra Ln.
Denton, TX 76201

Faith Christian Academy
1101 Audra Ln.
Denton, TX 76201

KILLEEN AREA:

Good Shepherd Christian School
Killeen, TX 76541

Seventh Day Adventist School
Killeen, TX 76541

Saint Joseph's Catholic School
Killeen, TX 76541

DEL RIO AREA:

Bethel Baptist Academy High
  School
700 Cantu Rd.
Del Rio, TX 78840

First Assembly Christian
  School
190 Western Dr.
Del Rio, TX 78840

Saint James Episcopal Day
  School
206 West Greenwood St.
Del Rio, TX 78840

Redeemer Episcopal School
Madison & Ferry Sts.
Eagle Pass, TX 78852

Sacred Heart Catholic School
209 East Greenwood St.
Del Rio, TX 78840

BIG SPRING AREA:

Big Spring Christian Academy
Industrial Park
Big Spring, TX 79720

Alpine Christian School
Highway 90 E.
Alpine, TX 79830

Saint Mary's Episcopal School
1005 Goliad St.
Big Spring, TX 79720

Immaculate Heart of Mary
  Catholic School
1009 Hearn St.
Big Spring, TX 79720

VICTORIA AREA:

Presbyterian Day School
2408 North Navarro St.
Victoria, TX 77901

Saint Michael's Episcopal
  Academy
2505 South College Ave.
Bryan, TX 77801

Saint Joseph Catholic High
  School
110 East Red River
Victoria, TX 77901

Saint Joseph's Catholic School
109 North Preston St.
Bryan, TX 77801

SHERMAN AREA:

Grayson Christian Academy
600 East Cherry St.
Sherman, TX 75090

Central Christian Academy
306 South Union St.
Whitesboro, TX 76273

Saint Luke's Parish Day School
P.O. Box 603
Denison, TX 75020

Saint Joseph's Catholic
  Academy
708 South Travis St.
Sherman, TX 75090

HARLINGEN AREA:

Valley Baptist Academy
3700 East Harrison St.
Harlingen, TX 78550

PORT ARTHUR AREA:

Garnet Avenue Christian
  School
6247 Garnet Ave.
Port Arthur, TX 77640

Nederland Baptist Schools
2005 Peterson St.
Nederland, TX 77627

United Christian Pentecostal
  Academy
2700 25th St.
Port Arthur, TX 77640

Trinity Lutheran School
2448 Fifth St.
Port Arthur, TX 77640

Bishop Byrne Catholic High
  School
Byrne Dr.
Port Arthur, TX 77640

TEXARKANA AREA:

Saint James Episcopal Day
  School
North State Line Blvd.
Texarkana, TX 75501

Reformed Baptist Christian
  School
3010 Main St.
Texarkana, TX 75503

BEEVILLE AREA:

Trinity Christian Academy
P.O. Box 686
Beeville, TX 78102

TEMPLE AREA:

Twin Cities Christian
  Academy
5505 Midway Dr.
Temple, TX 76501

UTAH

SALT LAKE CITY AREA:

Landmark Christian Academy
1680 West Stratford Ave.
Salt Lake City, UT 84119

Good Shepherd Christian
  School
859 South 800 E.
Salt Lake City, UT 84102

Galilean Elementary School
475 East First S.
Salt Lake City, UT 84111

Anchor Baptist Christian
  Academy
1880 East 5600 S.
Salt Lake City, UT 84121

Redeemer Lutheran Day
  School
1955 East Stratford Ave.
Salt Lake City, UT 84106

Christ Lutheran School
230 East 5600 S.
Murray, UT 84107

American Heritage Schools,
  Inc.
125 North 100 E.
Pleasant Grove, UT 84060

Salt Lake Adventist Jr.
  Academy
965 East 3370 S.
Salt Lake City, UT 84106

Rowland – Saint Mark's
  Episcopal Academy
205 First Ave.
Salt Lake City, UT 84103

Mount Vernon Academy
  Latter Day Saints
184 East Vine St.
Murray, UT 84107

Judge Memorial Catholic High
  School
650 South 1100 E.
Salt Lake City, UT 84102

Saint Vincent Catholic School
1385 Spring Ln.
Holladay, UT   84117

Saint Francis Xavier School
4501 West 5215 S.
Kearns, UT   84118

PROVO AREA:

Wasatch Presbyterian Academy
120 South 100 W.
Mount Pleasant, UT   84647

Seventh Day Adventist School
255 South 700 E.
Provo, UT   84601

OGDEN AREA:

Berean Baptist School
3846 Jackson Ave.
Ogden, UT   84403

Saint Paul Lutheran School
3329 Harrison Blvd.
Ogden, UT   84403

Seventh Day Adventist School
Ogden, UT   84403

Saint Joseph's Catholic High
  School
1790 Lake St.
Ogden, UT   84403

PRICE AREA:

Seventh Day Adventist School
Sunnyside, UT   84539

Notre Dame Catholic School
210 North 600 E.
Prince, UT   84501

CEDAR CITY AREA:

Beaver High School
  Latter Day Saints
Beaver, UT   84713

MOAB AREA:

Castle Valley Institute
  Seventh Day Adventist
Castle Valley, UT   84532

MINERAL WELL AREA:

Bible Baptist Academy
900 S. E. 6th Ave.
Mineral Well, UT   76067

VERMONT

BURLINGTON AREA:

Trinity Baptist Christian
  School
Route 2A
Williston, VT   05495

Rock Point Episcopal School
Institute Rd.
Burlington, VT   05401

Rice Memorial Catholic High
  School
Proctor Ave. Extension
South Burlington, VT   05401

Christ the King Catholic School
Locust St.
Burlington, VT   05401

RUTLAND AREA:

Vermont Christian School
190 Grove St., Box 274
Rutland, VT   05701

Mount Saint Joseph Catholic
  Academy
Box 540
Rutland, VT   05701

BENNINGTON AREA:

Green Mountain Christian
  School
School St.
Bennington, VT   05201

Sacred Heart Catholic School
School St.
Bennington, VT   05201

NEWPORT AREA:

Grace Christian School
Newport, VT   05855

Saint Paul's School
Newport, VT   05855

Sacred Heart Catholic High
  School
Newport, VT   05855

WINDSOR AREA:

Assist Christian School
Wilder, VT   05088

Sacred Heart Catholic School
11 Eldridge St.
(Lebanon)
New Hampshire, VT   03766

BARRE AREA:

Greater Barre Christian School
Websterville, VT   05678

Websterville Baptist Christian
  School
P. O. Box 1
Websterville, VT   05678

SAINT JOHNSBURY AREA:

Union Baptist School
130 Railroad St.
Saint Johnsbury, VT   05819

MONTPELIER AREA:

Life on Holiness Christian
  School
Mr. Stan Bettis
P. O. Box 778
Morrisville, VT   05661

Saint Michael's Catholic School
Montpelier, VT   05602

BRATTLEBORO AREA:

Saint Michael's Catholic School
Brattleboro, VT   05301

SPRINGFIELD AREA:

Vermont Academy
Saxton's River, VT   05154

VERGENNES AREA:

Champlain Valley Christian
  School
P. O. Box 153, New Haven Rd.
Vergennes, VT   05491

VIRGINIA

NORFOLK AREA:

Norfolk Christian Schools
255 Thole St.
Norfolk, VA 23505

Seaboard Christian Schools
  of Tidewater, Inc.
4700 Little John Dr.
Norfolk, VA 23513

Victory Christian Day School
3834 East Princess Anne Rd.
Norfolk, VA 23502

Victory Christian Day School
1520 Kennon Ave.
Norfolk, VA 23502

Bethany Christian School
  Free-Will Baptist
2430 Azalea Garden Rd.
Norfolk, VA 23513

Tidewater Christian Academy
  Assembly of God
5204 Elmhurst Ave.
Norfolk, VA 23513

Bayview Christian School
707 Bayview Blvd.
Norfolk, VA 23503

Azalea Garden School
  Church of God
5160 Beamon Rd.
Norfolk, VA 23513

Trinity Lutheran School
6001 Granby St.
Norfolk, VA 23505

Norfolk Catholic High School
6401 Granby St.
Norfolk, VA 23505

Saint Mary's Academy West
1300 Stockley Gardens
Norfolk, VA 23517

Saint Mary's Catholic Academy
1000 Holt St.
Norfolk, VA 23504

Christ the King Catholic
  School
3401 Tidewater Dr.
Norfolk, VA 23509

Holy Trinity Catholic School
154 West Government Ave.
Norfolk, VA 23503

Blessed Sacrament Catholic
  School
3611 Colley Ave.
Norfolk, VA 23508

VIRGINIA BEACH AREA:

Virginia Beach Baptist
  Christian Academy
3177 Virginia Beach Blvd.
Virginia Beach, VA 23452

Gateway Christian Schools
5473 Virginia Beach Blvd.
Virginia Beach, VA 23462

Tabernacle Baptist Christian
  School
717 North Whitehurst
  Landing Rd.
Virginia Beach, VA 23462

First Colonial Christian School
929 First Colonial Rd.
Virginia Beach, VA 23454

Kempsville Mennonite School
201 Overland Rd.
Virginia Beach, VA 23462

Friends School
1537 Laskin Rd.
Virginia Beach, VA 23451

Tidewater Jr. Academy
  Seventh Day Adventist
Centerville Turnpike
P.O. Box 62262
Virginia Beach, VA 23462

Saint Matthew's Catholic School
3316 Sandra Ln.
Virginia Beach, VA 23462

Saint Nicholas School of
  Religion
644 Little Neck Rd.
Virginia Beach, VA 23452

Saint Gregory's Catholic School
5345 Virginia Beach Blvd.
Virginia Beach, VA 23462

WILLIAMSBURG AREA:

Williamsburg Christian Academy
114 Palace Ln.
Williamsburg, VA 23185

Lightfoot Christian School
Lightfoot, VA 23090

Walsingham Catholic Academy
Jamestown Rd., Box 159
Williamsburg, VA 23185

NEWPORT NEWS AREA:

Northside Christian School
943 J. Clyde Morris Blvd.
Newport News, VA 23601

Warwick River Christian School
252 Lucas Creek Rd.
Newport News, VA 23602

Immanuel Baptist Christian
  Academy
69 Saunders Rd.
Newport News, VA 23602

Memorial Christian School
324 Newport News Ave.
Newport News, VA 23601

Denbigh Baptist Christian
  School
13010 Mitchell Point Rd.
Newport News, VA 23602

Orcutt Baptist Day School
653 Oyster Point Rd.
Newport News, VA 23602

Trinity Lutheran School
6807 Huntington Ave.
Newport News, VA 23607

Saint Andrew's Episcopal
   School
45 Main St.
Newport News, VA   23601

Peninsula Catholic High School
332 34th St.
Newport News, VA   23607

ALEXANDRIA AREA:

Metropolitan Christian Schools
P.O. Box 10274
5411 Franconia Rd.
Alexandria, VA   22310

Engleside Christian School
8428 Highland Ln.
Alexandria, VA   22309

Calvary Road Christian
   Schools
6811 Beulah St.
Alexandria, VA   22310

Calvary Christian School
Leesburg Pike & George Mason
   Dr.
Alexandria, VA   22302

Immanuel Christian School
5211 Braddock Rd.
Springfield, VA   22151

Immanuel Lutheran School
109 Belaire Rd.
Alexandria, VA   22301

Episcopal High School
1200 Quaker Ln.
Alexandria, VA   22302

Saint Stephen's Episcopal
   School
1000 Saint Stephen's Rd.
Alexandria, VA   22304

Grace Episcopal Day School
3601 Russell Rd.
Alexandria, VA   22305

Saint Agnes Episcopal School
Fontain St.
Alexandria, VA   22302

Bishop Ireton Catholic High
   School
201 Cambridge Rd.
Alexandria, VA   22314

Ascension Catholic Academy
4401 West Braddock Rd.
Alexandria, VA   22304

Saint Louis Catholic School
2901 Popkins Ln.
Alexandria, VA   22306

FREDERICKSBURG AREA:

Fredericksburg Christian
   School
1501 Washington Ave.
Fredericksburg, VA   22401

Payne Christian Academy
336 Riverside Dr.
Fredericksburg, VA   22401

Temple Baptist Christian
   School
504 White Oak Rd.
Fredericksburg, VA   22401

Fredericksburg Seventh Day
   Adventist School
1500 Stafford Ave.
Fredericksburg, VA   22401

Montfort Catholic Academy
700 Sunken Rd.
Fredericksburg, VA   22401

PORTSMOUTH AREA:

Portsmouth Christian School
3214 Elliott Ave.
Portsmouth, VA   23702

Central Baptist Schools
1200 Hodges Ferry Rd.
Portsmouth, VA   23701

Alliance Christian Schools
5803 Portsmouth Blvd.
Portsmouth, VA   23701

Bethany Baptist Christian
   School
4 South Colin Dr.
Off Portsmouth Blvd.
Portsmouth, VA   23701

Court Street Baptist Academy
Court & Queen Sts.
Portsmouth, VA   23704

Sweethaven Baptist Christian
   School
5100 West Norfolk Rd.
Portsmouth, VA   23703

Portsmouth Catholic High
   School
435 Washington St.
Portsmouth, VA   23704

Portsmouth Catholic School
2301 Oregon Ave.
Portsmouth, VA   23701

CHESAPEAKE AREA:

Chesapeake Christian School
1401 South Battlefield Blvd.
Chesapeake, VA   23320

South Norfolk Congregational
   Christian School
1030 Jackson St.
Chesapeake, VA   23324

Faith Baptist Christian School
1629 Jolliff Rd.
Chesapeake, VA   23321

Berean Christian Academy
2705 Taylor Rd.
Chesapeake, VA   23321

Bethel Christian Schools
938 Decatur St., Box 5068
Chesapeake, VA   23325

Good News Christian Schools
3252 Taylor Rd. at Bruce Rd.
Chesapeake, VA   23321

Mount Pleasant Christian Day
   School
1613 Mount Pleasant Rd.
Chesapeake, VA   23322

Bethel Christian Schools
1212 Willow Ave.
Chesapeake, VA   23325

Welcome Baptist Christian
School
1200 Kempsville Rd.
Chesapeake, VA   23320

Believer's Baptist Christian
School
4501 Portsmouth Blvd.
Chesapeake, VA   23321

Great Hope Baptist School
P. O. Box 15106
Chesapeake, VA   23322

HAMPTON AREA:

Hampton Christian High School
609 Aberdeen Rd.
Hampton, VA   23361

Mary Atkins Christian Day
School
2424 North Armistead Ave.
Hampton, VA   23366

Memorial Christian School
317 Lee St.
Hampton, VA   23669

Central Baptist Schools
3100 Butternut Dr.
Hampton, VA   23366

Bethel Christian Schools
1647 Briarfield Rd.
Hampton, VA   23369

Emmanuel Lutheran Day School
3311 Kecoughtan Rd.
Hampton, VA   23361

Gloria Dei Lutheran School
250 Fox Hill Rd.
Hampton, VA   23369

Seventh Day Adventist School
3400 Kecoughtan Rd.
Hampton, VA   23361

SUFFOLK AREA:

Suffolk Christian Schools
629 Turlington Rd.
Suffolk, VA   23434

RICHMOND AREA:

Richmond Christian School
400 Newby's Bridge Rd.
Richmond, VA   23234

The Collegiate Schools
North Mooreland Rd.
Richmond, VA   23231

Warwick Christian School
6255 Warwick Rd.
Richmond, VA   23224

Landmark Christian School
Creighton Rd., Box 62-A
Richmond, VA   23223

Fellowship Christian School
7101 South Laburnum Ave.
Richmond, VA   23231

Cumberland Christian Day
School
Cumberland St.
Richmond, VA   23220

Open Door Christian School
5327 Orcutt Ln.
Richmond, VA   23224

Grove Avenue Baptist School
8701 Ridge Rd.
Richmond, VA   23229

Hatcher Christian School
2320 Dumbarton Rd.
Richmond, VA   23228

Liberty Christian Schools
Box 502
Mechanicsville, VA   23111

Meadowood Christian School
Church of God
325 Azalea Ave.
Richmond, VA   23227

Luther Memorial School
1301 Robinhood Rd.
Richmond, VA   23227

Richmond Jr. Academy
Seventh Day Adventist
3809 Patterson Ave.
Richmond, VA   23221

Ephesus Jr. Academy
Seventh Day Adventist
37th St. & Midlothian
Richmond, VA   23224

Trinity Episcopal High School
Pittaway Rd.
Richmond, VA   23235

Saint Margaret's School
Water Ln.
Tappahannock, VA   22560

Saint Christopher's School
711 Saint Christopher's Rd.
Richmond, VA   23226

Saint Andrew's Parochial Day
School
227 South Cherry St.
Richmond, VA   23220

PETERSBURG AREA:

Graceland Christian School
233 South Adams St.
Petersburg, VA   23803

Faith Christian School
1226 West Roslyn Rd.
Colonial Heights, VA   23834

Broadway Christian School
15th Ave. & Broadway
Hopewell, VA   23860

West End Christian School
1600 Atlantic St.
Hopewell, VA   23860

Grace Christian School
1010 South Main St.
Blackstone, VA   23824

Saint James School
107 North 6th Ave.
Hopewell, VA   23860

LYNCHBURG AREA:

Lynchburg Christian Academy
701 Thomas Rd., Box 1111
Lynchburg, VA   24505

Timberlake Christian School
300 Horizon Dr.
Lynchburg, VA 24502

Temple Christian School
Box 40
Madison Heights, VA 24572

Gospel Fellowship Chapel
  Schools
Seminole Dr.
Madison Heights, VA 24572

Longwood Avenue Christian
  School
P.O. Box 608
Bedford, VA 24523

Hargrave Baptist Military
  Academy
Military Dr.
Chatham, VA 24531

Virginia Episcopal School
Virginia Episcopal School Rd.
Lynchburg, VA 24503

Holy Cross Catholic High
  School
2125 Langhorne Rd.
Lynchburg, VA 24501

ARLINGTON AREA:

Virginia Christian Academy
3020 Davis Ford Rd.
Woodbridge, VA 22191

Cherrydale Christian School
2321 North Military Rd.
Arlington, VA 22207

Trinity Temple Academy
13403 Boxter St.
Woodbridge, VA 22191

Evangel Christian School
14836 Ashdale Ave.
Dale City, VA 22193

Calvary Temple School
Sterling, VA 22170

Vienna Jr. Academy
340 Court House Rd., S.W.
Vienna, VA 22180

Our Savior Lutheran School
9th & South Taylor Sts.
Arlington, VA 22204

Bishop Denis J. O'Connell
  Catholic High School
6600 Little Falls Rd.
Arlington, VA 22213

Cathedral of Saint Thomas
  More Catholic School
101 North Thomas St.
Arlington, VA 22203

FAIRFAX AREA:

Fairfax Christian School
11121 Popes Head Rd.
Fairfax, VA 22030

Commonwealth Christian
  School
8822 Little River Turnpike
Fairfax, VA 22031

Fairfax Baptist Temple
  Academy
9524 Braddock Rd.
Fairfax, VA 22032

Way of Faith Christian Academy
8800 Arlington Blvd.
Fairfax, VA 22031

Leesburg Christian School
212 South King St.
Leesburg, VA 22075

Bethlehem Baptist Christian
  Academy
4501 West Ox Rd.
Fairfax, VA 22030

Immanuel Christian School
7210 Braddock Rd.
Annandale, VA 22003

Grace Baptist School
3149 Annandale Rd.
Falls Church, VA 22042

Manassas Christian School
8757 Signal Hill Rd.
Manassas, VA 22110

Fresta Valley Christian School
Beckham St.
Warrenton, VA 22186

Westminster School
3819 Gallows Rd.
Annandale, VA 22003

Grace Lutheran School
3233 Annandale Rd.
Falls Church, VA 22042

Saint Michael's Catholic School
Ravensworth Rd. & Michael's
  Ln.
Annandale, VA 22003

Saint Leo's Catholic School
3704 Old Lee Hwy.
Fairfax, VA 22030

Saint Philip's School
7506 Saint Philip's Ct.
Falls Church, VA 22042

CHARLOTTESVILLE AREA:

Heritage Christian School
1225 Park St.
Charlottesville, VA 22901

Piedmont Christian School
Box 51
Bumpass, VA 23024

Fork Union Baptist
  Military Academy
Fork Union, VA 23055

Blue Ridge Episcopal School
Dyke, VA 22935

Christchurch Episcopal School
Christchurch, VA 23031

ROANOKE AREA:

Roanoke Valley Christian
  Schools
6520 Williamson Rd., N.W.
Roanoke, VA 24019

Berean Baptist Christian
  Academy
447 Dalewood Ave.
Salem, VA 24153

Gospel Christian Academy
Route 3, Box 187A
Salem, VA 24153

Grace Academy
2731 Edgewood St., S.W.
Roanoke, VA 24015

Heritage School, Inc.
127 McClanghan St., S.W.
Roanoke, VA 24014

Roanoke Catholic High School
620 North Jefferson St.
Roanoke, VA 24016

DANVILLE AREA:

Danville Christian Schools
Highway 58 E.
P.O. Box 3427
Danville, VA 24543

Seventh Day Adventist School
212 Ingram Rd.
Danville, VA 24541

Sacred Heart Catholic School
708 Randolph St.
Danville, VA 24541

MARTINSVILLE AREA:

Martinsville Christian School
1425 Spruce St.
Martinsville, VA 24112

Stanleytown Christian Academy
Route 57 W.
Stanleytown, VA 24168

RADFORD AREA:

New River Christian Schools
Route 11 W.
Radford, VA 24141

Gateway Christian Academy
Luster's Gate
Blacksburg, VA 24060

Christiansburg Christian
 Academy
1125 Roanoke St.
Christiansburg, VA 24073

Granite Christian Academy
Route 2, Box 412
Wytheville, VA 24382

HARRISONBURG AREA:

United Christian Academy
P.O. Box 486
Stanardsville, VA 22973

Eastern Mennonite High School
Harrisonburg, VA 22801

Trinity Christian School
Highway 257
Bridgewater, VA 22812

Rockingham Christian School
P.O. Box 606
Harrisonburg, VA 22801

Berea Christian School
Route 3, P.O. Box 117
Dayton, VA 22821

WINCHESTER AREA:

Randolph Macon Academy
 United Methodist
Front Royal, VA 22630

Massanutten Military Academy
 United Church of Christ
Woodstock, VA 22664

ABINGDON AREA:

Southwest Virginia Christian
 Academy
Highway 11, P.O. Box 778
Glade Spring, VA 24340

Wise County Christian School,
 Inc.
Highway 23
Norton, VA 24273

Oak Hill Baptist Academy
Mouth of Wilson, VA 24363

Christian Mountain Mission
 School
Box 649
Grundy, VA 24614

BRISTOL AREA:

Gateway Baptist School
1864 Holston Dr.
(Virginia-Tennessee)
Bristol, VA 24201

Saint Anne's Episcopal School
Euclid Ave.
(Virginia-Tennessee)
Bristol, VA 24201

NORTON AREA:

Wise County Christian School
Route 1, P.O. Box 561
Norton, VA 24273

SUFFOLK AREA:

Suffolk Christian School
P.O. Box 217
Suffolk, VA 23434

WASHINGTON

SEATTLE AREA:

Seattle Christian School
19639 28th Ave., S.
Seattle, WA 98188

King's Garden High School
19303 Fremont Ave., N.
Seattle, WA 98133

Northgate Christian School
12345 8th St., N.E.
Seattle, WA 98125

Watson Groen Christian School
2400 N.E. 147th St.
Seattle, WA 98155

Echo Lake Christian School
1602 North 192nd St.
Seattle, WA 98133

Landgren Christian Academy
34424 First St.
Federal Way, WA 98003

Christian Education Center
3817 S.W. Oregon St.
Seattle, WA 98126

Green Lake Christian School
2004 North 75th St.
Seattle, WA 98103

Queen Anne Christian School
1716 Second Ave., N.
Seattle, WA 98109

Ranier Valley Christian School
7930 Ranier South Ave.
Seattle, WA 98118

West Seattle Christian School
4401 42nd Ave., S.W.
Seattle, WA 98116

Bellevue Christian High School
1601 98th St., N.E.
Bellevue, WA 98004

Carden Christian Academy
2029 132nd St., S.E.
Bellevue, WA 98004

Cascade Christian School
2315 173rd St., N.E.
Redmond, WA 98052

Renton Christian School
221 Hardie St., N.W.
Renton, WA 98055

Lake Boren Christian Center
 High School
12636 S.E. 89th Pl.
Renton, WA 98055

Auburn Valley Christian School
1312 2nd St., S.E.
Auburn, WA 98002

Maple Valley Christian School
16700 174th Ave., S.E.
Renton, WA 98055

Church Alive Christian School
 Assembly of God
4830 148th St., S.W.
Edmonds, WA 98020

Mountlake Christian Schools
23607 54th Ave., W.
Mountlake Terrace, WA 98043

The King's Temple Christian
 School
21705 58th St., W.
Mountlake Terrace, WA 98043

Liberty Christian School
1000 172nd St., S.W.
Lynnwood, WA 98036

Y.M.C.A. Technical Schools
909 Fourth Ave.
Seattle, WA 98104

Seattle Regular Baptist Schools
14660 18th Ave., S.W.
P.O. Box 66430
Seattle, WA 98166

Smith Bible Academy
1430 26th Ave.
Seattle, WA 98122

Saint James School
 Christian, Nondenominational
24447 94th Ave., S.
Kent, WA 98031

Kent View Christian School
930 East James St.
Kent, WA 98031

Landgren Christian Academy
25030 Military Rd., S.
Kent, WA 98031

Lutheran Bible Institute of
 Seattle
4221 228th St., S.E.
Seattle, WA 98188

Lutheran Bible Institute of
 Seattle
Providence Heights
Issaquah, WA 98027

Auburn Adventist Academy
5000 Auburn Way, S.
Auburn, WA 98002

Cypress Adventist School
21500 Cypress St.
Lynnwood, WA 98036

Lutheran High School of Seattle
4141 41st Ave., S.W.
Seattle, WA 98116

Amazing Grace Lutheran School
10056 Renton South Ave.
Seattle, WA 98178

Concordia Lutheran School
7040 36th St., N.E.
Seattle, WA 98105

Grace Lutheran School
2000 N.E. Perkins Way
Seattle, WA 98155

Hope Lutheran School
4446 42nd St., S.W.
Seattle, WA 98116

Calvary Lutheran School
439 164th St., N.E.
Bellevue, WA 98004

Pilgrim Lutheran School
1030 104th St.
Bellevue, WA 98004

Salem Lutheran School
9906 232nd St., S.W.
Edmonds, WA 98020

Holy Trinity Lutheran School
2009 South 260th St.
Kent, WA 98031

Saint Luke School
17533 Saint Luke Pl., N.
Seattle, WA 98133

Epiphany School
3710 East Howell St.
Seattle, WA 98122

Holy Names Catholic Academy
728 21st Ave., E.
Seattle, WA 98102

Immaculate Catholic High School
803 Terry Ave.
Seattle, WA 98104

Eastside Catholic High School
225 102nd St.
Bellevue, WA 98004

Saint Thomas Day School
84th St., N.E. & 12th
Medina, WA 98039

Saint Anthony Catholic School
4068 4th St.
Renton, WA   98055

Saint Pius X Catholic School
22105 57th St., W.
Mountlake Terrace, WA   98043

SPOKANE AREA:

Northwest Christian School
West 1412 Central St.
Spokane, WA   99208

Inland Empire School of the
  Bible
East 618 Baldwin Ave.
Spokane, WA   99207

Valley Christian School
South 2303 Bowdish Rd.
Spokane, WA   99206

Marshall Christian School
P.O. Box 60
Marshall, WA   99020

Spokane Jr. Academy
  Seventh Day Adventist
West 1505 Cleveland Ave.
Spokane, WA   99205

Spokane Valley School
  Seventh Day Adventist
North Pines Rd. & East
  Mission
Spokane, WA   99206

Spokane Lutheran School
West 4001 Fremont Rd.
Spokane, WA   99204

Saint Matthew's Lutheran
  School
North 6917 Country Homes
  Blvd.
Spokane, WA   99208

Gethsemane Lutheran School
East 11315 Broadway Ave.
Spokane, WA   99206

Saint George's Episcopal
  School
West 2929 Waikiki Rd.
Spokane, WA   99218

Gonzaga Catholic Preparatory
  School
East 1224 Euclid Ave.
Spokane, WA   99207

Saint John Bosco Catholic
  School
East 503 Liberty Ave.
Spokane, WA   99207

South Side Catholic Schools
East 1428 33rd Ave.
Spokane, WA   99203

WALLA WALLA AREA:

Liberty Christian School
P.O. Box 174
Walla Walla, WA   99362

Walla Walla Valley Academy
  Seventh Day Adventist
P.O. Box 457
College Place, WA   99324

DeSales Catholic Jr. & Sr.
  High School
919 East Sumach St.
Walla Walla, WA   99362

TACOMA AREA:

Tacoma Baptist High School
2052 South 64th St.
Tacoma, WA   98409

Parkland Christian Academy
620 134th St., S.
Tacoma, WA   98444

Heritage Christian School
  Bible Presbyterian
5412 67th St., W.
Tacoma, WA   98467

Genesis School of the Bible
226 166th St.
Spanaway, WA   98387

Life Christian School
1717 South Puget Sound
Tacoma, WA   98405

Peninsula Christian School
8601 Goodman Dr., N.W.
Gig Harbor, WA   98335

Palisades Baptist Academy
5015 S.W. Dash Point Rd.
Tacoma, WA   98422

Clover Creek Baptist School
3509 Military Rd., E.
Tacoma, WA   98446

Emmanuel Holiness Academy
714 East 50th St.
Tacoma, WA   98404

Tacoma Adventist School
1125 South 34th St.
Tacoma, WA   98408

Central Lutheran Christian Day
  School
409 Tacoma Ave., N.
Tacoma, WA   98403

Evergreen Lutheran High
  School
Barksdale & Steilacoom Rd.
Dupont, WA   98327

Concordia Lutheran School
202 East 56th St.
Tacoma, WA   98404

Parkland Lutheran School
South 123rd & Pacific Ave.
Tacoma, WA   98444

Lakewood Lutheran School
10202 112th Ave., S.W.
Tacoma, WA   98498

Good Shepherd Lutheran School
East 56th & East B Sts.
Tacoma, WA   98404

Faith Lutheran School
96th St. & A St.
Tacoma, WA   98444

Charles Wright Episcopal
  Academy
7723 Chambers Creek Rd.
Tacoma, WA   98467

Bellarmine Catholic High School
2300 South Washington St.
Tacoma, WA   98405

Marymount Catholic Military
  Academy
423 East 152nd St.
Tacoma, WA 98445

EVERETT AREA:

Everett Christian School
2221 Cedar St.
Everett, WA 98201

Silver Lake Christian School
2027 132nd St., S.E.
Everett, WA 98204

Arlington Christian School
724 East Highland Dr.
Arlington, WA 98223

Monroe Christian School
1009 West Main St.
Monroe, WA 98272

Oak Harbor Christian School
7171 700 West
Oak Harbor, WA 98277

Grace Baptist Academy
8521 67th Ave., N.E.
Marysville, WA 98270

Zion Lutheran Christian School
3923 103rd Ave., S.E.
Everett, WA 98205

Sky Valley School
  Seventh Day Adventist
200 Academy Way
Monroe, WA 98277

Seventh Day Adventist School
9610 48th Dr., N.E.
Marysville, WA 98270

Saint Mary Magdalen Catholic
  School
8615 7th Ave.
Everett, WA 98204

Immaculate Conception
  Catholic School
2508 Hoyt St.
Everett, WA 98201

VANCOUVER AREA:

Clark County Christian School
7915 N.E. Burton Rd.
Vancouver, WA 98662

Longview Christian Academy
2610 Ocean Beach Hwy.
Longview, WA 98632

Columbia Heights Christian
  Academy
3609 Columbia Heights Rd.
Longview, WA 98632

Columbia Ridge Baptist
  Academy
9914 S.E. 6th St.
Vancouver, WA 98664

Faith Temple School
2203 38th St.
Longview, WA 98632

Fir Grove School
  Seventh Day Adventist
2920 Falk Ave.
Vancouver, WA 98661

Seventh Day Adventist School
96 Garden St.
Kelso, WA 98626

Saint Joseph Catholic School
6500 Highland Dr.
Vancouver, WA 98661

Saint Rose Catholic School
2571 Nichols Blvd.
Longview, WA 98632

OLYMPIA AREA:

Evergreen Christian School
1000 Black Lake Blvd.
Olympia, WA 98502

Christian Life School
4205 Lacey Rd.
Lacey, WA 98503

Good Shepherd Christian Day
  School
1601 North St.
Olympia, WA 98501

Olympia Jr. Academy
  Seventh Day Adventist
1416 26th Ave., N.E.
Olympia, WA 98506

Saint Placid Catholic High
  School
4600 Martin Way
Olympia, WA 98506

MOUNTLAKE TERRACE AREA:

Heritage Christian School
12617 N.E. Hollyhills Dr.
Bothell, WA 98011

YAKIMA AREA:

Yakima Christian School
301 South 7th Ave.
Yakima, WA 98902

Central Christian Academy
701 South 3rd Ave.
Yakima, WA 98902

West Side Christian School
3414 Tieton Dr.
Yakima, WA 98902

Neighborhood Christian School
2805 Englewood Ave.
Yakima, WA 98902

Grace Evangelical Lutheran
  Christian Day School
1207 South 7th Ave.
Yakima, WA 98902

Yakima Jr. Academy
  Seventh Day Adventist
1206 Fruitvale Blvd.
Yakima, WA 98902

Saint Paul's School
1214 West Chestnut Ave.
Yakima, WA 98902

Saint Joseph's School
212 North 4th St.
Yakima, WA 98901

RICHLAND AREA:

Richland Christian Academy
2505 Duportall St.
Richland, WA 99352

West Side Church School
615 Wright Ave.
Richland, WA 99352

Tri-City Jr. Academy
  Seventh Day Adventist
4115 West Henry St.
Pasco, WA 99301

Bethlehem Lutheran School
1409 South Garfield St.
Kennewick, WA 99336

Christ the King Catholic
  School
1122 Long Ave.
Richland, WA 99352

Saint Patrick's Catholic
  School
West Park St. & North 14th
Pasco, WA 99301

WENATCHEE AREA:

Wenatchee Christian Academy
605 First St.
Wenatchee, WA 98801

Wenatchee Valley Christian
  School
1901 Rock Island Rd.
East Wenatchee, WA 98801

Bethesda Christian High
  School
301 North Chelan St.
Wenatchee, WA 98801

Upper Valley Christian
  School
111 Ski Hill Dr.
Leavenworth, WA 98826

ABERDEEN AREA:

Gray's Harbor Christian
  School
111 East Third St.
Aberdeen, WA 98520

Faith Christian School
1800 Coolidge Rd.
Aberdeen, WA 98520

Rhema Christian School
601 Karr St.
Hoquiam, WA 98550

Seventh Day Adventist School
3101 Cherry St.
Hoquiam, WA 98550

Saint Mary's Catholic School
518 North H St.
Aberdeen, WA 98520

BREMERTON AREA:

Bremerton Christian Academy
1904 8th St.
Bremerton, WA 98310

Bremerton Christian Schools
3670 Chico Way, N.W.
Bremerton, WA 98310

Forks Christian Academy
Mansfield Addition
Forks, WA 98331

Sequim Adventist School
Route 5, P.O. Box 350
Sequim, WA 98382

PULLMAN AREA:

Pullman Christian School
N.W. 115 State St.
Pullman, WA 99163

MOSES LAKE AREA:

Moses Lake Christian School
Craig & Larsen St.
Moses Lake, WA 98837

Light & Life Christian School
  Free Methodist
935 West Valley Rd.
Moses Lake, WA 98837

Adventist School
1023 North Stratford Rd.
Moses Lake, WA 98837

Saint Rose of Lima Catholic
  School
Ephrata, WA 98823

SUNNYSIDE AREA:

Sunnyside Christian School
811 North Ave.
Sunnyside, WA 98944

BELLINGHAM AREA:

Bellingham Christian School
1600 East Sunset Dr.
Bellingham, WA 98225

Assumption Catholic School
2116 Cornwall Ave.
Bellingham, WA 98225

Seventh Day Adventist School
910 North Forest St.
Bellingham, WA 98225

Langley Christian Schools
c/o H. Navis
P.O. Box 382
Lynden, WA 98264

Lynden Christian High School
515 Drayton St.
Lynden, WA 98264

Ebenezer Christian School
9390 Guide Meridian Rd.
Lynden, WA 98264

Covenant Christian School
9088 Northwood Rd.
Lynden, WA 98264

Lynden Christian Elementary
  School
408 First St.
Lynden, WA 98264

MOUNT VERNON AREA:

Mount Vernon Christian School
820 Blackburn Rd.
Mount Vernon, WA 98273

Arlington Christian School
724 East Highland Dr.
P.O. Box 125
Arlington, WA 98223

ROCHESTER AREA:

Faith Christian Academy
P.O. Box 501
Rochester, WA   98572

WEST VIRGINIA

CHARLESTON AREA:

Kanawha Christian Academy
529 Mary St.
Charleston, WV   25302

Elk Valley Christian School
P.O. Box 187
Elkview, WV   25071

Cross Lanes Christian School
5442 Big Tyler Rd.
Charleston, WV   25312

Fairhaven Christian School
689 Fairhaven Dr.
Charleston, WV   25306

Christian Academy
Box 418
Boomer, WV   25031

Charlestown Christian Academy
P.O. Box 4162
Charleston, WV   25304

Charleston Catholic High
  School
Virginia & Broad Sts.
Charleston, WV   25301

Saint Anthony Catholic School
1027 Sixth Ave.
Charleston, WV   25312

HUNTINGTON AREA:

Huntington Christian Academy
615 West 10th St.
Huntington, WV   25704

Mountain State Christian School
Martin's Ln.
Huntington, WV

Grace Christian School
1159 Adams Ave.
Huntington, WV   25704

Mountain State Bible School
P.O. Box 268
Culloden, WV   25510

Fellowship Christian School
P.O. Box 5627
Huntington, WV   25703

Saint Joseph's Catholic High
  School
600 13th St.
Huntington, WV   25701

WHEELING AREA:

Linsly Military Institute
  Christian, Nondenominational
Wheeling, WV   26003

Wheeling Country Day School
8 Park Rd.
Wheeling, WV   26003

Moundsville Christian School
4th St. & Annadale Ave.
Moundsville, WV   26041

Pipestem Christian School
Pipestem, WV   25975

Central Catholic High School
14th & East Off St.
Wheeling, WV   26003

Saint John's Central High
  School
37th & Guernsey Sts.
Wheeling, WV   26003

Bishop Donahue Memorial
  Catholic High School
325 Logan St.
McMechen, WV   26040

Cathedral Grade School
14th & Byron Sts.
Wheeling, WV   26003

Blessed Trinity Catholic
  School
111 North York St.
Wheeling, WV   26003

Saints James & John Catholic
  School
52 7th St.
Benwood, WV   26031

PARKERSBURG AREA:

Briscoe Run Academy
Route 1, P.O. Box 44
Parkersburg, WV   26101

Weirton Christian Academy
148 Main St.
Weirton, WV   26062

Williamstown Christian School
111 9th St.
Williamstown, WV   26187

Heritage Christian School
P.O. Box 445
Ravenswood, WV   26164

De Sales Heights Catholic
  Academy
3201 Fairview Ave.
Parkersburg, WV   26101

Saint Joseph Catholic School
Route 1, P.O. Box 199
Proctor, WV   26055

ELKINS AREA:

Randolph-Elkins Christian
  Academy
Ervin Ln.
Elkins, WV   26241

Don Bosco Catholic Agricultural
  School
Huttonsville, WV   26273

BUCKHANNON AREA:

Christian School
P.O. Box 596
Buckhannon, WV   26201

MORGANTOWN AREA:

Saint Francis Central Catholic
  School
375 Birch St.
Morgantown, WV   26505

FAIRMONT AREA:

Calvary Christian School
Route 3, P.O. Box 342-B2
Fairmont, WV   26554

Fairmont Catholic School
409 Jackson St.
Fairmont, WV 26554

Saints Peter & Paul
 Catholic School
Monongah, WV 26554

KEYSER AREA:

Keyser Christian School
1 North Main St.
Keyser, WV 26726

North Fork Christian School
Cabins, WV 26855

Christian Academy
Route 1
Summersville, WV 26651

Truth & Liberty School
2765 2nd St.
Hurricane, WV 25526

Saint Frances Catholic School
251 West Piedmont St.
Keyser, WV 26726

BECKLEY AREA:

Greater Beckley Christian
 Schools
P.O. Box 320
Prosperity, WV 25909

Appalachian Bible Institute
Bradley, WV 25818

Sophia Christian School
Sophia, WV 25921

Saint Francis de Sales
 Catholic School
614 South Oakwood Ave.
Beckley, WV 25801

CLARKSBURG AREA:

Emmanuel Christian School
1318 North 16th St.
Clarksburg, WV 26301

Notre Dame Catholic High
 School
127 East Pike St.
Clarksburg, WV 26301

Saint Mary's Catholic School
107 East Pike St.
Clarksburg, WV 26301

BLUEFIELD AREA:

Midway Christian Day School
417 Old Bramwell Rd.
Bluefield, WV 24701

Child Development Center,
 Inc.
301 Mahood St.
Princeton, WV 24740

Valley View Adventist School
Green Valley Rd.
Bluefield, WV 24701

MARTINSBURG AREA:

Martinsburg Christian
 Academy
U.S. Route 11
P.O. Box 1356
Martinsburg, WV 25401

Tri-State Christian School
P.O. Box 657
Charles Town, WV 25414

Rocky Noll School
 Seventh Day Adventist
Arden Rd.
Martinsburg, WV 25401

Saint Joseph's Catholic School
219 South Queen St.
Martinsburg, WV 25401

WHITE SULPHUR SPRINGS
AREA:

Greenbrier Valley Baptist
 School
Route 92 North
White Sulphur Springs, WV
24986

Mountain State Christian
 Schools
Route 2
Alderson, WV 24910

Ballard Christian School
Ballard, WV 24918

LOGAN AREA:

Triadelphia Christian Academy
Kistler, WV 25628

Beth Haven Christian School
Chauncey, WV 25612

West Virginia Training School
Point Pleasant Mission
2300 Lincoln Ave.
Point Pleasant, WV 25550

Sacred Heart Catholic School
126 West 4th Ave.
Williamson, WV 25661

WISCONSIN

MILWAUKEE AREA:

Milwaukee Christian Academy
1212 South 12th St.
Milwaukee, WI 53204

Milwaukee Christian School
14155 West Burleigh Rd.
Brookfield, WI 53005

Central Christian Schools
2600 South Sunny Slope Rd.
Milwaukee, WI

Heritage Christian Academy
8225 North 107th St.
Milwaukee, WI 53224

Christian Liberty Academy
3675 North Calhoun Rd.
Brookfield, WI 53005

Greendale Baptist Academy
5650 South 51st St.
Milwaukee, WI 53220

Pilgrim Baptist Christian
School
8731 West Burleigh Rd.
Milwaukee, WI 53222

Bethel Christian Academy
7711 West Luscher Ave.
Milwaukee, WI 53218

Christ the Lord Evangelical
Lutheran School
1650 North Brookfield Rd.
Brookfield, WI 53005

Saint John's Evangelical
Lutheran School
4001 South 68th St.
Milwaukee, WI 53220

Good Shepherd's Evangelical
Lutheran School
1337 South 100th St.
Milwaukee, WI 53214

North Trinity Evangelical
Lutheran School
6090 North 35th St.
Milwaukee, WI 53209

Saint Matthew's Evangelical
Lutheran School
8444 West Melvin St.
Milwaukee, WI 53222

Saint Philip's Evangelical
Lutheran School
2976 North First St.
Milwaukee, WI 53212

Fairview Evangelical Lutheran
School
137 North 66th St.
Milwaukee, WI 53213

Mount Lebanon Evangelical
Lutheran School
6000 West Hampton Ave.
Milwaukee, WI 53218

Pilgrim Evangelical Lutheran
School
6817 West Center St.
Milwaukee, WI 53210

Woodlawn Evangelical
Lutheran School
2217 South 99th St.
Milwaukee, WI 53227

Wisconsin Lutheran High
School
330 Glenview Ave.
Milwaukee, WI 53213

Milwaukee Lutheran High
School
9700 West Grantosa Dr.
Milwaukee, WI 53222

Christ Lutheran School
2229 West Greenfield Ave.
Milwaukee, WI 53204

Christ Memorial Lutheran
School
5719 North Teutonia Ave.
Milwaukee, WI 53209

Our Redeemer Lutheran
School
10025 West North Ave.
Milwaukee, WI 53226

Redemption Lutheran School
5641 North 68th St.
Milwaukee, WI 53218

Immanuel Lutheran School
4780 North 135th St.
Milwaukee, WI

Saint Paul's Lutheran School
3766 East Cudahy Ave.
Milwaukee, WI 53207

Saint Paul's Lutheran School
7823 West Grant St.
Milwaukee, WI 53219

Saint Paul Lutheran School
7821 West Lincoln Ave.
Milwaukee, WI 53219

Northwest Lutheran School
4119 North 81st St.
Milwaukee, WI 53222

Walther Memorial Lutheran
School
4040 West Fond du Lac Ave.
Milwaukee, WI 53216

Emmaus Lutheran School
2818 North 23rd St.
Milwaukee, WI 53213

Bethany Lutheran School
2004 North 33rd St.
Milwaukee, WI 53208

Bethlehem Lutheran School
2466 West McKinley Ave.
Milwaukee, WI 53208

Centennial Lutheran School
3558 South 24th St.
Milwaukee, WI 53221

Ebenezer Lutheran School
1127 South 35th St.
Milwaukee, WI 53215

Garden Homes Lutheran
School
2475 West Roosevelt Dr.
Milwaukee, WI 53209

Mount Olive Lutheran School
5301 West Washington Blvd.
Milwaukee, WI 53208

Hales Corners Lutheran School
5409 South 111th St.
Milwaukee, WI 53228

Milwaukee Seventh Day
Adventist School
10900 West Mill Rd.
Milwaukee, WI 53225

Sharon School
Seventh Day Adventist
1353 West Meinecke Ave.
Milwaukee, WI 53206

Divine Savior - Holy Angels
Catholic High School
4257 North 100th St.
Milwaukee, WI 53222

Dominican Catholic High
School
120 East Silver Spring Dr.
Milwaukee, WI 53217

RACINE AREA:

Racine Christian Academy
1250 Lathrop Ave.
Racine, WI 53405

Racine Christian School
912 Virginia St.
Racine, WI 53405

Union Grove Christian School
P.O. Box 103
Union Grove, WI 53182

Racine Apostolic Christian
School
P.O. Box 855
Racine, WI 64858

Racine Baptist School
4835 Taylor Ave.
Racine, WI 53403

Holy Trinity Community
School
2015 Franklin St.
Racine, WI 53403

Lutheran High School
251 Luedtke Ave.
Racine, WI 53405

Concordia Lutheran School
3350 Lathrop Ave.
Racine, WI 53405

Prince of Peace Lutheran
School
4340 Six Mile Rd.
Racine, WI 53402

Saint John's Lutheran School
510 Kewaunee St.
Racine, WI 53402

Trinity Lutheran School
2065 Geneva St.
Racine, WI 53402

Saint Catherine's Catholic
High School
1200 Park Ave.
Racine, WI 53403

MADISON AREA:

East Side Evangelical
Lutheran School
2310 Independence Ln.
Madison, WI 53704

Holy Cross Lutheran School
2670 Milwaukee St.
Madison, WI 53704

Christian Day School
Route Box 446
Muscoda, WI 53573

New Glarus Christian School
207 6th St.
Box 101
New Glarus, WI 53574

Seventh Day Adventist High
School
3801 Dutch Mill Rd.
Madison, WI 53716

Edgewood Sr. Catholic High
School
2219 Monroe St.
Madison, WI 53711

GREEN BAY AREA:

Bay City Baptist School
1840 Bond St.
Green Bay, WI 54303

First Evangelical Lutheran
School
743 South Monroe Ave.
Green Bay, WI 54301

Northeastern Wisconsin
Lutheran High School
1731 Saint Agnes Dr.
Green Bay, WI 54304

Redeemer Lutheran School
205 Hudson St.
Green Bay, WI 54303

Saint Paul Lutheran School
512 South Clay St.
Green Bay, WI 54301

Beth Haven Academy
901 Shawano Ave.
Green Bay, WI 54303

Seventh Day Adventist School
1422 Shawano Ave.
Green Bay, WI 54303

Catholic Central Grade School
139 South Monroe Ave.
Green Bay, WI 54301

WAUKESHA AREA:

Waukesha Christian Academy
Merril Hills Rd.
Waukesha, WI 53186

Calvary Christian School
9122 Racine Ave.
Sturtevant, WI 53177

Sonshine Christian
School
W224 N3297 Duplainville Rd.
Pewaukee, WI 53072

Friedens Evangelical Lutheran
School
5038 19th Ave.
Kenosha, WI 53140

Concordia Lutheran School
8500 Racine Ave.
Sturtevant, WI 53177

Eisonhouwer Middle School
4333 South Sunny Slope Rd.
New Berlin, WI 53151

Trinity Lutheran School
7937 Nicholson Rd.
Caledonia, WI 53108

Bethany Lutheran School
2110 75th St.
Kenosha, WI 53140

Saint Luke's Lutheran School
6712 30th Ave.
Kenosha, WI 53142

Trinity Lutheran School
1060 White Rock Ave.
Waukesha, WI 53186

Mount Calvary Lutheran School
1941 Madison St.
Waukesha, WI 53186

Kemper Hall Episcopal School
Third Ave.
Kenosha, WI 53140

Saint Joseph's Catholic High
  School
2401 69th St.
Kenosha, WI 53140

Catholic Memorial High
  School
601 East College Ave.
Waukesha, WI 53186

Holy Rosary Catholic School
4400 22nd Ave.
Kenosha, WI 53140

Saint Bonaventure Catholic
  High School
2017 Wisconsin St.
Sturtevant, WI 53177

WISCONSIN RAPIDS AREA:

Rapids Christian School
  Evangelical Free Church
611 Cook Ave.
Wisconsin Rapids, WI 54494

Saint Paul's Evangelical
  Lutheran School
311 14th Ave., S.
Wisconsin Rapids, WI 54494

Immanuel Lutheran School
111 11th St., N.
Wisconsin Rapids, WI 54494

Saint Peter's Lutheran School
1461 Grand Ave.
Schofield, WI 54476

Assumption Catholic High
  School
445 Chestnut St.
Wisconsin Rapids, WI 54494

Saints Peter & Paul Catholic
  School
1140 Second St., N.
Wisconsin Rapids, WI 54494

RANDOLF AREA:

Randolf Christian School
457 Second St.
Randolf, WI 53956

OSHKOSH AREA:

Bethel Baptist School
1331 High Ave.
Oshkosh, WI 54901

Trinity Evangelical Lutheran
  School
819 School Ln.
Oshkosh, WI 54901

Saint Peter Evangelical
  Lutheran School
6601 North French St.
Appleton, WI 54911

Mount Olive Evangelical
  Lutheran School
930 East Florida St.
Appleton, WI 54911

Bethlehem Evangelical
  Lutheran School
126 North Pine St.
Hortonville, WI 54944

Fox Valley Lutheran Sr.
  High School
2626 North Oneida St.
Appleton, WI 54911

Bethel Lutheran School
829 Appleton Rd.
Menasha, WI 54952

Grace Lutheran School
776 Birch St.
Neenah, WI 54956

Grace Lutheran School
919 Nebraska St.
Oshkosh, WI 54901

Luther Memorial Lutheran
  School
134 East 21st St.
Fond du Lac, WI 54935

Redeemer Lutheran School
606 Forest Ave.
Fond du Lac, WI 54935

Saint Peter's Lutheran School
35 East 2nd St.
Fond du Lac, WI 54935

Winnebago Lutheran
  Academy
475 Merrill Ave.
Fond du Lac, WI 54935

Faith Lutheran School
400 East Johnson St.
Fond du Lac, WI 54935

Martin Luther Lutheran
  School
436 South Lake St.
Neenah, WI 54956

Saint Paul Lutheran School
225 East Harris St.
Appleton, WI 54911

Trinity Lutheran School
10 Oak St.
Neenah, WI 54956

Trinity Lutheran School
300 Broad St.
Menasha, WI 54952

Riverview Lutheran School
136 West Seymour St.
Appleton, WI 54911

Seventh Day Adventist
  School
350 West Capitol St.
Appleton, WI 54911

Xavier Catholic High
  School
1600 West Prospect
Appleton, WI 54911

Catholic Central School
313 South State St.
Appleton, WI 54911

Saint Mary's Spring Catholic
High School
Route 4
Fond du Lac, WI 54935

Saint Joseph's Catholic School
95 East 2nd St.
Fond du Lac, WI 54935

Saints Peter & Paul Catholic
School
107 North Oak St.
Hortonville, WI 54944

Lourdes Catholic Academy
110 North Sawyer St.
Oshkosh, WI 54901

SUPERIOR AREA:

Twin Ports Baptist Academy
1831 East 4th St.
Superior, WI 54880

Cathedral School
1419 Baxter Ave.
Superior, WI 54880

Saint Francis Xavier Catholic
School
2411 East 4th St.
Superior, WI 54880

LA CROSSE AREA:

Faith Christian School
3615 South 28th St.
La Crosse, WI 54601

First Evangelical Lutheran
School
520 West Ave., S.
La Crosse, WI 54601

Luther High School
Wilson St.
Onalaska, WI 54650

Immanuel Lutheran School
Saint Paul & Avon Sts.
La Crosse, WI 54601

Mount Calvary Lutheran
School
1614 Park Ave.
La Crosse, WI 54601

Saint John's Lutheran
School
Route 1
La Crosse, WI 54601

Saint Paul's Lutheran School
1201 Main St.
Onalaska, WI 54650

Aquinas Catholic High
School
315 South 11th St.
La Crosse, WI 54601

Cathedral of Saint Joseph
the Workman School
1319 Ferry St.
La Crosse, WI 54601

Saint Pius X Catholic
School
3710 East Ave., S.
La Crosse, WI 54601

SHEBOYGAN AREA:

Sheboygan County Christian
High School
929 Greenfield Ave.
Sheboygan, WI 53081

Sheboygan Christian School
418 Geele Ave.
Sheboygan, WI 53081

Sheboygan Christian Academy
1552 South 9th St.
Sheboygan, WI 53081

Oostburg Christian School
610 Superior St.
Oostburg, WI 53070

Ebenezer Christian School
1556 North 16th St.
Sheboygan, WI 53081

Calvary Baptist High School
N84 W16971 Menomonee Ave.
Menomonee Falls, WI 53051

First Baptist Academy
224 Butternut St. at Sandra
West Bend, WI 53095

Calvary Baptist Christian Day
School
792 Milford St.
Watertown, WI 53094

Calvary Evangelical Lutheran
School
2132 North 27th St.
Sheboygan, WI 53081

Immanuel Evangelical Lutheran
School
1626 Illinois Ave.
Sheboygan, WI 53081

Grace Evangelical Lutheran
School
N87 W16173 Kenwood Blvd.
Menomonee Falls, WI 53051

Bethlehem Evangelical Lutheran
School
N84 W15252 Menomonee Ave.
Menomonee Falls, WI 53051

Zion Evangelical Lutheran
School
W188 N4868 Emerald Hills
Menomonee Falls, WI 53051

David's Star Evangelical
Lutheran School
Western Ave.
Jackson, WI 53037

Kettle Moraine Lutheran High
School
3399 Division Rd.
Jackson, WI 53037

Saint Paul's Lutheran School
Route 1
Sheboygan Falls, WI 53085

Saint Paul's Lutheran School
1810 North 13th St.
Sheboygan, WI 53081

Good Shepherd Lutheran
School
777 Indiana Ave.
West Bend, WI 53095

Immanuel Lutheran School
Route 2
Watertown, WI 53094

Trinity Lutheran School
801 South Fifth St.
Watertown, WI 53094

Trinity Lutheran School
824 Wisconsin Ave.
Sheboygan, WI 53081

Lutheran High School
107 Cedar St.
Sheboygan Falls, WI 53085

Bethlehem Lutheran School
1121 Georgia Ave.
Sheboygan, WI 53081

Seventh Day Adventist School
3910 Erie Ave.
Sheboygan, WI 53081

Saint John's Lutheran School
899 South 6th Ave.
West Bend, WI 53095

Saint John's Lutheran School
623 Congress St.
Newburg, WI 53060

Trinity Lutheran School
1268 Pleasant Valley Rd.
West Bend, WI 53095

Saint John's Lutheran School
317 North Sixth St.
Watertown, WI 53094

Saint Mark's Lutheran School
705 Cady St.
Watertown, WI 53094

Saint Peter's Lutheran School
Lebanon, WI 53047

Northwestern Episcopal
  Military and Naval Academy
550 South Lake Shore Dr.
Lake Geneva, WI 53147

Holy Name Catholic School
814 Superior Ave.
Sheboygan, WI 53081

Immaculate Conception
  Catholic School
2722 Henry St.
Sheboygan, WI 53081

Saint Anthony's Catholic
  School
N74 W13604 Appleton Ave.
Menomonee Falls, WI 53051

Saint Mary's Catholic School
N89 W16217 Cleveland Ave.
Menomonee Falls, WI 53051

Saint Frances Cabrini
  Catholic School
529 Hawthorne Dr.
West Bend, WI 53095

Holy Angels Catholic School
230 North 8th Ave.
West Bend, WI 53095

Saint Mary's Immaculate
  Conception Catholic School
415 Roosevelt Dr.
West Bend, WI 53095

Saint Bernard's Catholic
  School
111 South Montgomery St.
Watertown, WI 53094

Saint Henry's Catholic School
300 Cady St.
Watertown, WI 53094

JANESVILLE AREA:

Abundant Life Christian
  School
967 Benton Ave.
Janesville, WI 53545

Delavan Christian School
820 North Oak St.
Delavan, WI 53115

Saint Matthew's Evangelical
  Lutheran School
709 Milton Ave.
Janesville, WI 53545

Faith Christian Academy
1013 Henry Ave.
Beloit, WI 53511

Saint Paul's Evangelical
  Lutheran School
210 South Ringold St.
Janesville, WI 53545

Saint John's Evangelical
  Lutheran School
1006 Bluff St.
Beloit, WI 53511

Good Shepherd Lutheran School
2447 Park Ave.
Beloit, WI 53511

Woodland Adventist School
4324 Bingham Rd., Route 2
Janesville, WI 53545

Beloit Catholic High School
1221 Henry Ave.
Beloit, WI 53511

Saint Patrick's Catholic
  School
305 Lincoln St.
Janesville, WI 53545

Saint Mary's Catholic School
117 North Wisconsin St.
Janesville, WI 53545

WAUPUN AREA:

Waupun Christian School
520 McKinley St.
Waupun, WI 53963

Central Wisconsin Christian
  High School
Route 1, Box 342
Waupun, WI 53963

Poynette Christian School
Poynette, WI 53955

Merrywood Christian School,
  Inc.
Reedsburg, WI 53959

Wayland Baptist Academy
North University Ave.
Beaver Dam, WI 53916

Randolph Christian School
Route 1, Box 41
Randolph, WI 53956

Peace Lutheran School
1400 East 8th St.
Reedsburg, WI 53959

Campion Jesuit Catholic High
  School
300 East Campion Blvd.
Prairie du Chien, WI   53821

MANITOWOC AREA:

Immanuel Evangelical
  Lutheran School
916 Pine St.
Manitowoc, WI   54220

Saint John Evangelical
  Lutheran School
East Park 17th St.
Two Rivers, WI   54241

First German Evangelical
  Lutheran School
1025 South 8th St.
Manitowoc, WI   54220

Lutheran High School
4045 Lancer Circle
Manitowoc, WI   54220

Bethany Lutheran School
3209 Meadow Ln.
Manitowoc, WI   54220

Roncalli Catholic High School
2000 Mirro Dr.
Manitowoc, WI   54220

Saint Paul Catholic School
2411 Wollmer St.
Manitowoc, WI   54220

Saint Andrew's Catholic School
1808 South 14th St.
Manitowoc, WI   54220

Sacred Heart Catholic Center
2218 Washington St.
Two Rivers, WI   54241

WAUSAU AREA:

Christian Liberty Academy
P.O. Box 3
Tigerton, WI   54486

Our Savior's Evangelical
  Lutheran School
Wausau, WI   54401

Trinity Lutheran School
301 Elm St.
Athens, WI   54411

Zion Lutheran School
616 Grant St.
Wausau, WI   54401

Saint Frances Cabrini
  Catholic Middle School
321 Grand Ave.
Wausau, WI   54401

Saint Matthew Catholic School
225 South 28th Ave.
Wausau, WI   54401

Holy Name Catholic School
1122 South 9th Ave.
Wausau, WI   54401

EAU CLAIRE AREA:

Immanuel Lutheran High
  School
Eau Claire, WI   54701

Messiah Lutheran School
2015 North Hastings Way
Eau Claire, WI   54701

Baldwin Christian School
Route 1
Baldwin, WI   54002

Regis Catholic High School
Eau Claire, WI   54701

KAUKAUNA AREA:

Trinity Lutheran School
800 Augustine St.
Kaukauna, WI   54130

Mount Calvary Lutheran School
226 South Pine St.
Kimberly, WI   54136

Notre Dame of De Pere
  Catholic Upper School
517 Lewis St.
De Pere, WI   54115

Holy Name of Jesus
  Catholic School
614 East Kimberly St.
Kimberly, WI   54136

SAINT CROIX FALLS AREA:

Christian Fellowship Academy
P.O. Box 137
Centuria, WI   54824

WYOMING

CHEYENNE AREA:

Sunnyside Baptist School
Route 3, Box 1030B
Cheyenne, WY   82001

Our Savior Lutheran School
5101 Del Range Blvd.
Cheyenne, WY   82001

Trinity Lutheran School
1111 East 22nd St.
Cheyenne, WY   82001

Saint Mary's Catholic School
100 East 24th St.
Cheyenne, WY   82001

SHERIDAN AREA:

Sheridan Christian School
118 West 5th St.
Sheridan, WY   82801

Big Horn Christian Academy
Ranchester, WY   82839

Seventh Day Adventist School
Highway 14 E.
Sheridan, WY   82801

Holy Name Catholic School
121 South Connor St.
Sheridan, WY   82801

LARAMIE AREA:

Jane Ivinson Memorial Hall
  Episcopal School
601 Ivinson Ave.
Laramie, WY   82070

Saint Laurence Catholic School
608 South 4th St.
Laramie, WY   82070

CASPER AREA:

Riverview Baptist Schools
24th & Mulberry Sts.
P.O. Box 826
Casper, WY 82601

Grace Lutheran School
315 C Y Ave.
Casper, WY 82601

LANDER AREA:

King's Harvest School
Lander, WY 82520

Seventh Day Adventist School
202 Eugene St.
Lander, WY 82520

Saint Margaret's Catholic
   School
220 North 7th St., E.
Riverton, WY 82501

GILLETTE AREA:

Bible Baptist School
2300 Country Club Rd.
Gillette, WY 82716

Seventh Day Adventist
   School
East of Newcastle
Newcastle, WY 82701

ROCK SPRINGS AREA:

Big Horn School
Buffalo, WY 82834

Rock Springs Catholic
   School
615 Elias Ave.
Rock Springs, WY 82901

TORRINGTON AREA:

Valley Christian School
30th & East D Sts.
Torrington, WY 82240

Frontier School of the
   Bible
Lagrange, WY 82221

Saint Joseph's Catholic
   School
222 West Spruce St.
Rawlins, WY 82301

CODY AREA:

Grace Baptist School
P.O. Box 1145
Cody, WY 82414

Seventh Day Adventist
   School
17th & Charles Sts.
Worland, WY 82401

Seventh Day Adventist
   School
804 Road $8\frac{1}{2}$
Powell, WY 82435